"Vina Vinyāsa Yogena āsanadin na karayet"
O Yogī, do not do Āsana without Vinyāsa

— Vamana Rishi, *Yoga Korunta*

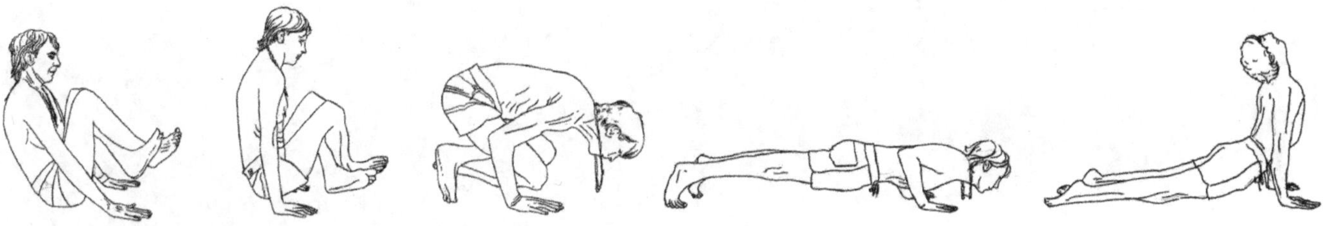

Also by David Garrigues

Teaching Yoga With Verbal Cues

Ecstatic Discipline: 46 Poems for Lovers of Haṭha Yoga

Vāyu Siddhi: Secrets of Yogic Breathing

Maps and Musings: Writings that Celebrate Haṭha Yoga and the Quest for Self Knowledge

ASHTANGA YOGA VINYĀSA

Movement, Breath, And Posture
In The Primary Series

DAVID GARRIGUES

Please email asanakitchen@gmail.com if you would like to reproduce any of this material for your own training or any other purpose.

Cover design by Ashley Low & Jaime Raposo
Book layout and design by Ashley Low & Joanna Darlington
Edited by Laura McNamara & Joy Marzec
Illustrations by Jo Mindhart & Bill Ross

DEDICATION

One evening in 1997, while I was in Mysore studying with Sri K. Pattabhi Jois, the founder of Ashtanga Yoga, I attended a conference in the front room of his old house in Laxmipuram. At one point, there was a lot of commotion about what constituted the method of Ashtanga and for a few moments everyone was talking loudly at the same time. I was sitting directly across from SKPJ and he looked into my eyes piercingly and held my gaze intently. He said, in his broken English, "Quickly you do, that's the method." He was speaking quietly, but it was as though his voice and his words were being directly transmitted to me and imprinting on my soul. It seemed as if that message was meant for my ears only.

"Why the word quickly?" I asked myself.

I was aware that his limited English was one reason he used the word quickly, but he meant far more than merely going through a series at a fast pace.

"Quickly you do, that's the method."

What Pattabhi Jois meant by these words has been at the forefront of my personal study for the past thirty years. Through intense research, I've discovered that quickly means sharp, with-it, all in—to be dynamic, confident, decisive, and sure in your actions, not fearful, doubtful, hesitant, or stuck in unconscious habit. In other words, quickly means VINYĀSA.

This book gives the earnest yoga student an unprecedented road map to the Vinyāsa system of Ashtanga Yoga. My intention is to teach you how to use the training ground of Vinyāsa to scale the heights of Āsana and Yoga. I've given exhaustive, loving attention to the details of every transition and breath in the Primary Series, and this includes the many extra, uncounted breaths and movements that are often found within a single Vinyāsa. This book is the first of its kind to provide a systematic approach to the study of Vinyāsa.

I'm not exaggerating when I say that to make this book has taken everything I've got— my body, my mind, my heart, and my soul. Maybe it would have been easy for someone else to write down all the ins and outs of the great Vinyāsa system of Ashtanga Yoga in an organized manner, but not for me. It was at least fifteen years ago when I naively started to articulate what I consider to be the full spectrum of the technology that falls under the heading: Vinyāsa in Ashtanga. Fortunately, I didn't realize the massiveness of the undertaking or I wouldn't have believed in myself enough to even make a try at it. But I withstood the searing heat of the long-term challenges. I rode the momentum gained by thinking that each one of the one hundred or more drafts was going to be the one, and I gathered steam by learning many new skills and growing tremendously as a writer and also as a student and teacher of yoga. Equally important is the fact that I couldn't have done it alone. I'm thankful for the help I've had from many students along the way, but the unswerving, over-the-top, outrageously generous trust and support of three guardian angels, Joanna Darlington, Ashley Low, and Laura McNamara, finally tipped the scales and made the impossible possible for me.

I also give thanks for the other impactful teachers that I've learned from: Sri T. Krishnamacharya, B.K.S. Iyengar, Marie Svoboda, Aadil Palkhivala, Richard Freeman, Chuck Miller, Tim Miller, and others. Without the unique gifts that I've received from each of these Yogīs, I wouldn't have been able to write this book. Richard Freeman turned me on to the endless creative possibilities that exist for articulating the technical, visual, poetic, energetic, and mystical language of Yoga.

Also, Marie Svoboda, the first teacher who truly lit the fire for yoga in my heart, had a wholly original approach to yoga based on the principal Vinyāsa tenet that says, the yogī is to value HOW to get into the pose more than being in the pose itself. Her teachings put in practice the saying: "The ends don't justify the means." To put it in Vinyāsa terms: the transition, movement, or action that takes you into your pose largely determines the quality, effectiveness, and beauty of your pose. Although I never heard her say the word Vinyāsa, her love of transitioning, and her nearly exclusive emphasis on the process of moving into a pose, embodied the intrinsic essence of Vinyāsa.

Beside me, I've long kept a handful of books on yoga philosophy and Haṭha Yoga, and the value I place on these treasures increases with the passage of time. I'm referring to *The Haṭha Yoga Pradīpikā, The Śiva Saṁhitā, The Bhagavad Gītā, The Yoga Vasiṣṭha, Patañjali's Yoga Sūtras, The Upanishads,* and other sacred texts. These books have helped me to know the magic of yoga both as a physical practice of Āsana, Prāṇāyāma, and Mudrās as well as a mystical science of the mind and Spirit. These stupendous books not only inspired me to practice yoga but also helped me find the courage to undertake the audacious task of offering my own writings on the subject. I feel eternally blessed that the Universe somehow contrived to allow me to share this resource with you. May it help you find your own individual path within the magical labyrinth of yoga.

David Garrigues
10/27/22

Pancha Bhutas
Five Elements: Earth, Fire, Water, Air, Space

ASHTANGA YOGA VINYĀSA

KEY TO THE GRID

This book is arranged in a grid structure in order to give you ready access to the many important layers of information that make up the Ashtanga system of Haṭha Yoga. Most of the information reads across the page from left to right. Examples include: the Vinyāsa position numbers, the photos and accompanying captions, and breathing cues in italics that are located just below the horizontal line. However, the bullet points in the columns are read vertically down the page.

POSTURE NAME IN SANSKRIT & ENGLISH

VINYĀSA POSITION/NUMBER IN SANSKRIT & ENGLISH

MACRO BREATHING CUE

MICRO BREATHING CUE

Macro breathing cues correspond to the general Vinyāsa count and help you keep track of the "official" breath protocol. In contrast, the micro breathing cues give you the extra, "unofficial," uncounted breaths that make up many of the Vinyāsas. The micro cues provide an encyclopedic breathing reference and allow the student to track every breath in the series from Sūrya Namaskāra to Śavāsana.

STATE OF THE ĀSANA

The shaded box indicates poses held for 5 to 8 breaths or more *(State of the Āsana)* and information like gazing point *(Dṛṣṭi)* and which side of the pose is being done.

VINYĀSA META VIEW

The Meta Views consist of technical, poetic, and inspiring tidbits that help the student absorb a set of universal Vinyāsa principles and gain insights into the profound wisdom of Yoga.

"FULL" VINYĀSA PROTOCOL

In Ashtanga, every pose has a set number of Vinyāsas or positions. The number of Vinyāsas for each posture is based on starting and ending in Samasthiti, as though doing Sūrya Namaskāra between every pose. If you do a practice according to the strict Vinyāsa count, it is called a "Full Vinyāsa." The typical daily Ashtanga routine is called a "Half Vinyāsa" because you do only some of the Vinyāsas that make up the overall count. This book is laid out according to the Half Vinyāsa practice, but the information for the Full Vinyāsa practice is provided at the beginning and end of every posture so a student can learn to properly count the Vinyāsas for each pose.

Ashtanga Yoga Vinyāsa

JĀNU ŚĪRṢĀSANA A (Head to Knee Pose A)

7 SAPTA
7TH POSITION, INHALE

Exhale

Crouch; energize limbs.

— Lower your hips into a poised squat and build up energy in your body, like a pitcher winds up to throw a baseball.

Inhale

Spring to Daṇḍāsana.

— Jump forward exuberantly and swing your legs through to Daṇḍāsana with a lively forward throw of your feet.

Free Breathing, Inhale

Root legs and arms, lift chest, and strike Setup!

— Take your right knee back to 90° and rotate your torso to the left.

— Reach forward with your arms and use your left hand to catch your right wrist around your left foot.

— Hold steady at the end Position.

— In the tiny pause, lift up your head and chest, stamp down your legs, and pull back towards you with your arms.

Vinyāsa Meta View
Playing with opposing forces allows you to discover the subtle energetic technique of Mudrā that serves to help you create internal awareness, the hallmark of meditation. An example of opposing forces in this pose is to fix your extended leg in position as you pull back towards you with your arms.

8 AṢṬAU
8TH POSITION, EXHALE

Exhale, 5 to 8 Breaths

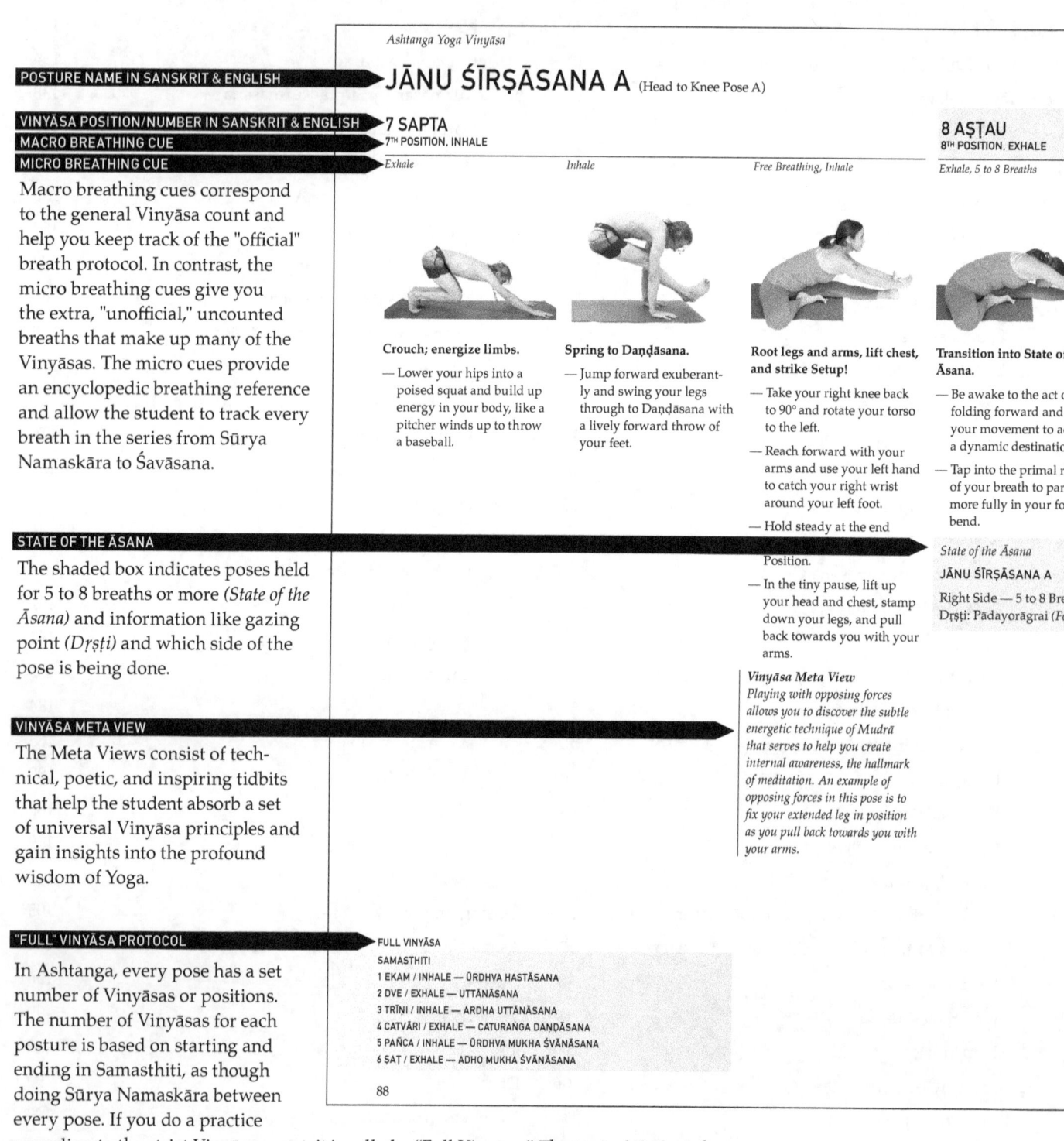

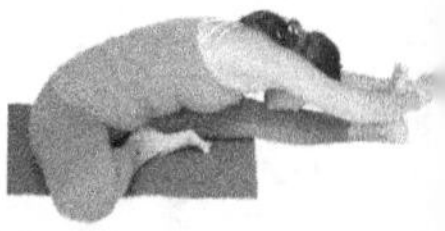

Transition into State of the Āsana.

— Be awake to the act of folding forward and use your movement to achieve a dynamic destination.

— Tap into the primal rhythm of your breath to participat more fully in your forward bend.

State of the Āsana
JĀNU ŚĪRṢĀSANA A
Right Side — 5 to 8 Breaths
Dṛṣṭi: Pādayorāgrai *(Foot)*

FULL VINYĀSA
SAMASTHITI
1 EKAM / INHALE — ŪRDHVA HASTĀSANA
2 DVE / EXHALE — UTTĀNĀSANA
3 TRĪṆI / INHALE — ARDHA UTTĀNĀSANA
4 CATVĀRI / EXHALE — CATURAṄGA DAṆḌĀSANA
5 PAÑCA / INHALE — ŪRDHVA MUKHA ŚVĀNĀSANA
6 ṢAṬ / EXHALE — ADHO MUKHA ŚVĀNĀSANA

88

Primary Series

9 NAVA
9TH POSITION, INHALE

Inhale

Return to Setup.

— Lift up your head and torso and pause at the halfway point.

— With speedy poise, anchor your thighs and pull up from the root of your spine.

— Drop all false imaginings and pierce through to Now in a glorious moment of illumination.

Exhale

Crouch!

— Sit up, lean back, and bend your knees. Lift up your feet, plant your hands on the ground in front of your hips, and pause.

— Charge your limbs and build up to a threshold of power; store up enough force within your body to propel a formidable jump-back move!

10 DAŚA
10TH POSITION, INHALE

Inhale

Spring!

— Stamp your hands down swiftly; lift up decisively and clear your body off the ground.

— Suck your feet back and begin to lean forward with your upper body.

11 EKĀDAŚA
11TH POSITION, EXHALE

Exhale

Jump Back.

— Bend your elbows, pivot in place, balance on your arms in midair as you lean forward and shoot your legs back.

— Continue to shift your chest forward and bend the elbows until your upper arm bones are parallel to the ground.

89

TIMELINE

This horizontal line helps you keep track of the Vinyāsa position, especially useful when a single Vinyāsa has more than one movement/column or continues on to the next page.

PHOTOS WITH CAPTIONS

The captions offer concise commands for each transition and position.

BULLET POINTS

The bullet points under the captions provide a more thorough set of instructions on the technical practicalities of transitioning into the pose while also pointing the student towards wider, deeper applications of the Haṭha Yoga technology. Highlights include: more detailed instructions on breathing and cues that speak to energetic, poetic, and mystical aspects of Ashtanga/Haṭha/Raja Yoga.

BOOK TERMINOLOGY

THREE BODY PLANES

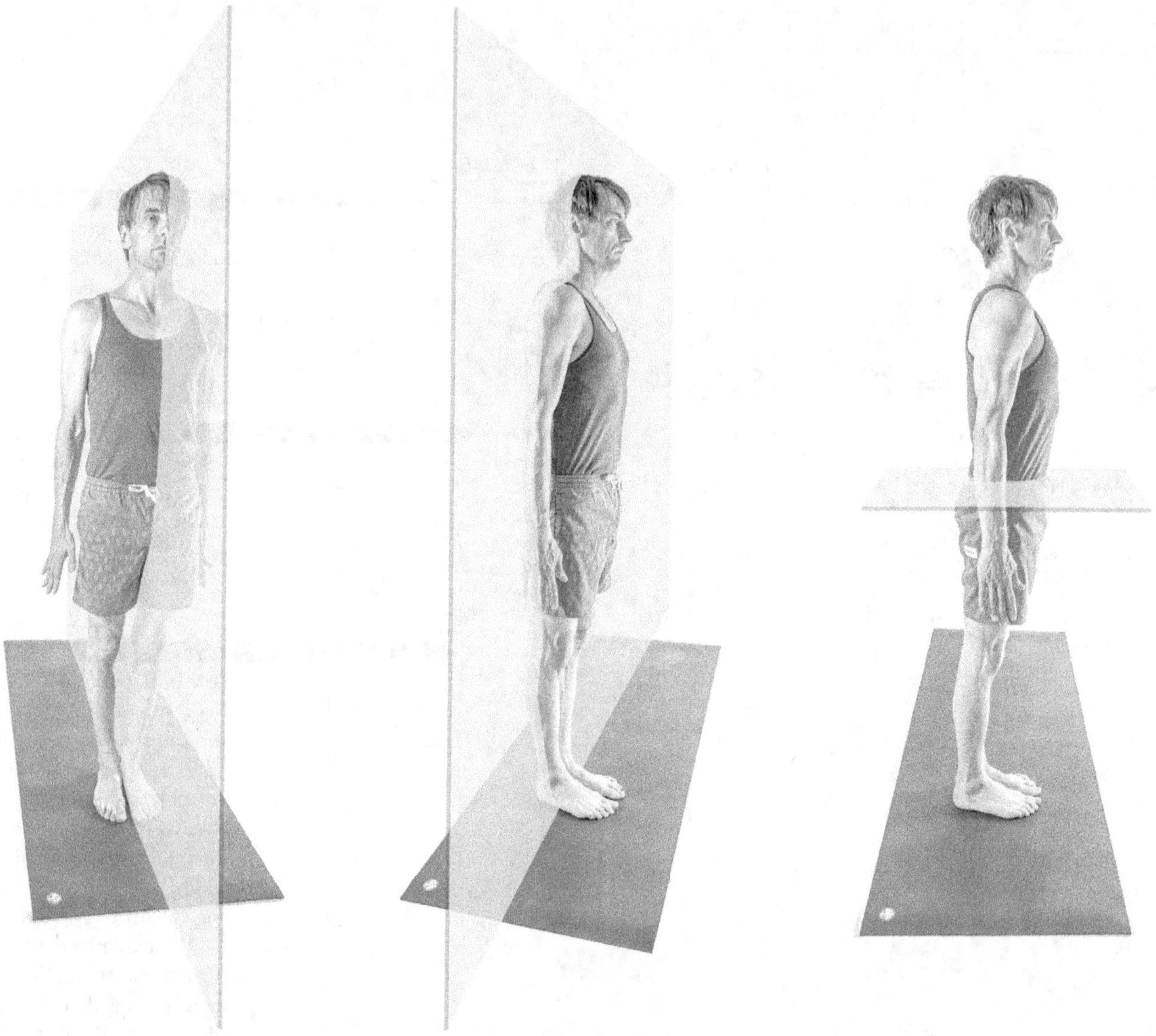

SAGITTAL / MEDIAN PLANE

The sagittal or median plane divides the body into right and left halves.

SIDE / FRONTAL PLANE

The side or frontal plane divides the body into front *(anterior)* and back *(posterior)* halves.

TRANSVERSE / HORIZONTAL PLANE

The transverse or horizontal plane divides the body into upper *(superior)* and lower *(inferior)* halves.

THE CROUCH & SPRING

Every Vinyāsa *(transition)* has three phases: Crouch, Spring, and Destination.

CROUCH / SETUP POSITION

Strike a formal Setup position. Store up energy within your body to get ready to take action—like bending back a bow to gather force before shooting an arrow.

SPRING / TRANSITION

Launch into skillful action. Execute a fearless move, a targeted gesture—like an arrow speeding through the air towards the chosen target with a sure, unalterable trajectory.

DESTINATION / STATE OF THE ĀSANA

Arrive in a distinct, chosen posture and commandingly bring all motion to a standstill—like piercing the bull's eye at the center of the target.

EXAMPLE #1

Crouch Spring Destination

EXAMPLE #2

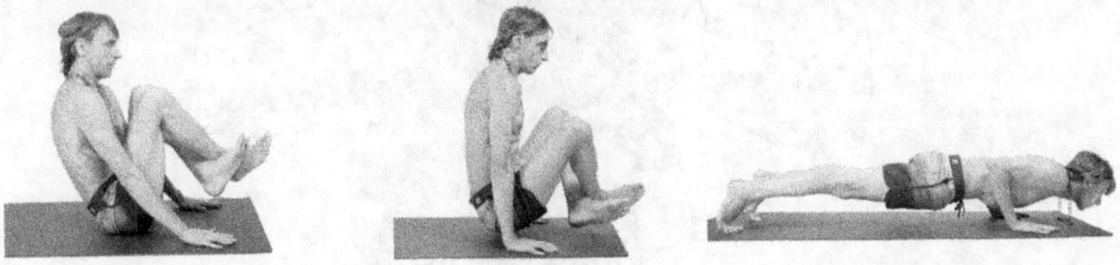

Crouch Spring Destination

EXAMPLE #3

Crouch Spring Destination

EXAMPLE #4

Crouch Spring Destination

Patañjali striking Samasthiti.

OPENING PRAYER*

Om

Vande gurūṇām caraṇāravinde

Sandarśita svātmasukhāvabodhe

Niḥśreyase jāṅgalikāyamāne

Saṁsāra hālāhala mohaśāntyai

Ābāhu puruṣākāraṃ

Śaṅkhacakrāsi dhāriṇam

Sahasra śirasaṃ śvetaṃ

Praṇamāmi Patañjalim

Om

—

Om

I praise the lotus feet of the Eternal Teacher who lives within the heart of every being,

who shows me the way to yoga, helps me be happy with me, and realize my essence as Self.

The Inner Teacher is me, as a shaman, the one who transforms the psychic wilderness into a refuge,

and alleviates confusion caused by drinking the poison of imbalanced attachment to worldly life.

His upper body has the shape of a human,

in his hands he holds the conch and the disc of light,

his lower body has the form of a snake whose head forms a hood of 1000 cobras,

I bow down to Patañjali.

Om

* It is customary for Ashtanga students to chant this invocation at the start of each practice. These two Ślokas *(stanzas or chants of praise)* are from two different sources. The first is the opening verse from Ādi Śaṅkara's *Yoga Tārāvali,* an important Haṭha Yoga text. The second comes from a commentary on *Patañjali's Yoga Sūtras* with Bhojavritti called *Rājamārtaṇḍa.*

SŪRYA NAMASKĀRA A (Sun Salutation A)

SAMASTHITI
0 POSITION

Free Breathing

Samasthiti.

— Stand tall, ground your feet, and brace your thighs.

— Lengthen your arms and reach down through your fingers.

— Pull up your navel and broaden your chest.

0 POSITION
Samasthiti
(Equal Standing Pose)
Dṛṣṭi: Agrataḥ *(Forward)*

1 EKAM
1ST POSITION, INHALE

Inhale

Sweep arms up overhead.

— Make your palms face out.

— Reach your arms up in the side plane, trace a semi-circle in the air with your hands, and pull your breath in evenly against resistance from your narrowed throat *(Ujjāyī Breathing).*

— Stop moving and finish inhaling at the same time.

— Stamp your hands together overhead and stack your wrists, elbows, shoulders, hips, knees, and ankles over each other with great precision.

Vinyāsa Meta View
Synchronize the smooth sound of your breath with the gesture of sweeping your arms up. Contemplate the action of pressing your hands together overhead as a Mudrā (Energetic Seal), a unique gesture of prayer, a humble offering to the Great Spirit. Devote yourself to the most plain and basic bodily tasks and gradually the magical potency of Vinyāsa will be revealed to you.

1ST VINYĀSA
Ūrdhva Hastāsana
(Raised Hands Pose)
Dṛṣṭi: Aṅguṣṭā Ma Dyai *(Thumbs)*

2 DVE
2ND POSITION, EXHALE

Exhale

Fold forward to 2nd Position.

— Project your torso forward and swoop down smoothly into your forward bend.

— As you move, hinge at your hips and rotate your pelvis around your stable femur heads within the hip sockets.

— Skillfully flush the air out of your lungs as you arrive in position and match the end of your exhalation with the end of your movement.

— Maintain your tall, sturdy legs; plant your hands on the ground to either side of your feet. Brace your arms and gently coax your head and torso closer to your legs.

— Generate an instance of pure stillness *(Nirodha—Cessation of Activity).*

2ND VINYĀSA
Uttānāsana
(Standing Forward Bend)
Dṛṣṭi: Nasagrai *(Nose)*

3 TRĪṆI
3RD POSITION, INHALE

Inhale

Lift up head and spine; strike Setup position.

— Sweep your torso up towards a horizontal plane and inhale by pulling your breath in across your narrowed throat *(Ujjāyī).*

— Fully extend your arms, roll back your shoulders, and press the ground firmly with your fingertips.

— Find contrast between rooting your limbs and elongating your spine.

— Hold steady in position briefly. Finish inhaling and properly appreciate the potent yet easily overlooked 3rd Vinyāsa of Sūrya Namaskāra.

3RD VINYĀSA
Ardha Uttānāsana
(Intense Stretch Pose at Halfway)
Dṛṣṭi: Broomadhya
(Eyebrow Center)

4 CATVĀRI

4TH POSITION, EXHALE

Exhale

Make a compact shape, a ready crouch.

— Bend your knees, keep your head up and your chest forward, lower your hips to a squat.

— Bring your thighs forward and suck your legs directly underneath your torso.

— Shift forward to the edge of imbalance.

Exhale (continued)

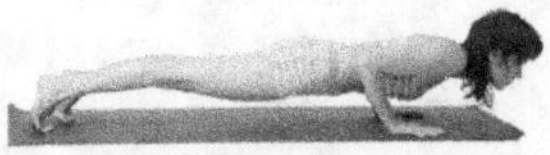

Jump or step back to Caturaṅga Daṇḍāsana.

Two ways to jump back:

1) Jump directly to Caturaṅga.
   - Swiftly bend your elbows.
   - Drive your legs back.
   - Arrive, and make a full stop in position.

2) Jump (or step back) to Plank Pose, then lower into Caturaṅga.
   - Hold steady for a brief moment in Plank Pose with straight arms.
   - Hinge at your elbows and come down into position.

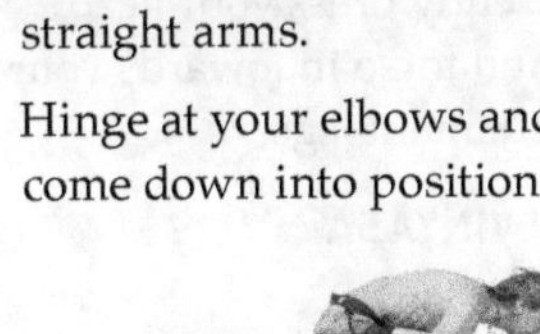

4TH VINYĀSA

Caturaṅga Daṇḍāsana
(Four-Limbed Staff Pose)

Dṛṣṭi: Nasagrai *(Nose)*

5 PAÑCA

5TH POSITION, INHALE

Inhale

Lift head, arch spine, press arms straight.

— To go from Caturaṅga Daṇḍāsana to Upward Dog Pose, lift up your head in a circle and arch your spine as you press your arms straight. Add maximum bracing power to your legs.

— As you repeat this challenging transition, work to establish a clear, momentum-generating rhythm that takes you from start to finish in a single, limb-lengthening, spine-arching, lung-filling power move.

5TH VINYĀSA

Ūrdhva Mukha Śvānāsana
(Upward Facing Dog Pose)

Dṛṣṭi: Broomadhya
(Eyebrow Center)

6 ṢAṬ

6TH POSITION, EXHALE

Exhale, 5 to 8 Breaths

Thrust hips back; strike Downward Dog.

— Swing your hips back, roll over the tops of your feet smoothly, and come to Downward Dog Pose in a sweep of power.

— As you strike your position, stamp down your hands, firm your arms, root your thighs back, and dip your spine down towards the ground boldly.

6TH VINYĀSA

State of the Āsana

ADHO MUKHA ŚVĀNĀSANA
(Downward Facing Dog Pose)

5 to 8 Breaths or more
Dṛṣṭi: Nābi Chakra *(Navel)*

SŪRYA NAMASKĀRA A (Sun Salutation A)

7 SAPTA

7TH POSITION, INHALE

Exhale

Crouch low and exhale thoroughly.

— Stamp the ground firmly with your hands, brace your arms, bend your knees, and come down into a poised squat.

— Hunker back through your hips, store up force in your legs and arms, and galvanize your center.

Vinyāsa Meta View
Don't hurry through the crouch. Stop in place and take the time to engage your whole body before you spring into action.

Inhale

Spring forward, head up, and strike Setup position.

— Jump forward fearlessly. Don't hold back! Bring your whole body with you and plant your feet on the ground between your hands.

— Fully extend your arms, go up on your fingertips, and lift your chest high.

— Project your spine forward into the space away from your tall, unmoving legs and come to a distinct standstill at the end point of your movement.

Vinyāsa Meta View
Commit to each transition in earnest and join in the great Vinyāsa game of Crouch and Spring!

7TH VINYĀSA
Ardha Uttānāsana
(Intense Stretch Pose at Halfway)
Dṛṣṭi: Broomadhya
(Eyebrow Center)

8 AṢṬAU

8TH POSITION, EXHALE

Exhale

Swoop down towards fixed legs and empty lungs.

— Fold forward with a decisive downward sweep of your head and torso.

— Make a playful, daring move out of bringing your torso towards your stubbornly rooted legs.

— Achieve a precise stopping point and instantly command your form.

— Light up your body with subtle actions such as:

- Keep your weight shifted forward.
- Stamp your hands down on either side of your feet.
- Brace your arms and legs.
- Gently press your head and torso in towards your adamant legs.

8TH VINYĀSA
Uttānāsana
(Standing Forward Bend)
Dṛṣṭi: Nasagrai *(Nose)*

9 NAVA

9TH POSITION, INHALE

Inhale

Stand up; reach arms overhead and fill up lungs.

— As you come to standing, reach your arms up and out to the sides in an expansive gesture. Stamp the earth with your feet and strengthen your legs "to the point of gnashing your teeth" as the *Yoga Vasiṣṭha* instructs in reference to the necessity for vigorous effort in practice and taking command of one's destiny.

— Instantly invest your whole body with great stopping power. Transform your legs, torso, pelvis, and arms into a daṇḍa, a strong, straight stick, an energetic lightning rod that enables you to conduct mighty Prāṇic forces throughout your structure.

— Create an Immovable Spot so legendary that the gods and goddesses up in the heavens take notice and rain down flowers upon you.

9TH VINYĀSA
Ūrdhva Hastāsana
(Raised Hands Pose)
Dṛṣṭi: Aṅguṣṭā Ma Dyai
(Thumbs)

SAMASTHITI
0 POSITION

Exhale

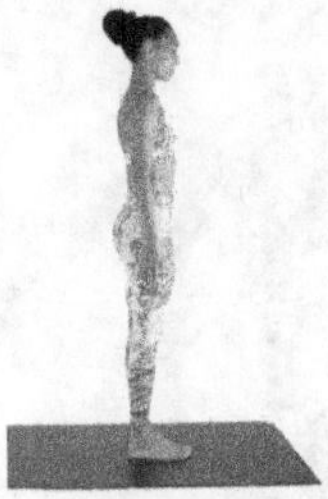

Glide arms down to Samasthiti with sound breathing *(Ujjāyī).*

— As you swim your arms down, probe the side plane with your reach and find the full extent of your wingspan.

— Make the great gesture of your arms steady and even in order to make your out-breath steady and even.

— As you exhale, create a smooth, aspirant sound, "HAM."

— As you arrive in Tāḍāsana *(Mountain Pose)*, internalize your senses, steady your mind, and perceive the magic in the basic act of standing.

0 POSITION
Samasthiti
(Equal Standing Pose)
Dṛṣṭi: Agrataḥ *(Forward)*

SŪRYA NAMASKĀRA B (Sun Salutation B)

SAMASTHITI
0 POSITION

Free Breathing

Samasthiti.

— Stand supremely rooted and tall like a great tree. Show the Universe the beauty of a human being.

0 POSITION
Samasthiti
(Equal Standing Pose)
Dṛṣṭi: Agrataḥ
(Forward)

1 EKAM
1ST POSITION, INHALE

Inhale

Bend knees and reach arms up overhead.

— Bend your knees, lower your pelvis vertically toward your heels, and come into a generous half-squat as you sweep your arms up on a diagonal line in front of the vertical axis.

— Drive your shins, knees, and thighs dramatically forward. Shift your pelvis, torso, head, and arms forward too.

— Stamp your hands together and shoot your arms up with enough force to launch your body to the moon while rooting your legs so that you remain tethered to the beloved Earth.

Vinyāsa Meta View
When striking Utkaṭāsana, synchronize lowering your hips into a half-squat with reaching up through your arms. Bend your knees at the same speed as you reach up. Stop your hips and legs in place at the same time as you stop your arms in place. O Yogī! When all your parts work together as a team, clear intention and internal focus, coordination, and discernment are your rewards!

1ST VINYĀSA
Utkaṭāsana
(Fierce Pose)
Dṛṣṭi: Aṅguṣṭā Ma Dyai
(Thumbs)

2 DVE
2ND POSITION, EXHALE

Exhale

Sweep down into a forward bend.

— From your half-squat position, simultaneously project your spine forward into the space ahead of you and straighten your legs. Then, swoop your head and torso down and maintain your tall, rooted legs.

— Arrive in position and decisively stop in place by stamping down your hands, bracing your arms and legs, and rounding your spine into flexion.

2ND VINYĀSA
Uttānāsana
(Standing Forward Bend)
Dṛṣṭi: Nasagrai *(Nose)*

3 TRĪṆI
3RD POSITION, INHALE

Inhale

Lift up chest, extend arms, and ground legs.

— Lift up your head and project your spine forward with a rhythmic gesture as you fill your lungs to the brim.

3RD VINYĀSA
Ardha Uttānāsana
(Intense Stretch Pose at Halfway)
Dṛṣṭi: Broomadhya
(Eyebrow Center)

4 CATVĀRI
4TH POSITION, EXHALE

Exhale

Lower hips, lean forward, and crouch.

— Bend your knees, bring your thighs forward, and coil your body into a low, compact shape.

— Lean forward, place weight on your arms, and get ready for action.

Vinyāsa Meta View
Transition into each pose in three phases:

1) Start from a poised crouch.

2) Execute an uninterrupted move.

3) Arrive in a fully realized form.

Exhale (continued)

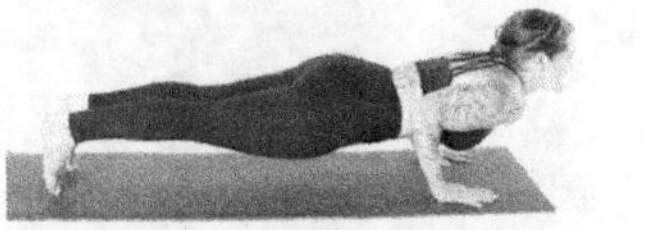

Spring to the Stick Shape!

— As you jump, bend your elbows, project your chest forward, and drive your legs back.

— Strike Four-Limbed Staff Pose; stop all movement as you skillfully empty your lungs.

4TH VINYĀSA
Caturaṅga Daṇḍāsana
(Four-Limbed Staff Pose)

Dṛṣṭi: Nasagrai *(Nose)*

5 PAÑCA
5TH POSITION, INHALE

Inhale

Lift up head, straighten arms, and open chest.

— Lift your head by tracing a circle across the sky with your nose.

— Arch your spine by expanding your chest mightily.

— Upon arrival in position:

- Root down through your sturdy arms and lift your head and spine up off your shoulders.
- Invest your legs with great stopping power.
- Cast your gaze up, over, and back to complement reaching back through your legs. Think: head back, legs back, spine forward!

5TH VINYĀSA
Ūrdhva Mukha Śvānāsana
(Upward Facing Dog Pose)

Dṛṣṭi: Broomadhya
(Eyebrow Center)

6 ṢAṬ
6TH POSITION, EXHALE

Exhale

Swing hips back to Down Dog.

— Project your pelvis back with enough force to roll over the tops of your feet smoothly and empty your lungs completely.

— Anticipate stepping your right foot forward into a lunge.

6TH VINYĀSA
Adho Mukha Śvānāsana
(Downward Facing Dog Pose)

Dṛṣṭi: Nābi Chakra *(Navel)*

SŪRYA NAMASKĀRA B (Sun Salutation B)

7 SAPTA
7TH POSITION, INHALE

Inhale

Step, lunge, reach up arms, stamp palms together.

— Angle your left heel in to 45° and step your right foot between your hands.

— Before coming upright, fully commit to your lunge. Make your right thigh parallel to the ground and vertically line up your right knee over your right ankle.

— Come upright continuing to lunge and sweep your arms up to the vertical axis.

— As you arrive in position, create subtle alignment throughout your body.

— Ground both legs, bring your left hip forward towards square, and infinitely extend your back leg.

— Anchor your coccyx and pull up your navel.

— Widen your mid-back and suck your lower front ribs down.

— Take your head back and shift your sternum forward.

— Rocket your arms vertically upward and stamp your hands together in a gesture of prayer.

7TH VINYĀSA
Vīrabhadrāsana A
(Warrior A Pose)
Dṛṣṭi: Aṅguṣṭā Ma Dyai
(Thumbs)

8 AṢṬAU
8TH POSITION, EXHALE

Exhale

Plant hands, step back to plank, and bend elbows.

— Bring your hands to the ground on either side of your right foot, step back to Plank Pose, and hold steady for a split second with your arms fully extended. In Plank, charge your limbs with vitality and formalize your Daṇḍa *(Stick Shape)* with swiftness.

— Bend your elbows and strike Four-Limbed Staff Pose as you sweep the air out of your lungs "with proper tact" as instructed in the *Haṭha Yoga Pradīpikā* in reference to breathing skillfully in practice.

8TH VINYĀSA
Caturaṅga Daṇḍāsana
(Four-Limbed Staff Pose)
Dṛṣṭi: Nasagrai (Nose)

9 NAVA
9TH POSITION, INHALE

Inhale

Arch spine, press arms straight, strike Up Dog Pose.

— With precise timing, push back your toes and lift up your head, then arch your spine as you extend your arms and legs.

— At the peak of the pose, come to a clean stop. Fully embody this legendary backbend by the following actions:

- Anchor your legs.
- Root your arms.
- Pull up your navel.
- Puff your chest.
- Cast your gaze up, over, and back.

9TH VINYĀSA
Ūrdhva Mukha Śvānāsana
(Upward Facing Dog Pose)
Dṛṣṭi: Broomadhya
(Eyebrow Center)

10 DAŚA
10TH POSITION, EXHALE

Exhale

Pull hips back to destination.

— Sweep your hips back dynamically and at the same time take charge of your exhalation.

— Arrive instantly in Downward Dog and anticipate stepping forward with your left leg.

10TH VINYĀSA
Adho Mukha Śvānāsana
(Downward Facing Dog Pose)
Dṛṣṭi: Nābi Chakra *(Navel)*

11 EKĀDAŚA

11TH POSITION, INHALE

Inhale

Step, lunge, and reach up arms; strike second side.

— Angle your right heel in 45° and step your left foot between your hands.

— Lunge deeply, lower your left thigh parallel to the ground, and vertically line up your knee over your ankle.

— Fix your lower body in position, bring your torso upright, and sweep your arms up overhead.

— As you arrive in Warrior A Pose, stamp your hands together and reach vertically upward with enough force to pierce the sky-dome with your arrow-like arms.

— Take your head back, gaze up past your thumbs, and project your collarbones forward.

— Pull up your abdomen and lift your pelvis up off of your grounded legs.

11TH VINYĀSA

Vīrabhadrāsana A

(Warrior A Pose)

Dṛṣṭi: Aṅguṣṭā Ma Dyai *(Thumbs)*

12 DVĀDAŚA

12TH POSITION, EXHALE

Exhale

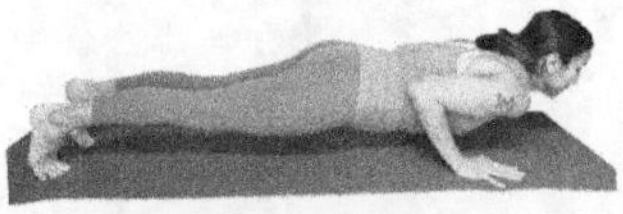

Step to Plank and lower to Caturaṅga Daṇḍāsana.

— Stamp down your hands and step back to a virtuous Plank Pose with your arms fully extended.

— Bend your elbows and come down to Caturaṅga Daṇḍāsana maintaining integrity throughout your body masses.

— Upon arrival in position, light up the horizontal axis that spans the core of your body from your feet to your head.

12TH VINYĀSA

Caturaṅga Daṇḍāsana

(Four-Limbed Staff Pose)

Dṛṣṭi: Nasagrai *(Nose)*

13 TRAYODAŚA

13TH POSITION, INHALE

Inhale

Circle up with head, bow spine, and stop in Up Dog.

— Draw a circle in the air with your nose as you lift your head, press your arms straight, and coil your spine into a satisfying bow shape within your torso.

— Come to a clean stopping place with your legs and arms fully extended and your arched spine centered between your four strong limbs.

13TH VINYĀSA

Ūrdhva Mukha Śvānāsana

(Upward Facing Dog Pose)

Dṛṣṭi: Broomadhya

(Eyebrow Center)

14 CATURDAŚA

14TH POSITION, EXHALE

Exhale, 5 to 8 Breaths

Go from Up Dog to Down Dog with economy.

— Sweep your hips back forcefully, generate momentum to roll over the tops of your feet dexterously, and come to Downward Dog Pose with supreme confidence.

Vinyāsa Meta View

Economy is a word you'll find in this book. In reference to Vinyāsa, economy means:

- *Be efficient in your use of motion or effort.*
- *Pre-arrange your Setup position so that only a minimal amount of movement is needed to transition into your pose.*
- *Find the shortest, most direct route between the Setup position and the State of the Āsana.*
- *Eliminate hesitation, doubt, fear, deliberation, irresolution.*
- *Set your foundation and avoid repositioning during your movement.*
- *Cultivate subtle connections between your: 1) Crouch 2) Spring 3) Destination.*

14TH VINYĀSA

State of the Āsana

ADHO MUKHA ŚVĀNĀSANA

(Downward Facing Dog Pose)

5 to 8 Breaths or more

Dṛṣṭi: Nābi Chakra *(Navel)*

SŪRYA NAMASKĀRA B (Sun Salutation B)

15 PAÑCADAŚA
15TH POSITION, INHALE

Exhale

Sink down into a crouch; prepare to spring.

— Lower your body towards the earth, tuck your thighs up underneath your torso, and send your out-breath down your spine to your center. Build up energy, like an archer making a bow taut before launching an arrow.

Inhale

Leap forward and strike Setup position.

— Jump purely forward. Commit your whole body to the leap and plant your feet on the ground between your hands.

— Lift up your head and extend your arms; project your spine forward into space away from your tall, sturdy legs.

— Swiftly embody this all-important Setup and make ready to forward bend.

Vinyāsa Meta View
Part of the genius of the Ashtanga Vinyāsa system is the formal Setup position that comes before each pose. The prep pose helps you charge up your body, connect with your breath, and get ready to move dynamically and skillfully into the State of the Āsana. For example, in this position, strike the Setup by jumping forward, planting your feet, lifting your head and spine up to a halfway point, rooting your limbs, and lengthening your spine. By formalizing these actions, you'll be ready to forward bend and strike your pose. O Yogī, remember well the pose that comes before the pose is surpassingly great—as the connoisseur of Vinyāsa knows!

15TH VINYĀSA
Ardha Uttānāsana
(Intense Stretch Pose at Halfway)

Dṛṣṭi: Broomadhya
(Eyebrow Center)

16 ṢOḌAŚA
16TH POSITION, EXHALE

Exhale

Fold forward to Uttānāsana.

— Sweep your head and torso down towards your rooted legs, like closing a jackknife.

— As you fold forward, exhale with a dynamic rhythm.

— Plant your hands on the ground outside of your feet and brace your arms.

— Shift forward to a precipice. Vertically stack your hips, knees, and ankles; find great stability on the edge of imbalance.

16TH VINYĀSA
Uttānāsana
(Standing Forward Bend)

Dṛṣṭi: Nasagrai *(Nose)*

17 SAPTADAŚA
17TH POSITION, INHALE

Inhale

Bend knees, squat, reach arms up, and stamp hands.

— With a rhythmic inhalation, simultaneously swing your torso upright, bend your knees, lower your hips into a half-squat, and reach out to the sides and up with your arms.

— Drive your knees forward, sink your pelvis towards your heels, and weight your thighs.

— Extend your arms as you reach up and stamp your hands together overhead at a clear stopping point just in front of the vertical axis.

— Breathe in smoothly throughout the entire transition. See your continuous breath as a way to assemble this series of movements into a cohesive, whole-body gesture.

17TH VINYĀSA
Utkaṭāsana
(Fierce Pose)

Dṛṣṭi: Aṅguṣṭā Ma Dyai
(Thumbs)

SAMASTHITI
0 POSITION

Exhale

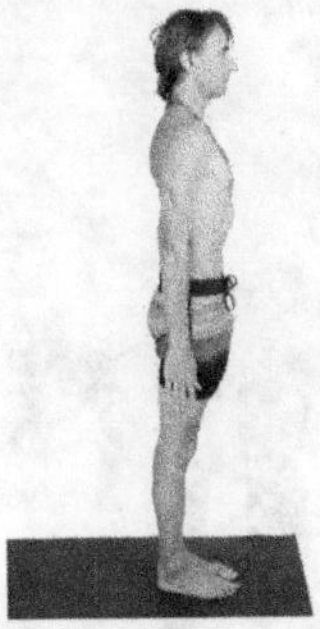

Swim arms down, extend legs, and exhale; strike destination.

— Stand up in slow motion by driving down through your feet, adding weight to your thighs, and thrusting up through your head and spine.

— Glide your arms down in the side plane at the same speed as you straighten your legs and empty your lungs.

— Focus your mind and senses inside your body. Exclude everything from your consciousness except the eternal flame of the Self dwelling within the Cave of your Heart.

0 POSITION
Samasthiti
(Equal Standing Pose)
Dṛṣṭi: Agrataḥ *(Forward)*

PĀDĀṄGUṢṬHĀSANA (Big Toe Pose)

SAMASTHITI
0 POSITION

Samasthiti *(Complete Standing).*

— Stand tall, root your legs, and get ready for a mini Crouch and Spring move.

— Strike Samasthiti by alchemically mixing earth, water, fire, air, and space within your very own body.

Vinyāsa Meta View
If you look carefully with both your outer and inner eyes, you'll see that beyond the apparent variety and diversity in the world, there are only the same Five Elements everywhere—Earth, Water, Fire, Air, and Space—and nothing more.

Yes! You and this world are composed of just five essential ingredients and these you must work tirelessly to embody and express in your Āsanas, Prāṇāyāma, and Mudrās.

Learn to see only pure expressions of Earth, Water, Fire, Air, and Space in everything that you do and make and know, and you'll soon become an Āsana wizard and be on your way to finding your own little original station in this life.

1 EKAM
1ST POSITION, INHALE

Exhale

Bring hands to waist and lower hips into a crouch.

— As you exhale down to the root of your spine, stamp your feet, bend your knees, lower your hips into a half-squat, and store up strength in your legs.

— Make ready to spring.

Vinyāsa Meta View
Don't fail to honor the small moves and less flashy positions that make up the core of the Vinyāsa matrix.

Inhale

Hop feet apart; strike the vertical Setup position.

— Separate your feet hip width apart, extend your legs, pull up your navel, lift your sternum, and look up.

— Activate your whole body en masse and prepare for a dynamic forward fold.

Exhale, Inhale

Sweep down to the Setup; grip big toes.

— Empty your lungs, hinge at your hips, fold, and stop in place at a halfway point.

— Catch your big toes with your middle and index fingers.

— Shift forward to the edge of imbalance and strike the Setup position.

— Prepare for your forward bend with the following actions:

- Extend your arms and legs, pull up on your toes with your fingers, and project your spine boldly forward.
- Skillfully breathe in, suck your belly into a hollow, raise Śakti from the root, and get ready for high action.

2 DVE
2ND POSITION, EXHALE

Exhale, 5 to 8 Breaths

Fold forward and flush lungs.

— Sweep your head and torso down towards your fixed legs.

— Grip your toes firmly, lengthen your legs, and remain committed forward as you execute your tiny yet bold move into the State of the Āsana.

— Upon arrival: make your legs tall and strong, brace your arms akimbo, and release your spine from tail to head.

State of the Āsana

PĀDĀṄGUṢṬHĀSANA

5 to 8 Breaths or more
Dṛṣṭi: Nasagrai *(Nose)*

3 TRĪṆI
3RD POSITION, INHALE

Inhale

Lift up head and return to Setup position.

— Shift forward, lift up your torso, and project your spine boldly into the space away from your anchored legs.

— Redouble the grip on your toes, fully extend your arms, and create a clean stop at the auspicious halfway station between forward folding and standing.

— Root your thighs to add power to projecting your spine forward.

— Stay in place while setting up the next pose, Pāda Hastāsana; breathe freely.

FULL VINYĀSA

SAMASTHITI

PĀDA HASTĀSANA (Hand to Foot Pose)

1 EKAM

1ST POSITION, INHALE

Inhale

Take hands under feet; lift head and chest.

— Stand directly on your hands and shift forward to the edge of imbalance.

— Stamp your feet down, lengthen your legs and arms, and pull up through your head and torso.

— Elongate your spine and fill up your lungs at the same time.

— Commit your whole body to this Setup position and you'll soon discover why such a seemingly humble shape is so highly prized among lovers of Haṭha Yoga.

— Get ready to fold.

2 DVE

2ND POSITION, EXHALE

Exhale, 5 to 8 Breaths

Forward bend.

— Remain forward on the edge of imbalance as you fold and draw your torso towards your unmoving legs.

— Vertically stack your hips, knees, and ankles instead of fearfully pushing your hips back.

— Find a natural stopping place for your head and torso. Alternate between these two opposite ways of expressing your pose:

1) Engage your whole body in a subtle effort to close the gap between your torso and legs while retaining the height of your pelvis and the rootedness of your legs.

2) Release your spine and head in a downward direction, like a free-flowing waterfall cascading down.

— Create Absorption *(Samādhi)* as you hold steady. Watch your breath deepen and the field of your mind become spacious without effort.

State of the Āsana

PĀDA HASTĀSANA

5 to 8 Breaths or more
Dṛṣṭi: Nasagrai *(Nose)*

3 TRĪṆI

3RD POSITION, INHALE

Inhale

Strike Setup position.

— Lift your head, pull up through your extended arms, and stamp down on your hands with your feet.

— Pause, shift forward, and commit your body to this unusual position.

Vinyāsa Meta View

The act of stamping your feet with your hands and pulling up through your arms is a Mudrā (Energetic Seal) that helps you call up Prāṇa (Life Force) inside your body and awaken Buddhi (Discernment).

Exhale

Bring hands to waist; hold in position for complete exhale.

— Use this unlikely intermediate position to catch the elusive prize of Uḍḍīyāna Bandha *(Belly Flying Up Lock)*. Here are the steps:

- Stop cleanly at the halfway point and stay put.
- Direct the force of your out-breath down your spine to your pelvic floor.
- Grip your waist with your hands and brace your arms.
- Root back your thighs and project your spine forward in rapid succession.
- Hold steady with patience and marvel as your entire abdomen "Flies Up" into a hollow.

SAMASTHITI
0 POSITION

Inhale

Root legs and sweep torso up to standing.

— From the halfway point, inhale and swing your body upright with a sure move.

— Seek maximal length through your spine and legs as you bring your head and torso up from horizontal to vertical.

— Visualize drawing a large-diameter quarter circle in the air with your head as you come up.

Exhale

Bend knees and lower hips into a half-squat.

— Make a skillful crouch and build up energy for your spring move.

Inhale

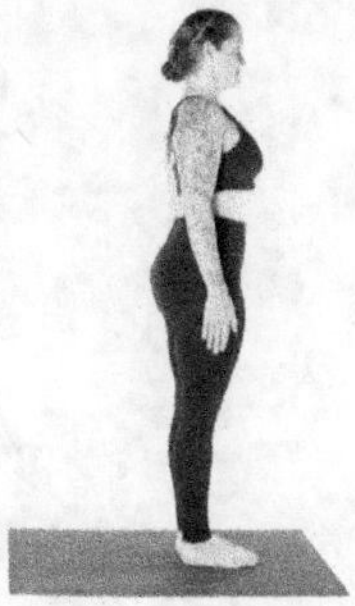

Strike Samasthiti Pratibhā!

— Hop your feet together dexterously, extend your arms and legs, and instantly strike a tall, delightful stance along the vertical axis.

Vinyāsa Meta View

The Sanskrit word "Pratibhā" is one of the greatest words ever. It means:

1) To manifest instantly.

2) To appear suddenly.

3) Brilliancy of conception.

4) To shine, appear bright, or luminous.

5) Boldness, confidence.

6) Genius.

Strike your Āsana PRATIBHĀ! Manifest a brilliantly conceived form instantly. Embody your shape boldly and swiftly, like a lightning bolt flashing across the night sky.

UTTHITA TRIKOṆĀSANA (Extended Triangle Pose)

SAMASTHITI
0 POSITION

Samasthiti.

— Stand as an act of total awakening. Find freedom within the rigor and structure of the form.

— Express the single vertical line well and soon you'll know the secret for drawing forth the intrinsic beauty of every pose.

1 EKAM
1ST POSITION, INHALE

Exhale

Crouch and get ready for action.

— Lower your hips into a generous half-squat and sweep your arms up to a horizontal axis with your fingers touching together in front of your sternum.

Inhale

Spring out to the right and extend arms!

— Jump your legs wide as you cast your arms away from each other in the side plane and land nimbly on the balls of your feet in a parallel stance.

Inhale (continued)

Angle feet and rotate legs; strike Setup.

— Angle your right leg out 90° and your left foot in 10°.

— Externally rotate your legs, level your pelvis, and make your spine tall along the vertical axis.

— Root your feet, ground your thighs, lift your navel, and open your chest.

— Fully extend your legs and arms; animate your entire skeleton to prepare for moving into Triangle Pose on the first side.

2 DVE
2ND POSITION, EXHALE

Exhale, 5 to 8 Breaths

Ground legs, swoop down, and grip big toe.

— Tip your pelvis to the side and reach out through your right arm.

— As you come down, use your well-anchored legs and arms to help you project your spine out into space.

— Catch your right big toe with your fingers or plant your right hand on the ground beside your front leg.

— Vertically stack your left hand, elbow, and shoulder.

— Reach straight up through the top arm expressing a gesture of continuous extension.

— Rotate your chest upwards any amount and turn your head to look up as a result of your spine's rotation.

— Gaze up past the thumb of your top arm.

State of the Āsana

UTTHITA TRIKOṆĀSANA

Right Side —
5 to 8 Breaths or more
Dṛṣṭi: Hastāgrai *(Hand)*

3 TRĪṆI
3RD POSITION, INHALE

Inhale

Sweep body upright and return to Setup.

— Keeping your legs anchored, pull up through your top arm and come to vertical in a single move synchronized with a sure inhalation.

Inhale (continued)

Switch feet and create Setup for second side.

— Angle your left leg out 90° and your right foot in 10°.

— Root your feet and externally rotate your thighs.

— Pull up your navel, lift your chest, brilliantly extend your arms and legs, and gear up for your move.

4 CATVĀRI
4TH POSITION, EXHALE

Exhale, 5 to 8 Breaths

Swoop down, grip big toe, strike second side.

—Tilt your pelvis to the left, reach out through your left arm, and lengthen your left side waist.

— Swoop your torso down and stop in place when you achieve a horizontal spinal line from your tail to your head.

—Reach down with your left hand and grip your left big toe.

—Reach up vertically through your right arm along a line that extends from your right shoulder through your right fingertips.

—Root your legs, lengthen your spine from tail to head, and rotate your chest upwards with a corkscrewing action.

—Turn your head and gaze up past your right thumb.

State of the Āsana

UTTHITA TRIKOṆĀSANA

Left Side —
5 to 8 Breaths or more
Dṛṣṭi: Hastāgrai *(Hand)*

5 PAÑCA
5TH POSITION, INHALE

Inhale

Return to the Setup position.

— Root down through your extended legs, pull up through your top arm, and draw your body upright as you fill your lungs to capacity.

FULL VINYĀSA

SAMASTHITI

Free Breathing

Switch feet.

— Get ready for the first side of Parivṛtta Trikoṇāsana.

PARIVṚTTA TRIKOṆĀSANA (Revolved Triangle Pose)

1 EKAM

1ST POSITION, INHALE

Inhale

Lengthen limbs, square hips, lift up spine; strike Setup.

— Angle your right leg out 90° and your left leg in 45°.

— Externally rotate your right thigh, internally rotate your left thigh, and square your hips and shoulders.

— Stamp down your feet, root your thighs, extend your legs, and channel weight into your lower body.

— Revolve your torso to the right and cast both arms up to the sky with surprising force.

— Pull up your navel and open your chest.

— Prepare for a dynamic forward bend.

Vinyāsa Meta View
Vinyāsa and Āsana mastery involve pre-arranging your pose before you actually move into it. It is wise to take full advantage of the tiny moment before you launch into action. Prepare, organize, and get ready!

2 DVE

2ND POSITION, EXHALE

Exhale, 5 to 8 Breaths

Swoop down, plant left hand, and twist.

— Hinge at your hips, tip your pelvis forward, and sweep your torso down to a horizontal axis with a sure move.

— Balance with poise as you firmly stamp your left hand or fingertips on the ground beside your right leg and reach up vertically through your top arm.

— Invest your legs and pelvis with great stopping power in order to both lengthen and rotate your spine.

— Twist evenly from tail to head. Focus on rotating your upper spine to open your chest towards the sky and win freedom to turn your head to the right and look up past your top thumb.

Vinyāsa Meta View
Use your stay in Triangle Pose to recite this Mantra that is given specially to lovers of Haṭha Yoga:

Limbs stop, spine goes.
Limbs stop, spine goes.

State of the Āsana

PARIVṚTTA TRIKOṆĀSANA

Right Side — 5 to 8 Breaths
Dṛṣṭi: Hastāgrai *(Hand)*

3 TRĪṆI

3RD POSITION, INHALE

Inhale

Pull up through top arm, stand up, turn feet parallel.

— To exit your pose skillfully: strike the earth with your feet, keep your legs maximally long and strong, reach up through your top arm, and hoist your torso up to the vertical Setup position with surprising speed and ease.

— Pull the air into your lungs against resistance from your throat *(Ujjāyī)* as you come up.

Inhale (continued)

Angle feet, reach arms overhead, strike Setup.

— Angle your left leg out 90° and your right leg in 45°.

— Perform the following premeditated actions:

- Externally rotate your front thigh and internally rotate your back thigh.
- Square your hips and shoulders.
- Extend your legs and reach up through your arms with astounding power.
- Expand your chest and pull up your navel.

FULL VINYĀSA

SAMASTHITI

4 CATVĀRI
4TH POSITION, EXHALE

Exhale, 5 to 8 Breaths

Rotate spine and come down into twist on the second side.

— Tip your pelvis forward and lower your torso towards the horizontal axis with a sure move.

— Plant your right hand or fingertips on the ground beside your front leg and reach up vertically through your top arm.

— As you arrive in position: plant your feet, brace your legs, and stabilize your pelvis. Do the work of anchoring your lower body to lengthen your spine and enhance your twist.

— Rotate your spine evenly from tail to head and also place extra emphasis on rotating your upper spine so that you can open your chest, turn your head freely, and gaze up past the thumb of your top arm.

Vinyāsa Meta View
Striking a masterful pose comes more easily when you formulate a clear Setup position and execute a confident transition.

State of the Āsana

PARIVṚTTA TRIKOṆĀSANA

Left Side — 5 to 8 Breaths
Dṛṣṭi: Hastāgrai *(Hand)*

5 PAÑCA
5TH POSITION, INHALE

Inhale

Pull up with top arm, come upright, make feet parallel.

— Plant your feet, stubbornly root your legs, and draw upon the power of the earth to sweep your body up to standing.

— Fully commit to your gesture and enlist participation from every tiniest corner of your body and mind.

SAMASTHITI
0 POSITION

Exhale

Crouch!

— Gently squeeze the air out of your lungs as you bend your knees and strike a sumo wrestler-like crouch.

Inhale

Spring to destination.

— Leap or step dynamically to the front of your mat.

— Arrive in Samasthiti with speedy skill and cause all thoughts to vanish.

— Reclaim your senses *(Pratyāhāra, Fifth Limb of the Eightfold Path of Yoga)* by turning them inward. Direct the flow of seeing, hearing, and feeling towards the inner world. Allow your mind to withdraw into the far interior of your body and take refuge in your Heart Center.

UTTHITA PĀRŚVAKOṆĀSANA (Extended Side Angle Pose)

SAMASTHITI
0 POSITION

Samasthiti.

— Send roots down into the earth through your feet and anchor your legs.

— Watch your spinal column wind vertically upwards, expressing its four natural curves with elegance and purpose, like smoke spiraling up from a fire and fearlessly merging into limitless space.

1 EKAM
1ST POSITION, INHALE

Exhale

Crouch, store up force, get ready to jump.

— In the same poised act: lower your hips into a half-squat and swing your hands in front of your chest with fingertips touching and forearms lined up along a horizontal axis.

Inhale

Spring to the right!

— Jump into a wide stance with feet parallel as you cast your arms away from each other in the side plane.

— Land nimbly on the balls of your feet with your arms horizontally extended.

Vinyāsa Meta View
A wise yogī brings a high degree of athleticism to this series of tiny leaps that make up the Vinyāsas of the standing poses. Benefits that result from becoming a skilled and nimble leaper include:

- *Strengthens the legs, arms, belly, and heart.*
- *Sharpens the mind, improves balance, and develops skill in risk-taking.*
- *Cleanses all body systems.*

Inhale (continued)

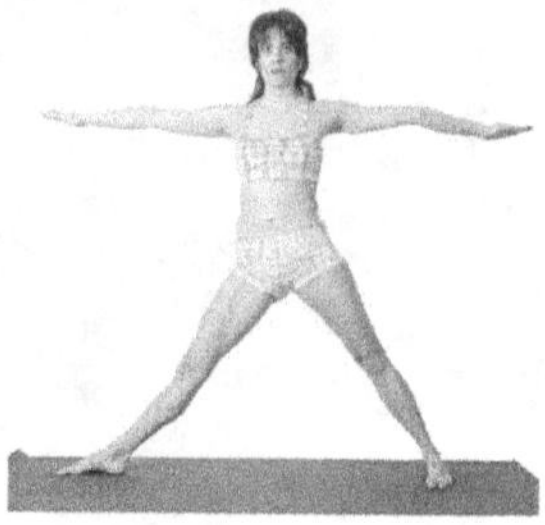

Angle feet; strike Set-up position.

— Angle your right leg out 90° and your left foot in 10°.

— Externally rotate your front thigh until the kneecap faces up and externally rotate your back thigh until the kneecap faces to the side.

— Lengthen your legs and spread your arms wide.

— Make your spine tall, pull up your navel, and anchor your tail.

— Skillfully negotiate the essential variables that go into setting up your pose.

2 DVE
2ND POSITION, EXHALE

Exhale, 5 to 8 Breaths

Lunge and swing left arm on the diagonal.

— Do this transition in two distinct parts:

1) Lunge to the right and strike Warrior II Pose for a brief moment.
2) Swing your left arm over your left ear and plant your right hand on the ground beside your right foot.

— In the pose, arrange your body along a diagonal line that starts with your back leg and extends through your top arm.

— Press your right outer knee against your right arm and root your back leg.

— Turn your chest up towards the sky by rotating your spine. Look upwards in front of your top arm and then gaze at your palm.

State of the Āsana
UTTHITA PĀRŚVAKOṆĀSANA
Right Side —
5 to 8 Breaths or more
Dṛṣṭi: Hastāgrai *(Hand)*

3 TRĪṆI
3RD POSITION, INHALE

Inhale

Return to the straight-legged Setup position.

— To maximally work your legs as you exit, stamp down your feet, root your thighs in position, then pull up through your top arm and strike Warrior II Pose for a brief moment.

— Next, straighten your front leg decisively, return to the Setup, and regain the original power stance that you started with.

Inhale (continued)

Switch feet and prepare to lunge to the left side.

— Angle your left leg out 90° and your right foot in 10°.

— Externally rotate your thighs, level your pelvis, and lift your chest.

— Lengthen and strengthen your arms and legs.

— Appreciate this excellent pre-position that you strike in anticipation of going into your pose.

4 CATVĀRI
4TH POSITION, EXHALE

Exhale, 5 to 8 Breaths

Lunge to left; sweep right arm on diagonal.

— Lunge to the left into Warrior II Pose and pause for a brief moment to establish your foundation.

— Then, with your legs rooted like tree trunks, swing your right arm over your right ear and reach up on a diagonal line that compliments the angle of your back leg.

— Plant your left hand outside your left foot and press your left leg against your firm left arm.

— Elongate your spine along the diagonal line that is formed by your back leg, torso, and top arm.

State of the Āsana

UTTHITA PĀRŚVAKOṆĀSANA

Left Side —
5 to 8 Breaths or more
Dṛṣṭi: Hastāgrai *(Hand)*

5 PAÑCA
5TH POSITION, INHALE

Inhale

Sweep body up to standing, feet parallel.

— Keep your lower body fixed in position while you pull up through your top arm and strike Warrior II Pose for a brief moment.

— Straighten your front leg and turn your feet to parallel.

— Prepare for the first side of Parivṛtta Pārśvakoṇāsana.

FULL VINYĀSA

SAMASTHITI

PARIVṚTTA PĀRŚVAKOṆĀSANA (Revolved Side Angle Pose)

1 EKAM
1ST POSITION, INHALE

Inhale

From previous position, stand tall.

— Maintain upright position with your legs in a wide stance.

— Extend limbs.

Inhale (continued)

Angle feet, rotate spine to right, windmill arms.

— Angle your right leg out 90° and your left leg in 45°.

— Bring your left hip forward and square your pelvis.

— Turn your torso to face your right leg; externally rotate your front thigh and internally rotate your back thigh.

— Stretch your arms horizontally away from each other and use them to help rotate your spine.

— Galvanize your body's forces and transform a mere position into a Yantra *(Magical Shape).*

2 DVE
2ND POSITION, EXHALE

Exhale, 5 to 8 Breaths

Lunge, twist, swing right arm on diagonal.

— Perform the following actions:

- Bend your right knee and lower your right thigh into a lunge while allowing your back heel to lift up slightly.
- Bring your torso down towards your right leg; rotate your spine to the right.
- Hook your left arm around your outer right knee and plant your left fingertips on the ground outside your right foot.
- Cast your right arm diagonally up over your right ear.
- Suck your right hip inward and continue to lunge deeply as you lengthen and root your back leg.

State of the Āsana

PARIVṚTTA PĀRŚVAKOṆĀSANA

Right Side —
5 to 8 Breaths or more
Dṛṣṭi: Hastāgrai *(Hand)*

3 TRĪṆI
3RD POSITION, INHALE

Inhale

Return to the Setup position.

— Come up to standing, extend your limbs, and strike the original Setup position.

Inhale (continued)

Angle feet, rotate spine to left, windmill arms.

— Angle your left leg out 90° and your right leg in to 45°.

— Square your hips and turn your torso to face your left leg.

— Externally rotate your front thigh and internally rotate your back thigh.

— Lengthen your arms horizontally away from each other and use them to enhance your twist.

Vinyāsa Meta View
Value pre-arranging your body in the Setup as much as being in the pose. This leads to Āsana mastery and offers you a potent, secret means of becoming more skillful in all of your actions.

FULL VINYĀSA

SAMASTHITI

4 CATVĀRI
4TH POSITION, EXHALE

Exhale, 5 to 8 Breaths

Lunge and twist on the way into position.

— Lunge deeply with your left leg and allow your back heel to come off the ground. Lower your torso, rotate your spine to the left, and hook your right arm around your outer left knee. Plant your right fingertips outside your left foot and reach your left arm diagonally up over your left ear.

— Stop in place and find these subtle pairs of opposites to balance your twist:

- Actively lunge through your front leg and root your back thigh.
- Push your left knee outward and tuck your left hip inward.
- Reach up and away with your top arm and lengthen your back leg in an opposite direction along the same diagonal line.

State of the Āsana

PARIVṚTTA PĀRŚVAKOṆĀSANA

Left Side —
5 to 8 Breaths or more
Dṛṣṭi: Hastāgrai *(Hand)*

5 PAÑCA
5TH POSITION, INHALE

Inhale

Return to Setup.

— Root your feet, strengthen your legs, and come up to standing with a gesture.

SAMASTHITI
0 POSITION

Exhale

Make feet parallel and crouch!

— Turn your feet to parallel, bend your knees into a powerful half-squat, and keep your arms extended along a horizontal axis.

— Make ready to leap buoyantly to the front of your mat.

Inhale

Spring to Samasthiti.

— Leap forward, command your landing, playfully strike the ground with your feet, and make a tall vertical pose instantly.

— Send a wave of awakened Life Force coursing up the Central Axis from your feet to the Thousand-Petaled Lotus Flower at the crown of your head.

PRASĀRITA PĀDOTTĀNĀSANA A (Wide-Legged Intense Forward Bend Pose A)

SAMASTHITI
0 POSITION

Samasthiti.

— Stand tall; visualize the Central Prāṇic Nāḍī *(Suṣumṇā)* situated in the middle of your body. This principal Energy Pole is as thin as a spider's thread and difficult to detect.

— Meditate upon this healing Pillar of Light, wake up to the world within your own body, and discover the magical realms of pure consciousness beyond ordinary thought.

1 EKAM
1ST POSITION, INHALE

Exhale

Crouch and get ready to leap.

— Lower your hips into a half-squat as you sweep your arms up and touch your fingers together in front of your chest.

— Pause; find a dynamic position on the edge of imbalance.

— Store up forces within your bones and become like a loaded spring before you leap into action.

***Vinyāsa* Meta View**
Take to the high art of Vinyāsa; create a conscious and playful position of risk whenever you crouch. Use risk to make yourself ready for action.

Inhale

Spring out to the right.

— Create a nimble but powerful landing. Touch down buoyantly on the balls of your feet and stamp down through your legs with earth-shaking power.

— In the same act, create a stance that is light like a cat and supremely grounded like a sumo wrestler on the ready.

Inhale (continued)

Hands to waist, brace legs, and open chest.

— Plant your feet with hands to waist, firm your limbs, and lift up your navel.

— Open your chest and drink in a full draft of Prāṇa.

— Get ready for a dynamic move.

2 DVE
2ND POSITION, EXHALE

Exhale, Inhale

Swoop down, plant hands, strike Setup.

— Hinge at your hips, bend forward, and stop with precision when your spine reaches a horizontal axis.

— Pause with tall, rooted legs and plant your hands on the ground. Fully extend your arms with your shoulders, elbows, and wrists in a vertical stack.

— Add great stopping power to your limbs to freely project your spine forward into space.

***Vinyāsa* Meta View**
The above halfway position is a crouch, a preparatory pose that you strike to build up energy in anticipation of boldly swooping your head down to the ground. Striking a Setup position followed by putting a commanding move in play is important because a doubtful transition leads to a doubtful pose, whereas a confident transition leads to a confident pose.

3 TRĪṆI
3RD POSITION, EXHALE

Exhale, 5 to 8 Breaths

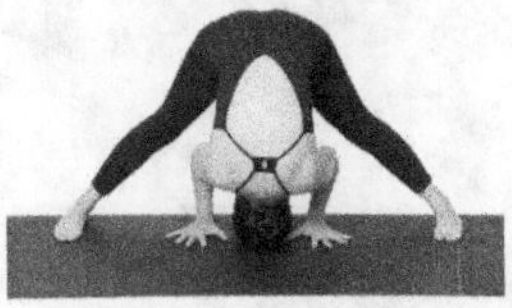

Bring head to ground between feet.

— Fold forward dynamically with a tiny, rhythmic swoop move.

— In a coordinated set of actions: stamp down your hands and feet, brace your arms and legs, round your spine into flexion, and plant your head on the ground.

— Walk your hands back and vertically stack elbows over wrists.

— Create five equal points of contact with the earth: your two feet, your two hands, and your head.

— Take note that as a round, weighted object, your head can be an important part of your foundation.

State of the Āsana

PRASĀRITA PĀDOTTĀNĀSANA A

5 to 8 Breaths or more
Dṛṣṭi: Nasagrai *(Nose)*

4 CATVĀRI
4TH POSITION, INHALE

Inhale

Lift head; strike halfway Setup position.

— Raise your spine up to horizontal and extend your arms. Stop in place and instantly stabilize your limbs.

— Vertically align your hips, knees, and ankles and also your shoulders, elbows, and wrists.

— Center your spine nicely between your four limbs.

— Hold steady as you brace your limbs, project your spine forward, and inhale.

Exhale

Hands to waist and hold at halfway Setup.

— Stay put with patience and direct the flow of your exhalation down your spine to its base.

— Use this unlikely position to catch the Belly Flying Up Gesture.

- Grip your waist with your hands.
- Exhale skillfully down the Central Axis to your pelvic floor.
- Brace your limbs; project your spine spine forward.
- Effortlessly suck your belly into a hollow.

Vinyāsa Meta View
Yogīs know this halfway Setup position as an oasis, one of many auspicious stopping points in the Primary Series where it's easy to drink deep from the secret well of Bandhas and gain great vitality.

5 PAÑCA
5TH POSITION, INHALE

Inhale

Come upright.

— Sweep yourself up to standing by elongating your spine and rooting your legs with an awakened breath.

— Pause, exhale with hands to waist, and anticipate Prasārita Pādottānāsana B.

PRASĀRITA PĀDOTTĀNĀSANA B (Wide-Legged Intense Forward Bend Pose B)

1 EKAM
1ST POSITION, INHALE

Inhale

Remain in a wide stance with hands to waist.

— Stamp down your feet with vigor, lengthen and strengthen your legs, grip your waist firmly with your hands, and brace your arms.

— Lift the pit of your abdomen and broaden your chest.

Inhale (continued)

Reach arms away from each other.

— Extend your arms with a mighty reach in the side plane and send lines of energy flowing out from your shoulders to your fingers.

— By the skill of your gesture, fill up your lungs to capacity.

2 DVE
2ND POSITION, INHALE

Exhale, Inhale

Return hands to waist and pause.

— Remain in your wide-legged stance with your arms akimbo and build up energy for your forward fold.

— Stamp down your feet, anchor your legs, brace your arms, pull up your navel, and open your chest generously.

— Inhale deeply and come to a peak of readiness before you fold forward.

3 TRĪṆI
3RD POSITION, EXHALE

Exhale, 5 to 8 Breaths

Sweep down in a semicircle and empty lungs.

— Boldly project your spine forward into space as you come down like a graceful diver executing a swan dive.

— Finish by rounding your spine and planting your head on the ground in line with your feet.

— When you arrive in position:

- Shift forward to place equal weight on your head and feet.
- Grip your waist with your hands to create a Mudrā *(Energetic Seal).*
- Add bracing power to your arms and legs; steady your body, breath, and mind.

State of the Āsana

PRASĀRITA PĀDOTTĀNĀSANA B

5 to 8 Breaths or more
Dṛṣṭi: Nasagrai *(Nose)*

4 CATVĀRI

4TH POSITION, INHALE

Inhale

Come up to standing with a gesture.

— Come up all at once. Make it a game to stand up in a single, reverse swoop synchronized with the suction force of your inhalation.

PRASĀRITA PĀDOTTĀNĀSANA C (Wide-Legged Intense Forward Bend Pose C)

1 EKAM

1ST POSITION, INHALE

Inhale

Maintain wide stance, hands to waist.

— Create a wide-legged version of Samasthiti with hands to waist.

— Anchor your feet, add great bracing power to your thighs, and firm your pelvis.

— Actively grip your waist with your hands and stabilize your arms akimbo.

— Pull up your navel and expand your chest greatly.

Vinyāsa Meta View
To become a connoisseur of the foundation of each pose, make the connection that your legs and arms work together as a team to provide the structure for your posture. In this instance, enjoy grounding your legs, making a powerful stance that supports your pelvis, torso, and head. Also, appreciate the auxiliary support that comes from firmly gripping your waist with your hands and bracing your arms. Finally, finish building your foundation by activating your four limbs as an ensemble.

Inhale (continued)

Reach arms out and fill up lungs.

— Stretch your arms out away from each other in the side plane. Be thorough about it; reach away through your arms from shoulder to fingertips.

— Allow this tiny gesture of extension to grow in importance by thinking of it as a Prāṇāyāma exercise, a device to fill up your lungs more thoroughly.

2 DVE

2ND POSITION, EXHALE

Exhale, Inhale

Clasp fingers behind back; remain upright.

— Extend your arms behind you and interlock your fingers.

— Roll back your shoulders and lengthen the line that spans from your shoulders to your fingers.

— Create a spirited Setup position and prepare to forward bend with the following actions:

- Firm your legs.
- Pull up your navel.
- Expand your chest.
- Picture the move that you are about to enact.

Vinyāsa Meta View
Begin the whole process of making your pose by asking the question, "What is my vision for my form?" Before you do the physical pose, take the time to create a mental picture of the shape you intend to make. Dream about the form and visualize what constitutes right effort or creative expression. Ponder questions such as,"What's the goal? What constitutes an ideal or very good pose? How shall I configure my arms and legs in relationship to the ground? How can I orient my spine in order to gain optimal support from my limbs?" Then translate your vision into a physical form, manifest your image, and suit your actions to your vision.

3 TRĪṆI

3RD POSITION, EXHALE

Exhale, 5 to 8 Breaths

Fold forward and bring head to ground.

— Sweep your head and torso down, brace your legs, and place the back of your head on the ground.

— As you arrive and strike your pose, shift forward and distribute your weight evenly between your head and your two feet.

— Lift up your pelvis and ground your legs as you reach away with your arms.

— Press down through your arms and work to bring your clasped hands towards the ground.

State of the Āsana

PRASĀRITA PĀDOTTĀNĀSANA C

5 to 8 Breaths or more
Dṛṣṭi: Nasagrai *(Nose)*

4 CATVĀRI

4TH POSITION, INHALE

Inhale

Hands to waist; sweep body upright all at once.

— Pull your body up to standing with a confident move.

— As you strike a vertical stance, bring your hands to your waist, exhale, and stand firm.

Vinyāsa Meta View

Deliberately play with a transition each time you repeat it. Be creative and daring! Exercise your power to joyously command your body! Use dynamic movement to strike a dynamic pose. Determine to single out each try, to express something new in each Crouch, Spring, and Destination. Speed up or slow down. Strike a form with dramatic propulsive power, like a stinging bee, or be light like a butterfly fluttering on a leaf. Don't get stuck in ignorance or habit! Use your study of Vinyāsa to stop resisting the law of constant change! By putting your body in motion and stopping at will with great skill, join the universe in its never-ending dance of changing forms.

PRASĀRITA PĀDOTTĀNĀSANA D (Wide-Legged Intense Forward Bend Pose D)

1 EKAM
1ST POSITION, INHALE

Inhale

Sustain wide stance with hands to waist.

— Plant your feet on this earth with the authority of I amness and fire up your legs with the healing power of enthusiasm.

2 DVE
2ND POSITION, EXHALE

Exhale, Inhale

Sweep down to halfway Setup position; empty lungs.

— Project your spine forward as you fold and stop at halfway.

— Grip your big toe knobs and shift forward to the edge of imbalance.

— Pause and animate your Setup position. *(inhale)*

— Ground your legs, lift up your torso, and straighten your arms.

— Press your thighs back and project your spine forward into the space away from your fixed legs.

— Strike your Setup to create a trustworthy transition and an auspicious pose.

Vinyāsa Meta View
The Haṭha Yoga Pradīpikā lists daring and courage as two of the six keys to speedy success in yoga. To be bold and daring requires that you possess the power to take risks and to act in the face of your fears. Fortunately, the arena of Vinyāsa (Transitioning) exists for you to practice risk-taking and thereby routinely meet your fears. Use your Setup to be bold, to summon courage. Then, follow through with an instance of pure action, let fly your move, test your skill in balalnce, find the edges of your strength and flexibility!

3 TRĪṆI
3RD POSITION, EXHALE

Exhale

Lower head to ground between feet.

— Swoop down confidently!

— Deftly squeeze the air out of your lungs and plant your head on the ground between your feet.

— Grip your toes, strengthen your arms, and shift your body subtly forward.

— Lift your pelvis, lengthen your legs, and perfect your balance.

State of the Āsana

PRASĀRITA PĀDOTTĀNĀSANA D

5 to 8 Breaths or more
Dṛṣṭi: Nasagrai *(Nose)*

4 CATVĀRI
4TH POSITION, INHALE

Inhale

Lift head up, lengthen spine, extend arms, and stop.

— Thrust upward through your head and spine, straighten your arms, grab on to your big toes, and light up your position at halfway.

Exhale

Hold steady at halfway with hands to waist; exhale.

— Stay put for the entire duration of your out-breath.

— Drive your breath down the spine to your navel and anchor your legs.

— Utilize the great stopping power of your legs to shoot your spine forward and hollow out your belly all at once.

5 PAÑCA

5TH POSITION, INHALE

Inhale

Stand up and breathe in.

— From the halfway point, swing yourself up to the original, powerful, wide-legged standing position with a well-timed inhalation.

Vinyāsa Meta View

Savor the tiny move knowing that Yama, God of Death, is always near.

SAMASTHITI

0 POSITION

Exhale

Crouch!

— Coil your body into a dynamic crouch and call upon Agni to awaken your inner fire.

Vinyāsa Meta View

Be loyal to Agni, God of Fire, by working to master the Crouch and Spring with each transition and you'll gain the power to:

- *Digest whatever you ingest, material or psychic.*
- *Perform Tapas (Austerities); purify body and mind.*
- *Burn up yesterday's mistakes with the fire of today's skillful action.*
- *Ignite your creativity, galvanize your energies, take to your special work.*
- *Motivate yourself to attain heights beyond your limits.*
- *Focus your mind on what matters; be one-pointed!*
- *Shine with enthusiasm and awakened consciousness.*
- *Reduce aversion, hate, envy, fear, anger, sadness, and divisiveness to ashes.*
- *Clear the field of your mind and perceive what is right, suitable, and beautiful.*
- *Remain rooted in the central seat of your spiritual essence.*

Inhale

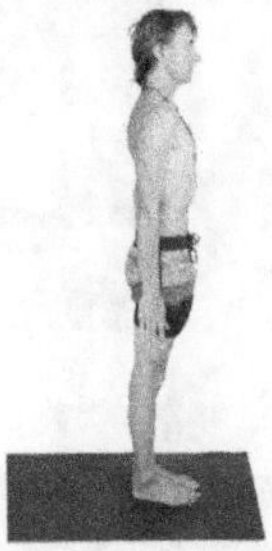

Spring to destination.

— Jump or step dynamically to the front of your mat.

Fire Element

PĀRŚVOTTĀNĀSANA (Side Intense Forward Bend Pose)

SAMASTHITI
0 POSITION

Samasthiti.

— Stand firm with your attention absorbed inside your body. Invest your legs and arms with great stopping power.

— Then, follow this auspicious teaching from the *Śvetāśvatara Upanishad:* "When he keeps his body straight, with the three sections erect (head, torso, pelvis) and draws the senses together with mind into his heart, a wise man shall cross all the frightful rivers with the boat consisting of the image of Self."

1 EKAM
1ST POSITION, INHALE

Exhale

Coil body into a crouch.

— Bend your knees and lower your hips into a half-squat as you sweep your arms up in front of you.

— Connect with the ground, store up force in your limbs, and be nimble on your feet.

— Get ready to spring out to the side with a targeted burst of power.

Inhale

Leap out to the right and throw arms open.

— Dexterously jump or step to the right while casting your arms out into the side plane with a powerful gesture of extension.

— Land nimbly on the balls of your feet rather than back on your heels.

— Arrive in a wide stance with your feet parallel and your pelvis, torso, and head well centered above your adamant legs.

Inhale (continued)

Arms behind back, angle feet, square hips, lift chest.

— Roll back your shoulders and flip your hands together behind you in a gesture of prayer.

— Angle your right leg out 90° and your left leg in 45°. Square your hips and shoulders.

— Plant your feet, ground your thighs, and lengthen your legs.

— Brace your arms and press your hands into each other.

— Skillfully draw your breath in against resistance from your constricted throat *(Ujjāyī Prāṇāyāma).*

— Charge up your entire structure, summon swiftness of mind, and get ready to enact a great forward-bending move.

2 DVE
2ND POSITION, EXHALE

Exhale, 5 to 8 Breaths

Lower head or chin to right shin.

— Swoop down with a speedy move. Trust your strong, adamant legs and let fly a confident gesture. Touch your head to your shin without any doubt.

— Stamp your hands together, lift your elbows, and brace your arms.

State of the Āsana

PĀRŚVOTTĀNĀSANA

Right Side — 5 to 8 Breaths
Dṛṣṭi: Nasagrai *(Nose)*

3 TRĪṆI
3RD POSITION, INHALE

Inhale

Circle head and torso up to standing.

— Root down through your legs and expertly draw the air into your lungs as you sweep yourself upright all at once.

Vinyāsa Meta View
Actions like stamping the ground with your feet, lengthening your legs, bracing your arms, pressing your hands, and drawing in your breath skillfully against resistance from your throat are all examples of Mudrās or gestures that help you tap into the power of the Earth element. Beyond being physical gestures, these Mudrās are also prayers, devices to help you in your quest to know your secret essence that is none other than the Self, author of all creation, soul of every living thing.

Inhale (continued)

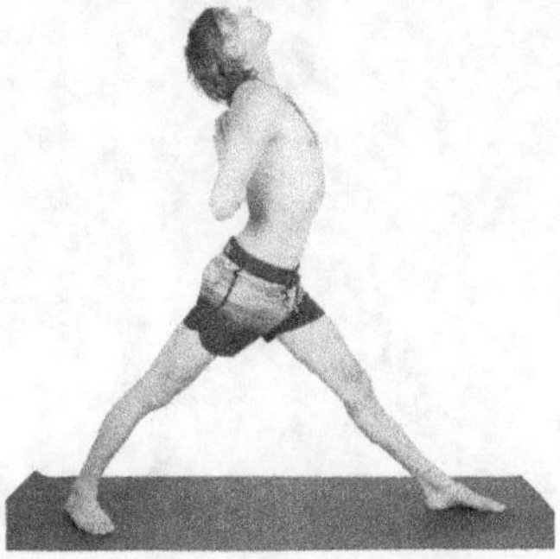

Angle feet, rotate legs, square hips, create Setup position.

— Angle your left leg out 90° and your right leg in 45°. Externally rotate your front leg and internally rotate your back leg. Square your hips and shoulders.

— Plant your feet, root your thighs, and lengthen your legs.

— Lift your belly and expand your chest. With hands positioned at the sweet spot between your shoulder blades, actively stamp your hands together and also push them forward into your back in an effort to help lengthen your thoracic spine and open your chest.

— Hold in position, galvanize your forces, and get ready to gesture daringly.

4 CATVĀRI
4TH POSITION, EXHALE

Exhale, 5 to 8 Breaths

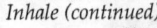

Swoop down.

— Project your spine forward while you come down; focus on striking a decisive end point as you touch your head to your shin.

Vinyāsa Meta View
By repeatedly taking a chance and executing your transition as a dynamic, whole-body gesture, you can gain skill in balance, build core strength, and learn to light up the subtle energy circuits (Nāḍīs) within you.

State of the Āsana

PĀRŚVOTTĀNĀSANA

Left Side — 5 to 8 Breaths
Dṛṣṭi: Nasagrai *(Nose)*

PĀRŚVOTTĀNĀSANA (Side Intense Forward Bend Pose)

5 PAÑCA
5TH POSITION, INHALE

Inhale

Come up to standing.

- Swing your body upright with speedy skill and pull the air in against resistance from your narrowed throat.
- Use rhythm to come up and make a clean, percussive stop at your chosen destination.

SAMASTHITI
0 POSITION

Exhale

Crouch!

- Make your feet parallel, release your arms, and bend your knees into a low crouch.

Inhale

Spring to Samasthiti.

- Jump or step dynamically to the front of your mat.
- Strike Samasthiti and delight in attending to the fiery Middle Axis *(Suṣumṇā).*

UTTHITA HASTA PĀDĀṄGUṢṬHĀSANA (Extended Hand to Big Toe Pose)

SAMASTHITI
0 POSITION

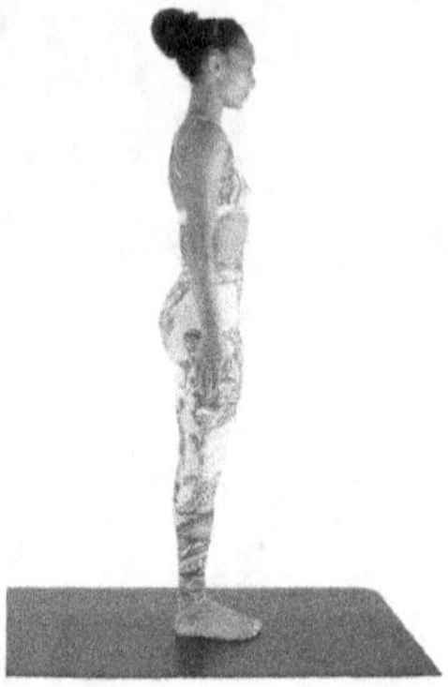

Samasthiti.

— Stand tall, strong, and awake.

— Withdraw your mind and senses; apply yourself well to the yoga of standing.

— Be an able sentinel guarding the inner fortress, warding off unwanted desires, those thieves that steal away your breath, siphon off your vitality, and snatch up your equanimity.

1 EKAM
1ST POSITION, INHALE

Inhale

Swing right leg up and catch big toe.

— Swing your right leg up in front of you and grip your right big toe.

— Before you bend forward, patiently express your Setup position with the following actions:

- Kick forward and up through your right foot; extend your right leg brilliantly as you brace your right arm and resist the forward thrust of your leg.
- Stand tall on your left leg and powerfully ground your left thighbone.
- Vertically stack your head, torso, pelvis, and standing leg.
- Grip your left side waist with your left hand and stabilize your left arm.
- Energize your skeletal lines en masse and know the power of striking a skillful Setup position.

— *Pro tip:* when you play opposing actions off each other, for example, boldly kicking forward with your leg versus tenaciously resisting with your arm—Voilà! Like magic, unsteadiness is transformed into adamant stability.

2 DVE
2ND POSITION, EXHALE

Exhale, 5 to 8 Breaths

Lift right leg and bow head.

— Fold forward with a mighty swoop and lift up your right leg with intensity.

— Lift your leg up to meet your head instead of bowing your head to meet your leg.

— As you bow, avoid:

1) Shifting your pelvis back.
2) Lowering your extended leg.
3) Bending your standing leg.

— In short, remain as upright as possible as you work to touch your head to your extended leg.

State of the Āsana

UTTHITA HASTA PĀDĀṄGUṢṬHĀSANA

Right Side — 5 to 8 Breaths
Dṛṣṭi: Pādayorāgrai *(Foot)*

3 TRĪṆI
3RD POSITION, INHALE

Inhale

Sweep torso upright to a clean stop and hold.

— Come up with economy and instantly animate your body along the vertical axis. This means stand tall, redouble the grip on your big toe, and renew your effort to kick forward with the right leg as you pull back in resistance with your right arm.

4 CATVĀRI
4TH POSITION, EXHALE

Exhale, 5 to 8 Breaths

Take leg out to right side.

— Circle your right leg out to the right with a playful throw and stop with precision when you reach the side plane.

— Stabilize your torso as you turn your head to the left and cast your gaze to the left.

— Actively kick out through your fully extended right leg and pull back towards you with your fully extended right arm. Awaken these opposing forces to create more steadiness and ease.

State of the Āsana

UTTHITA HASTA PĀDĀṄGUṢṬHĀSANA

Right Side — 5 to 8 Breaths
Dṛṣṭi: Pārśva *(Side)*

5 PAÑCA
5TH POSITION, INHALE

Inhale

Return right leg to center and strike Setup.

— With a move, return your right leg to the front by boldly sending your leg hurling through space to your chosen destination.

— Stop your leg movement with command, then pause and re-establish the upright Setup position.

— Lengthen your right leg and arm, lift your chest, strongly pull up your navel, and cause the great bird of Prāṇa to fly up the Middle Channel *(Suṣumṇā).*

6 ṢAṬ
6TH POSITION, EXHALE

Exhale

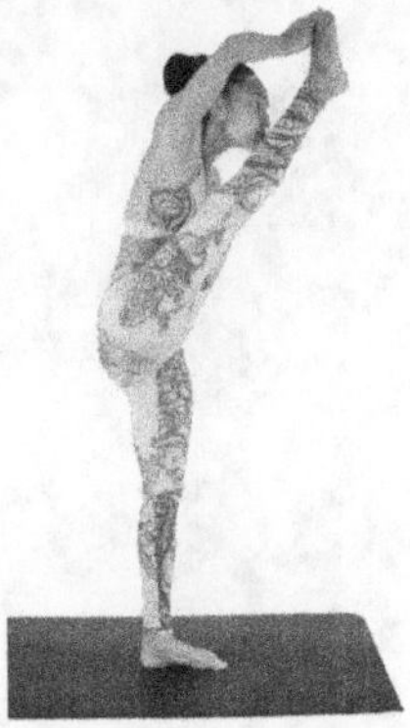

Kick up through right leg and bow forward.

— To execute this transition with Āsana savvy, follow this basic plan just before you bow forward:

1) Lift up your right leg any little bit.
2) Stubbornly stabilize your pelvis on the vertical axis.
3) Keep your standing leg maximally tall.

— As you go into action and fold forward, make a heroic effort to prioritize the three projects above instead of merely trying to get your head to your leg.

7 SAPTA
7TH POSITION, INHALE

Inhale

Return upright to Setup.

— Come up decisively; hold on to your big toe for a moment and extend your limbs brilliantly. Become a lover of expressing the upright root position.

UTTHITA HASTA PĀDĀṄGUṢṬHĀSANA (Extended Hand to Big Toe Pose)

5 to 8 Breaths

Bring hands to waist and lift up right leg.

— Release your big toe, take your hands to your waist, and powerfully lift up your extended leg.

— Hold steady and meet the challenge of keeping your body masses (head, torso, pelvis, standing leg) aligned in a vertical stack over one another.

— Kick forward through your right leg and stubbornly maintain its height.

State of the Āsana

UTTHITA HASTA PĀDĀṄGUṢṬHĀSANA

Right Side — 5 to 8 Breaths
Dṛṣṭi: Pādayorāgrai *(Foot)*

8 AṢṬAU

8TH POSITION, INHALE

Exhale

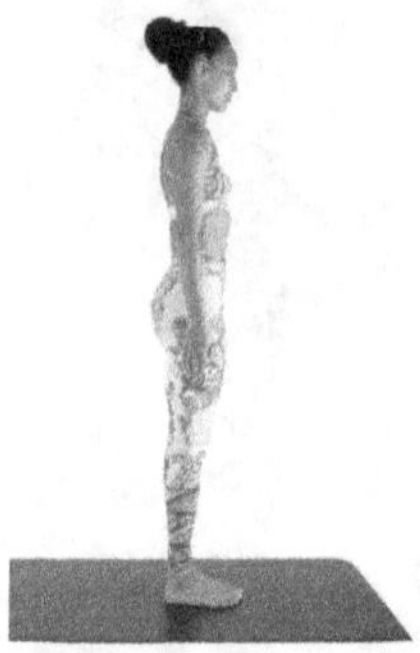

Return to Equal Standing.

— Bring your right leg down to Samasthiti, mother of all forms.

Inhale

Hoist left leg up and grip left big toe.

— Lift up your left leg, use the middle and index fingers of your left hand to catch a firm hold on your left big toe.

— Straighten both legs and fully extend your left arm.

— Grip your right side waist with your right hand and brace your right arm.

— Bring your Setup position to life. Thrust forward through your left leg with a mighty kick and pull back with your extended left arm.

— Powerfully straighten your standing leg and vertically align your head, torso, and pelvis.

Vinyāsa Meta View
Properly value each Setup position and joie de vivre will be a frequent visitor in your Āsana world.

9 NAVA

9TH POSITION, EXHALE

Exhale, 5 to 8 Breaths

Elevate left leg and bow head; strike destination.

— As you bow forward, pull up strongly with your left arm and thrust up through your left leg.

— Avoid pushing your pelvis back or lowering your left leg as you bow. Stubbornly resolve to keep your standing leg well grounded.

State of the Āsana

UTTHITA HASTA PĀDĀṄGUṢṬHĀSANA

Left Side — 5 to 8 Breaths
Dṛṣṭi: Pādayorāgrai *(Foot)*

10 DAŚA
10TH POSITION, INHALE

Inhale

Come upright to the beloved Setup position.

— Lift your head and torso up to the vertical axis and grip your big toe.

— Kick forward with your left leg and strengthen your left arm in a play of opposites.

— Charge your limbs with vital energy. Pull up from the Root Support *(Mūlādhāra)* at the base of the Great Axis and delight in awakening your spine.

11 EKĀDAŚA
11TH POSITION, EXHALE

Exhale, 5 to 8 Breaths

Sweep leg out to the side.

— Take a chance and boldly cast your leg out to the side with a lively throw.

— Actively lengthen your left leg and brace your left arm as you execute the transition—this is how to add stability to your gesture.

— Stop cleanly when your leg reaches the side plane.

Vinyāsa Meta View
Make it a game to move with confidence and stop with confidence. Use repetition to overcome timidity, doubt, or fear of falling.

State of the Āsana

UTTHITA HASTA PĀDĀṄGUṢṬHĀSANA

Left Side — 5 to 8 Breaths
Dṛṣṭi: Pārśva *(Side)*

12 DVĀDAŚA
12TH POSITION, INHALE

Inhale

Deftly swing your left leg to the front and hold.

— Return your left leg to the center with a circular throw of your foot.

— To keep your body steady, kick away through your left leg and resist with your left arm as you boldly swing your leg to the destination. Actively playing with opposites is critical to developing skill in balance.

— Upon arrival, strike the upright root Setup position with renewed vigor.

13 TRAYODAŚA
13TH POSITION, EXHALE

Exhale

Lift up left leg and bow forward.

— Lift up your left leg to any little degree as you bow forward, rather than focusing on lowering your head to your leg.

— Exhale as you bow. Sweep the air out of your lungs and send Life Force traveling down your spine to its base.

UTTHITA HASTA PĀDĀṄGUṢṬHĀSANA (Extended Hand to Big Toe Pose)

14 CATURDAŚA
14TH POSITION, INHALE

Inhale

Come up to the vertical axis and hold steady.

— Return upright and continue to hold on to your big toe.

— Steady your limbs and send a surge of Awakened Energy up the Axis from the root of your spine to your Heart Center.

5 to 8 Breaths

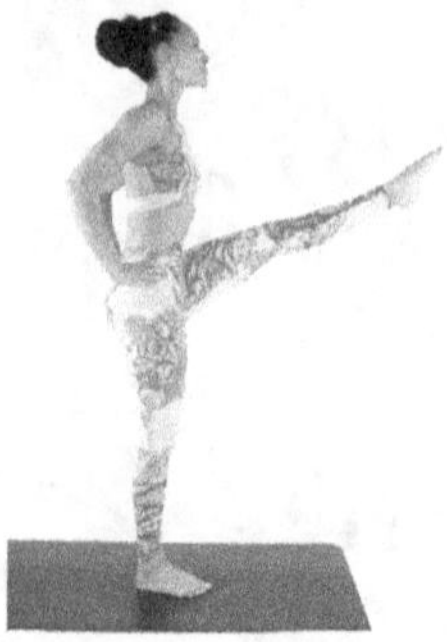

Bring hands to waist; maintain height of left leg.

— Release your toe and take your hands to waist.

— Kick forward and upward through your extended leg and patiently hold your position.

State of the Āsana

UTTHITA HASTA PĀDĀṄGUṢṬHĀSANA

Left Side — 5 to 8 Breaths
Dṛṣṭi: Pādayorāgrai *(Foot)*

SAMASTHITI
0 POSITION

Samasthiti.

— Root your feet into the earth and press your thighbones deeper into your legs. Use your well grounded legs to create a bouyant pelvis and pull up from the Root Support *(Mūlādhāra)* at the base of your spine.

— Send the mighty Kuṇḍalinī Force, made of subtle vitality, up the Axis. Join in the timeless ecstatic dance of the universe and know the unity of all life.

ARDHA BADDHA PADMOTTĀNĀSANA (Half Bound Lotus Stretching Pose)

SAMASTHITI
0 POSITION

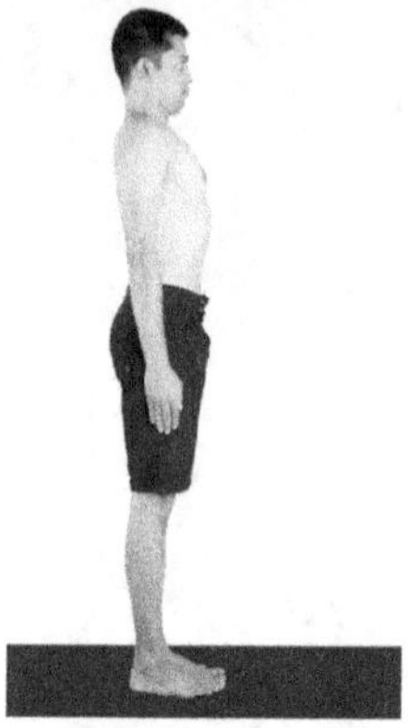

Samasthiti.

— Stand rooted in place with a steady mind.

— Lock the three Bandhas along the Glorious Axis *(Suṣumṇā Nāḍī).*

1 EKAM
1ST POSITION, INHALE

Free Breathing

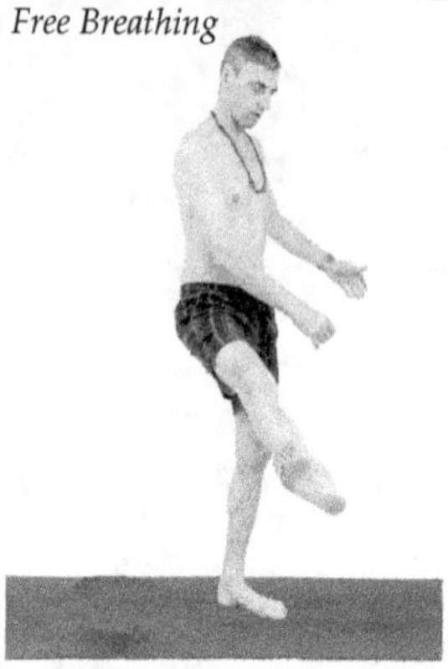

Turn right leg out and flip right foot into Half Lotus.

— To take your right foot into Half Lotus, perform a dynamic Flip Move with your foot and shin.

Flip Move instructions are:

— Stand upright. Lift your right foot off the ground; bring the foot six inches forward and six inches out to the right, keeping the leg fully extended.

— Turn your leg out by externally rotating your thighbone in the hip socket so that your kneecap faces to the side.

— Swing your right foot as high up your right thigh as possible.

— Ideally, by your leg action, you would fully achieve Half Lotus, but chances are you'll need to catch your foot with your hands at the end of the move and raise it up into position.

Inhale

Right leg to Half Lotus, bind foot with hand, strike Setup.

Upon achieving Half Lotus:

— Swing your right arm behind you and catch your right foot with your right hand.

— Pause and embody your Setup position with the following actions:

1) Entrust your weight to your standing leg and lift up your sternum.
2) Stabilize your pelvis at neutral by sucking up your belly and anchoring your coccyx.
3) Lengthen your right thigh in a downward direction from hip to knee and gently press your right knee back.

— Take charge of these actions, command your Setup, and be ready to fold forward boldly.

2 DVE
2ND POSITION, EXHALE

Exhale, 5 to 8 Breaths

Root standing leg and swoop down.

— Launch your torso forward into space confidently and come down curling your spine into flexion as you lower your head and torso towards your shin.

— As you stop in position, center your weight directly over your standing leg. Lift your pelvis, straighten the leg, and root your left arm.

***Vinyāsa* Meta View**
As a discerning yogī, perceive the fact that grounding your limbs elicits a response from your spine. It's a matter of planting your limbs in order to gesture with your spine. Here, in this pose, the gesture of the spine is a combination of releasing the whole column downward, waterfall-like, from tail to head, and actively sucking your torso towards the standing leg.

State of the Āsana

ARDHA BADDHA PADMOTTĀNĀSANA

Right Side — 5 to 8 Breaths
Dṛṣṭi: Nasagrai *(Nose)*

3 TRĪṆI
3RD POSITION, INHALE

Inhale, Exhale

Come up and pause at the halfway point.

— Lift up your head and chest, fully extend your left arm, and stop in place to define your Setup position.

— In the pause, ground your limbs and project your spine forward boldly.

— Zoom your out-breath down the length of your spine and scoop out your abdomen.

— A connoisseur of Mudrās knows that adopting this unlikely halfway position makes it easy to perform the Belly Flying Up Lock *(Uḍḍīyāna Bandha)*.

4 CATVĀRI
4TH POSITION, INHALE

Inhale

Return to standing and retain Bound Half Lotus.

— Return to standing and keep a grip on your Half Lotus foot.

— Pause and balance on one leg for a glorious moment.

5 PAÑCA
5TH POSITION, EXHALE

Exhale

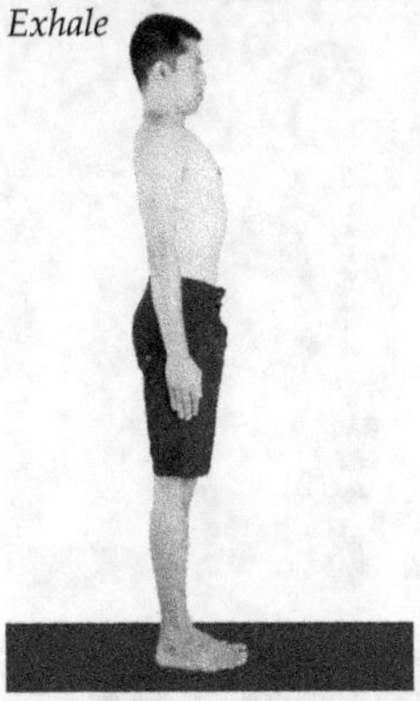

Release Lotus; return to Equal Standing.

— To release your Bound Half Lotus, let go of your foot with your hand, hinge at your right knee, execute a playful frog-like kick move with your right foot, and strike the root Yantra, Samasthiti.

ARDHA BADDHA PADMOTTĀNĀSANA (Half Bound Lotus Stretching Pose)

6 ṢAṬ

6TH POSITION, INHALE

Free Breathing

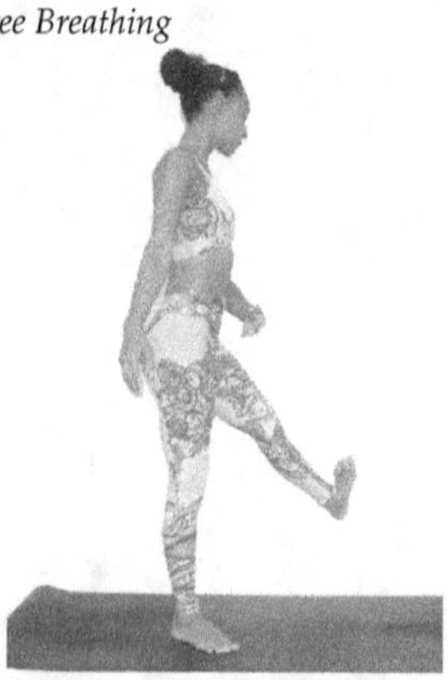

Flip left foot into Half Lotus.

— Bring your left foot into Half Lotus by strategically flipping your foot into position.

Flip Move instructions are:

— Stand upright. Lift your left foot just off the ground. Bring the foot six inches forward and six inches out to the left and keep the leg fully extended.

— Externally rotate your femur in the hip socket and turn your leg out so your kneecap faces to the side.

— Once you have your left leg positioned, swing your left foot onto the front of your right thigh.

— Ideally, you would achieve Half Lotus solely with the gesture of your leg, but you'll probably need to catch your foot with your hands and raise the foot up towards your navel into Half Lotus.

Inhale

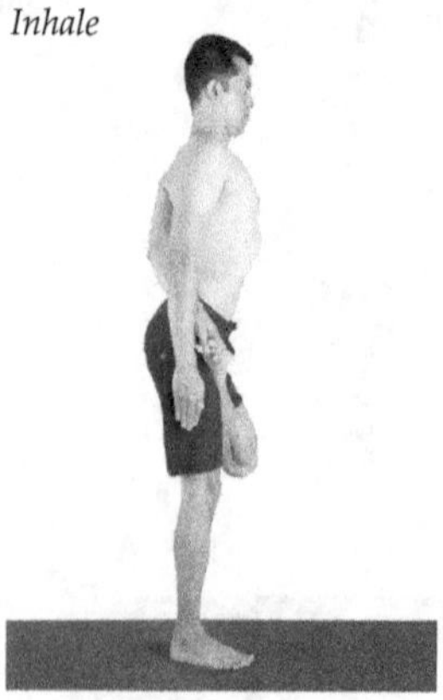

Swing left arm behind back and bind left foot.

Upon achieving Half Lotus:

— With rythm, throw your left arm behind your back and grip your left foot with your left hand.

— Pause and fully embody your Setup position with the following actions:

- Stamp your right foot down; stand firm on your right leg.
- Weight your tailbone and pull up your navel.
- Stabilize your pelvis, lengthen your left thigh, and press your left knee back.
- Get ready to test your skill in balance.

7 SAPTA

7TH POSITION, EXHALE

Exhale, 5 to 8 Breaths

Forward bend.

— Project your torso forward into space, then swoop down boldly. Plant your right hand on the ground outside your right foot and create a clean stop in a definite position.

— Swiftly introduce the following refinements:

- Shift forward to the edge of imbalance and vertically stack the hip, knee, and ankle of your standing leg.
- Engage in a continuous process of lengthening your standing leg.
- Press your left heel up into your belly as a device to trigger Uḍḍīyāna Bandha.
- Go with gravity; release your spine from tail to head in a waterfall-like, downward flow of energy.

State of the Āsana

ARDHA BADDHA PADMOTTĀNĀSANA

Left Side — 5 to 8 Breaths
Dṛṣṭi: Nasagrai *(Nose)*

8 AṢṬAU

8TH POSITION, INHALE

Inhale

Lift up to the halfway point and pause.

— When you stop at halfway, you are perfectly positioned to perform a vanishing act with your belly *(Uḍḍīyāna Bandha)*. The instructions are:

- Fix your foundation by lifting your head and chest high and rooting your limbs.
- Brace your right arm.
- Project your spine forward.
- Exhale down the length of your spine.
- Scoop out your abdomen into Uḍḍīyāna Bandha!
- Watch your mind fly into the auspicious void beyond all thought.

9 NAVA

9TH POSITION, INHALE

Inhale

Come up to standing; stop in place and hold.

— Come upright, keep your bind, and stand firmly on one leg for a distinct moment.

SAMASTHITI

0 POSITION

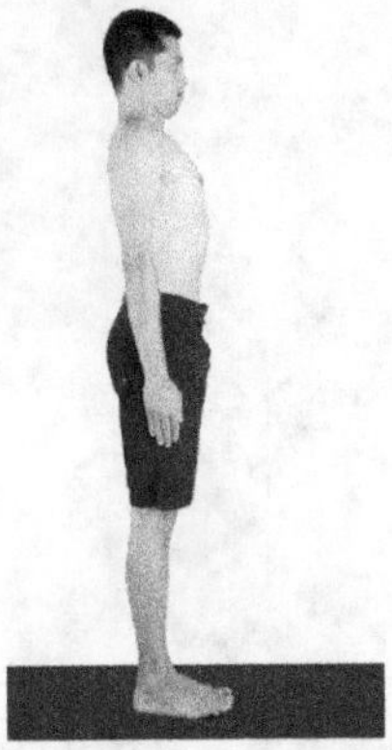

Samasthiti.

— Release your foot, strike the great Yantra, and dive into Universal Consciousness.

UTKAṬĀSANA (Fierce Pose)

SAMASTHITI
0 POSITION

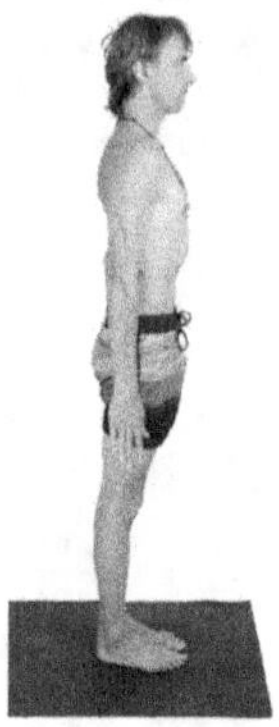

Stand tall, firm legs and arms, awaken center.

— Pull up your navel, cast your senses inward, and dive your body, mind, and soul into the limitless space of your Heart Center.

1 EKAM
1ST POSITION, INHALE

Inhale

Reach up; stamp hands together overhead.

— In a single move synchronized with the swift, sweeping sound of your inhalation, reach your arms up to the vertical axis.

2 DVE
2ND POSITION, EXHALE

Exhale

Fold forward into Uttānāsana.

— Elongate your spine as you fold forward.

— At the end of your move, stabilize your limbs, round your spine into flexion, and benevolently squeeze all the air out of your lungs.

3 TRĪṆI
3RD POSITION, INHALE

Inhale

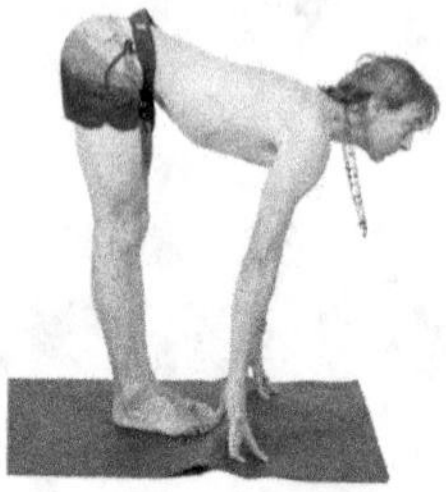

Lift up chest, extend arms, and stop.

— Lift your torso up towards horizontal, brace your arms, and press the earth with your fingertips.

— Stamp back your thighbones and project your spine far ahead out into space.

— Fill up your lungs to the brim; tank up on Prāṇa by pulling the air in against resistance from your narrowed throat.

4 CATVĀRI
4TH POSITION, EXHALE

Exhale

Crouch; prepare to jump back.

— Lower your hips towards the ground and suck your thighs underneath your torso.

— Shift your body forward, putting weight into your hands and arms.

— Embody this position well. Create a poised crouch and be ready for action.

Exhale (continued)

Jump or step back to Four-Limbed Staff Pose.

— Keep your body shifted forward.

— Swiftly bend your elbows as you shoot your legs straight back behind you.

— Arrive in the Horizontal Stick Shape and cleanly stop all movement.

Vinyāsa Meta View
Another equally important way to approach the jump-back move is to step or hop to Plank Pose, pause briefly with your arms straight, then bend your elbows and lower to Caturaṅga Daṇḍāsana.

5 PAÑCA
5TH POSITION, INHALE

Inhale

Rise up to Upward Facing Dog.

— Lift up your head in a circle, arch your spine, press your arms straight, and manifest your intention to create a magnificent backbend.

— Reach back strongly through your legs from your hips to your toes.

6 ṢAṬ
6TH POSITION, EXHALE

Exhale

Sweep hips back to Downward Facing Dog.

— Visualize your exhalation as a gust of wind that sweeps down the length of your torso from your collarbones to your pelvic floor.

— The source of your breath is Vāyu, Vedic God of the Wind, messenger of the Gods, pursing his lips and "whoosh"—blowing your hips back to Down Dog with an irresistible, benevolent force.

Vinyāsa Meta View
Vāyu (to blow, Air Element) is known for his great strength. He can summon enough wind force to uproot trees, blow down buildings, or wipe out any obstacle in his path. Vāyu's power serves to remind you of the astounding power of your own breath. However, most people rarely even notice their breath or consciously tap this mighty inner resource. Fortunately, the Vinyāsas of the Primary Series are specifically designed to help you wake up your breath and draw forth the latent Power (Life Force) housed in your center.

Air Element

UTKAṬĀSANA (Fierce Pose)

7 SAPTA
7TH POSITION, INHALE

Exhale

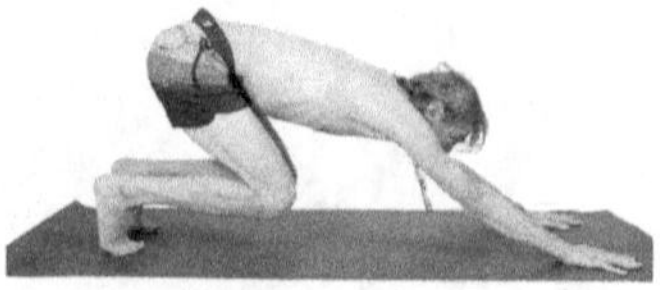

Crouch low.

— Lower your pelvis, hunker back, and press the ground with your hands.

— Gather power by activating your limbs and exhaling down your spine.

— Make a targeted forward leap.

Inhale, 5 to 8 Breaths

Spring forward, squat, and stamp hands together.

— Jump and plant your feet. Come upright, lower your hips into a half-squat, and reach up through your arms along a diagonal line in front of the vertical axis.

— Strike a form worthy of the word Utkaṭā—Fierce! Hunker down and make gravity your ally; connect to the earth with your feet and add weight to your thighs.

— Pull up your navel. Send a spectacular ascending force up through your spine and arms.

— Cause Śakti to rocket up the Middle Nāḍī and meet beloved Śiva in the Thousand-Petaled Lotus Flower at the crown of your head.

State of the Āsana

UTKAṬĀSANA

5 to 8 Breaths or more
Dṛṣṭi: Ūrdhva *(Upward)*

8 AṢṬAU
8TH POSITION, INHALE

Exhale

Bring hands to the ground and lean forward.

— To exit, bend your knees and lower your hips as you bring your hands to the ground.

— Keep your head up, lean forward, and add weight to your arms. Find power in your center and make ready to spring.

Inhale

Hop up and balance on arms.

— Jump up with a committed move. Keep your knees bent, sweep your feet up to a point directly over your hips, and skillfully balance on your arms.

— Remain suspended in a poised, upside-down position for a moment or two.

— Keep your heels to your seat in a squatting version of a handstand, or fully extend your legs into a proper handstand.

— If you can't balance on your arms, stay put in your crouch. Keep your hips low, tuck your legs up underneath you, shift forward, and rely on the strength of your arms to support you.

9 NAVA
9TH POSITION, EXHALE

Exhale

Strike destination.

— To lower from a handstand to Caturaṅga:
- Lean forward.
- Bend your elbows with control.
- Allow your legs to free fall to the ground in slow motion.
- Create a firm, nimble landing.

— In the gap before inhaling or moving, experience the interior field of your body as filled with nothing but pure space.

10 DAŚA
10TH POSITION, INHALE

Inhale

Lift head and straighten arms to Up Dog.

— Make a circle with your head and spine, open your chest, extend your arms with a press move, and reach back through your legs.

— Add weight and grounding power to your limbs to project your chest forward and achieve a satisfying spinal arch.

11 EKĀDAŚA
11TH POSITION, EXHALE

Exhale

Pull back through hips to Down Dog.

— Take aim, then swing your body back with a determined move, and arrive in Downward Dog all at once.

— Prepare for the first side of Vīrabhadrāsana A.

FULL VINYĀSA

12 DVĀDAŚA / INHALE — ARDHA UTTĀNĀSANA

13 TRAYODAŚA / EXHALE — UTTĀNĀSANA

SAMASTHITI

VĪRABHADRĀSANA A - B (Warrior Pose A - B)

7 SAPTA
7TH POSITION, INHALE

Inhale

Step right foot forward and lunge.

— Angle your left heel in 45° and step your right foot forward between your hands.

— Before you lift your arms and torso up, position your lower body in place with these actions:

1) Plant your foot on the ground between your hands.
2) Lower your right thigh into a deep lunge and line up your knee over your ankle.
3) Extend your back leg and root down your back foot (especially the ball of your big toe).

Inhale (continued), 5 to 8 Breaths

Come upright and reach arms overhead.

— Bring your torso upright, continue to lunge, and move your back hip forward towards square.

— Reach up overhead with your arms and stamp your hands together firmly on the vertical axis.

— Take your head back, gaze up past your thumbs, and draw your sternum forward.

— Widen your mid-back and center your rib cage evenly over your pelvis.

State of the Āsana

VĪRABHADRĀSANA A

Right Side — 5 to 8 Breaths
Dṛṣṭi: Ūrdhva *(Upward)*

8 AṢṬAU
8TH POSITION, EXHALE

Inhale

Return to Setup position and pause.

— Straighten your front leg, lift your hips, and define the Setup position for a brief moment.

Inhale (continued)

Switch feet and prepare for the second side.

— Stop well, galvanize your forces, and animate your whole skeleton.

— Angle your left leg out 90° and your right leg in 45°.

— Brilliantly extend your legs and arms.

— Bring your right hip towards square, lengthen your tail, and suck up your navel.

— Lift up your spine, open your chest, and send a mighty ascending force up your arms and out through your fingertips.

— Become ready to lunge with the commitment of a fencer on the attack.

FULL VINYĀSA

SAMASTHITI
1 EKAM / INHALE — ŪRDHVA HASTĀSANA
2 DVE / EXHALE — UTTĀNĀSANA
3 TRĪṆI / INHALE — ARDHA UTTĀNĀSANA
4 CATVĀRI / EXHALE — CATURAṄGA DAṆḌĀSANA
5 PAÑCA / INHALE — ŪRDHVA MUKHA ŚVĀNĀSANA
6 ṢAṬ / EXHALE — ADHO MUKHA ŚVĀNĀSANA

Exhale, 5 to 8 Breaths

Lunge deeply and strike Warrior A on the left side.

— Decisively lower your left thigh into a deep lunge. Track your left knee and thigh directly forward.

— Aim to make your thigh parallel to the ground.

— Lengthen and strengthen your back leg and bring your right hip towards square.

— Float your spine upwards and lift your pelvis up off your rooted legs.

— Stamp your hands together overhead, and with the limitless extent of your upward arm reach, contemplate infinity.

— Physically activate your body to awaken your center and cause Kuṇḍalinī to fly up the Middle Channel.

State of the Āsana

VĪRABHADRĀSANA A

Left Side — 5 to 8 Breaths
Dṛṣṭi: Ūrdhva *(Upward)*

9 NAVA

9TH POSITION, INHALE

Inhale, 5 to 8 Breaths

Transition to Warrior B on the same side.

— To go from Warrior A to Warrior B: keep your left thigh rooted in position, lower your arms to the horizontal plane, open your right hip (away from square), and extend your right leg.

— Pull up your navel strongly and lengthen your tailbone.

— Vertically align your head, torso, and pelvis.

— Reach both arms away from each other in the side plane.

— Turn your head to the left and cast a soft, steady gaze past the fingers of your left hand.

State of the Āsana

VĪRABHADRĀSANA B

Left Side — 5 to 8 Breaths
Dṛṣṭi: Hastāgrai *(Hand)*

10 DAŚA

10TH POSITION, EXHALE

Inhale

Come up, switch feet, and strike Setup on second side.

— Straighten your left leg and reverse your feet. Keep your legs extended as part of striking the Setup position.

— Angle your right leg out 90° and your left foot in 15°.

— Externally rotate your thighs, pull up your navel, and float the core of your heart.

— Reach through your arms in opposite directions along the horizontal axis and brace your legs.

Vinyāsa Meta View
Attending to your Setup position allows you to prepare your pose in advance. Adopt this method in earnest and you'll soon know the secret to creating a steady and agreeable form, no matter how difficult the pose.

Exhale, 5 to 8 Breaths

Lunge with the right leg and strike Warrior B.

— With a sure move, lunge to the right, lower your hips, and strike an adamant stance.

— Make your right thigh parallel to the ground and vertically stack the knee over the ankle.

— To establish a strong connection to the earth, lengthen and strengthen your back leg in contrast to lunging with your front leg.

— Add power to your foundation by pulling in opposite directions through your arms along the horizontal axis.

— Vertically stack your head and torso over your pelvis.

— Imagine your chest is a sun whose rays emanate outward in all directions sending healing light to all corners of space. By the purity of your efforts, light up this vast, wild cosmos.

State of the Āsana

VĪRABHADRĀSANA B

Right Side — 5 to 8 Breaths
Dṛṣṭi: Hastāgrai *(Hand)*

VĪRABHADRĀSANA A - B (Warrior Pose A - B)

11 EKĀDAŚA
11TH POSITION, INHALE

Inhale

Plant hands, right knee to upper arm, and arm balance.

— Plant your hands on the ground to either side of your right foot.

— Suck your right knee to the back of your right upper arm and lift up your right foot towards your right buttock.

— Lean forward, clear your left leg off the ground, and momentarily balance on your arms *(Eka Pāda Bakāsana).*

Vinyāsa Meta View

Alternate way to transition from Vīrabhadrāsana B: Step to Plank and pause.

— *Plant your hands on the ground to either side of your right foot and step back to Plank.*

— *Hold in the straight-armed, straight-legged position for a brief moment.*

— *Stabilize your head, torso, and pelvis accurately along the horizontal axis.*

12 DVĀDAŚA
12TH POSITION, EXHALE

Exhale

Jump back to Caturaṅga Daṇḍāsana.

— Remain forward and shoot your legs back as you bend your elbows; lower yourself to Caturaṅga Daṇḍāsana.

— Fully prostrate and transform your body into Prasad, a blessed offering to the Great Spirit.

13 TRAYODAŚA
13TH POSITION, INHALE

Inhale

Press the ground; inhale to Up Dog.

— Lift up your head, straighten your arms, root your legs, and make a graceful circular arch with your spine.

— Use timing, rhythm, and momentum to execute this move.

14 CATURDAŚA
14TH POSITION, EXHALE

Exhale

Flow back to Down Dog with a power move.

— Catapult your hips back playfully and discover the elemental force of the Wind *(Vāyu)* that is woven, "warp and woof," into your every breath.

Vinyāsa Meta View

The yoginī Gārgī asked the sage Yājñavalkya questions about the ultimate source of this world using weaving as an analogy in which the warp (threads that run lengthwise) and the woof (threads that run across) make up the fabric.

Gārgī: "On what are the worlds of the sun woven, warp and woof?"

Yājñavalkya: "On the worlds of the stars, Gārgī."

Gārgī: "On what then are the worlds of the stars woven, warp and woof?"

Yājñavalkya: "On the worlds of the gods, Gārgī."

Gārgī: "On what then are the worlds of the gods woven, warp and woof?"

Yājñavalkya: "On the worlds of Brahman (Self), Gārgī."

Gārgī: "On what then are the worlds of Brahman woven, warp and woof?"

Yājñavalkya: "Don't ask too many questions or your head will shatter apart. You are asking too many questions about a deity one should not ask too many questions about."

Thereupon Gārgī fell silent.

— Excerpt from the Bṛihadāraṇyaka Upanishad (Verse 3.6.1).

FULL VINYĀSA

15 PAÑCADAŚA / INHALE — ARDHA UTTĀNĀSANA
16 ṢOḌAŚA / EXHALE — UTTĀNĀSANA
SAMASTHITI

PASCHIMOTTĀNĀSANA A - B (Intense Western Stretching Pose A - B)

7 SAPTA

7TH POSITION, INHALE

Exhale

Crouch.

— Turn your attention to the all-important Crouch before the Spring!

— Playfully lower your body towards the earth and practice the great skill of exhaling.

— Hunker back by driving your hips away from your rooted hands.

— Pointedly store up force in your legs and belly; prepare in earnest for a great leap.

Inhale

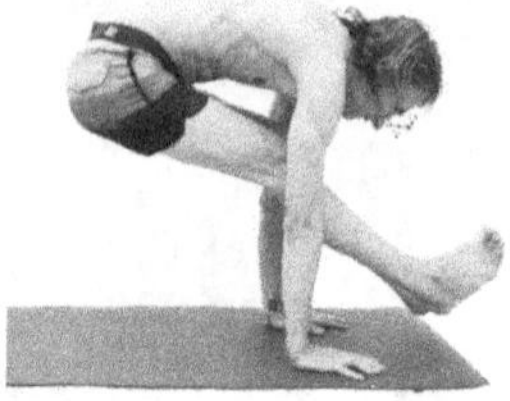

Spring forward!

— Like a pouncing cat, jump forward suddenly.

5 to 8 Breaths

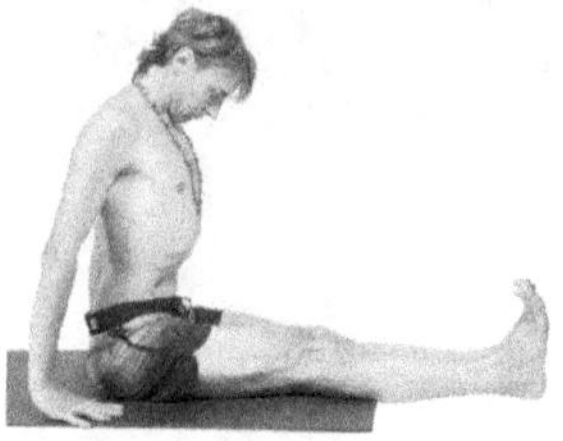

Take Staff Pose and hold steady.

— Swiftly animate your body in Daṇḍāsana with these actions:

- Stamp down your thighs and channel weight into your legs.
- Plant your hands on the ground beside your hips and brace your arms.
- Pull up your navel, expand your chest, and lower your chin.

State of the Āsana

DAṆḌĀSANA

5 to 8 Breaths or more

Dṛṣṭi: Pādayorāgrai *(Feet)*

Inhale

Grip toes; strike Setup position.

— Reach forward, grip your big toes, and get ready for action.

— Stamp down your thighs and lengthen your legs from your hips to your feet.

— Pull back with your arms, lift your chest mightily, and fly your belly into a hollow.

— Understand the wisdom of getting ready for action before taking action.

Vinyāsa Meta View

Dear student, let me tell you just how important the Setup position is: like your shadow always follows you, the pose always follows the Setup. To take it one step further, the greater hidden Self that dwells within you is the source of your smaller, physical self, just like the Setup position is the profound, hidden source of the pose.

FULL VINYĀSA

SAMASTHITI

1 EKAM / INHALE — ŪRDHVA HASTĀSANA

2 DVE / EXHALE — UTTĀNĀSANA

3 TRĪṆI / INHALE — ARDHA UTTĀNĀSANA

4 CATVĀRI / EXHALE — CATURAṄGA DAṆḌĀSANA

5 PAÑCA / INHALE — ŪRDHVA MUKHA ŚVĀNĀSANA

6 ṢAṬ / EXHALE — ADHO MUKHA ŚVĀNĀSANA

8 AṢṬAU
8TH POSITION, EXHALE

Exhale, 5 to 8 Breaths

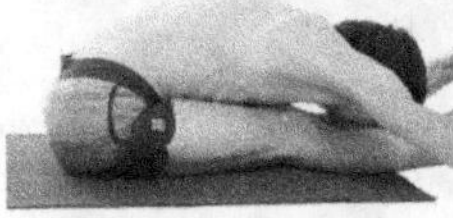

Fold forward.

— Sweep your head down towards your rooted legs, like closing a jackknife.

— As you come down and stop in place, squeeze all of the air out of your lungs.

— Upon arrival, increase the weight of your legs, arms, head, and torso.

— Befriend gravity, love the elemental quality of Earth, and find pure inertia as your means of entering a state of yoga.

— Gaze toward your feet or forward along your shins or look down.

State of the Āsana

PASCHIMOTTĀNĀSANA A

5 to 8 Breaths or more
Dṛṣṭi: Pādayorāgrai *(Feet)*

9 NAVA
9TH POSITION, INHALE

Inhale

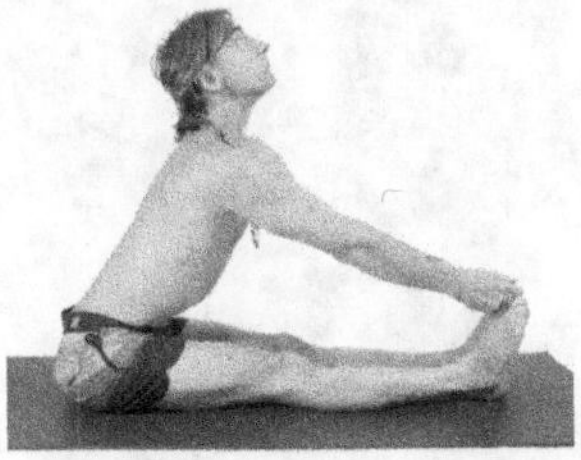

Lift head, extend arms, and pause.

— With a purposeful move, ground your legs, lift up your torso, pull back with your arms, and make a dynamic stop in place.

Exhale, Inhale

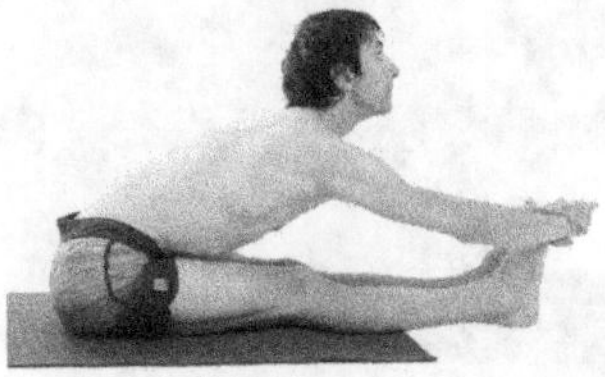

Reach forward; take the Setup for Paschimottānāsana B.

— Catch your wrist around the balls of your feet and pause.

— To animate your Setup position:

1) Stamp down your legs and pull back towards you through your arms.

2) Lift up your head, expand your chest, and pull up your belly.

Exhale, 5 to 8 Breaths

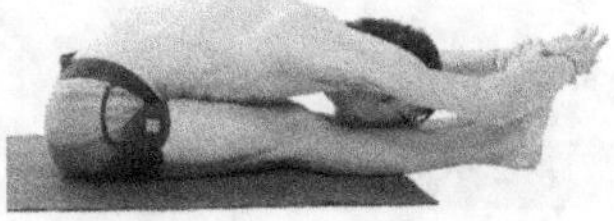

Fold forward with a clear exhalation.

— Sweep your head down towards your legs in time with flushing the air out of your lungs.

— Find a clear stopping place and create dynamic stillness with the following actions:

- Lengthen and strengthen your legs.
- Firm up the connection between your hands/wrists and balls of your feet.
- Lift up your elbows to a middle point and brace your arms.
- Elongate your spine while allowing your body masses to increase in weight and drop.
- Send the flow of your breath up (inhale) and down (exhale) the length of your spine.
- Wake up your sleeping center and cause Life Force to flow within Suṣumṇā Nāḍī.

State of the Āsana

PASCHIMOTTĀNĀSANA B

5 to 8 Breaths or more
Dṛṣṭi: Pādayorāgrai *(Feet)*

PASCHIMOTTĀNĀSANA A - B (Intense Western Stretching Pose A - B)

10 DAŚA
10TH POSITION. INHALE

Inhale

Lift up chest, return to Setup position, and pause.

— Hold on to your wrist, pull back on your feet with your interlocked hands, and stop at a halfway point.

— Instantly stabilize your limbs and lengthen your spine.

— Lift the pit of your abdomen and find the Belly Flying Up Lock.

Vinyāsa Meta View
Distinctly stopping at the halfway point and animating your body each time you exit a seated forward bend is difficult to achieve, but by practicing this method many Yoga Siddhas have gained superpowers such as: Vāyu Siddhi (Breathing Power), Agni Siddhi (Fire Making Power), and Pṛthivī Siddhi (Grounding Power).

Exhale

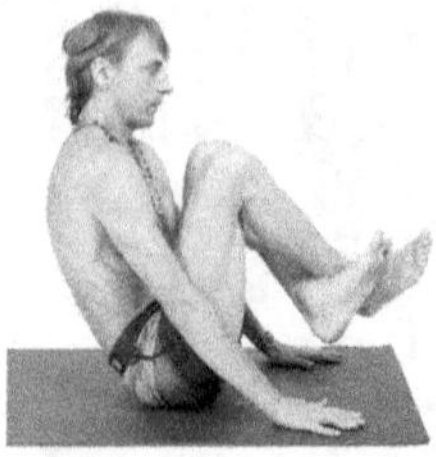

Breathe out and prepare to lift up.

— Sit up and lean back, bend your knees, and cross your ankles.

— Lift up your feet, keep your seat down, and plant your hands on the ground in front of your hips.

— Stop in this position to build up energy; anticipate the supreme power move that you are about to enact.

11 EKĀDAŚA
11TH POSITION. INHALE

Inhale

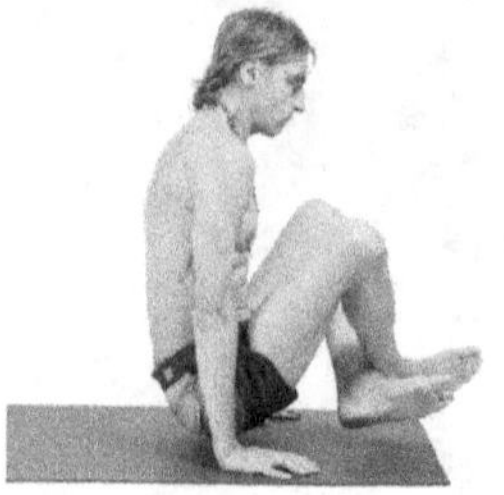

Strike the ground and lift up!

— Stamp down with your hands and lift up your seat and feet equally.

— Suck your feet back and begin to lean forward with your head and chest.

12 DVĀDAŚA
12TH POSITION. EXHALE

Exhale

Jump back.

— Bend your elbows, pivot on your arms, swing your upper body forward and down as you drive back with your feet and legs.

Exhale (continued)

Stop in place and finish exhaling.

— As you arrive, swiftly invest your whole body with great stopping power.

— Control the positioning of your head, torso, pelvis, and legs and achieve a gravity-defying daṇḍa.

— By creating a cessation of bodily movement and thought activity, become mesmerized, transported, enraptured.

13 TRAYODAŚA

13TH POSITION, INHALE

Inhale

Circle up to the peak of Upward Dog.

— Lift up your head, arch your spine, and root down through your extended arms.

— Take your head up, over, and back with a spiral gesture as you reach back through your legs from hips to toes.

— Strike a snake-like form.

14 CATURDAŚA

14TH POSITION, EXHALE

Exhale

Come to Down Dog all at once.

— Swing your hips back with great rhythm and ride the wave of energy all the way back to Downward Dog without interruption.

— Upon arrival, pause. Take an extra breath or two in Downward Dog whenever you like. Reset your position like returning to Samasthiti between standing postures.

FULL VINYĀSA

15 PAÑCADAŚA / INHALE — ARDHA UTTĀNĀSANA
16 ṢOḌAŚA / EXHALE — UTTĀNĀSANA
SAMASTHITI

PURVOTTĀNĀSANA (Intense Eastern Stretching Pose)

7 SAPTA
7TH POSITION, INHALE

Exhale

Crouch!

— Hunker back with great earnestness; repeatedly take to expressing the animal crouch. Plunge wholeheartedly into the adventure of your practice, like a child at play, fully immersed in a world of make-believe.

Inhale

Jump through feetfirst; sit down.

— Leap purely forward, not up.

— Aim to land your feet well in front of your hands.

Exhale

Take hands back and strike Setup position.

— Plant your hands on the ground about twelve inches behind your hips with fingers facing forward.

— Extend your arms, root down through your thighs, and straighten your legs.

— Keep your hips down. Lift your chest and use vacuum suction to draw your spine into an arch within your torso.

— Store up great quantities of Life Force within your entire body and make ready to lift up to a reverse plank pose.

8 AṢṬAU
8TH POSITION, INHALE

Inhale, 5 to 8 Breaths

Rise up, expand chest, and lengthen limbs.

— Lift up your head, brace your arms, throw open your chest, and suck your spine up into a bow shape within your torso.

— Upon arrival, lengthen your legs and ground your thighs.

— Take your head back freely and increase the height of your dome-shaped chest.

— Circle your nose up and over; cast your gaze back and down towards the ground.

State of the Āsana

PURVOTTĀNĀSANA

5 to 8 Breaths or more
Dṛṣṭi: Broomadhya
(Eyebrow Center)

FULL VINYĀSA

SAMASTHITI
1 EKAM / INHALE — ŪRDHVA HASTĀSANA
2 DVE / EXHALE — UTTĀNĀSANA
3 TRĪṆI / INHALE — ARDHA UTTĀNĀSANA
4 CATVĀRI / EXHALE — CATURAṄGA DAṆḌĀSANA
5 PAÑCA / INHALE — ŪRDHVA MUKHA ŚVĀNĀSANA
6 ṢAṬ / EXHALE — ADHO MUKHA ŚVĀNĀSANA

9 NAVA

9TH POSITION, EXHALE

Inhale

Return to Setup and pause.

— Learn to go from the State of the Āsana to the original Setup position with economy.

— Lower your hips to the ground, keep your chest open, and finish by bringing your head upright.

Exhale

Prepare to jump back.

— Make a crouch: lean back, bend your knees, lift your feet off the ground, cross the ankles, and plant your hands on the ground in front of your hips.

— Coil your spine into flexion and get ready for a mighty lift up.

10 DAŚA

10TH POSITION, INHALE

Inhale

Lift up with a burst of power.

— Strike down with your hands and lift up your seat and feet equally.

— Suck your feet back and lean forward with your head and chest.

11 EKĀDAŚA

11TH POSITION, EXHALE

Exhale

Jump back.

— Bend your elbows with speed, pivot on your arms, project your chest forward, and drive your legs back.

PURVOTTĀNĀSANA (Intense Eastern Stretching Pose)

Exhale (continued)

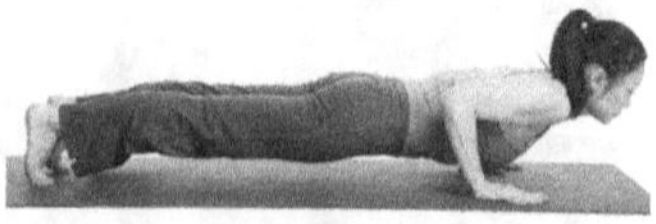

Stop in Caturaṅga and empty lungs.

— Strike a fully animated pose instantly.

— In the same rhythmic act, finish emptying your lungs with a flourish and stop your body's motion with pinpoint precision.

Vinyāsa Meta View
Student: How do I finish my exhale with a flourish?

Teacher: Research! Speed up the very end of your out-breath and engage all the breathing musculature within your torso. You can also add a flourish by expelling the air from your lungs with the badassery of a dragon and visualizing the air eddying or making a high-powered swirl as it exits your nostrils.

12 DVĀDAŚA
12TH POSITION, INHALE

Inhale

Transition to Up Dog and fill up lungs.

— To come into your pose, practice making a full-body gesture. Think of integrating the actions of your lower body, your center, and your upper body.

- To work your lower body: push your toes back into a point, extend your ankles, and root back through your legs from your hips to toes.
- To work your center: dive your coccyx down and pull up your navel.
- To work your upper body: lift up your head in a circle, expand your chest greatly, coil your spine, and extend your arms with a press move.

13 TRAYODAŚA
13TH POSITION, EXHALE

Exhale

Stop in Down Dog.

— Swing your hips back dexterously and use momentum to roll over the tops of your feet.

— Keep your arms and legs extended during your move.

Vinyāsa Meta View
An expert in Haṭha Yoga knows that Down Dog is a good shape for performing the Belly Flying Up Gesture, Uḍḍīyāna Bandha. The method is as follows:

1) *Strike an adamant pose and invest your limbs with great stopping power.*
2) *Lengthen your spine.*
3) *Skillfully sweep your exhale along the length of your spine to the base of your pelvis.*
4) *Then, before you inhale, pull up your navel and watch your abdomen fly into a hollow shape, like a greyhound dog's belly.*

FULL VINYĀSA
14 CATURDAŚA / INHALE — ARDHA UTTĀNĀSANA
15 PAÑCADAŚA / EXHALE — UTTĀNĀSANA
SAMASTHITI

ARDHA BADDHA PADMA PASCHIMOTTĀNĀSANA

(Half Bound Lotus Western Stretching Pose)

7 SAPTA

7TH POSITION, INHALE

Exhale

Crouch!

— Lower your hips towards the ground as you root down through your hands.

— Hunker back and build up energy in your legs.

— Make ready to launch your legs forward with skillful swiftness.

— Delight in building your crouch as a form of bodily prayer. Rally all your forces so that you are ready to commit to each bold move with full faith.

Inhale

Jump through to Daṇḍāsana.

— Jump forward with economy. Direct the force of your leap and project your feet ahead into the space in front of your hands.

Free Breathing

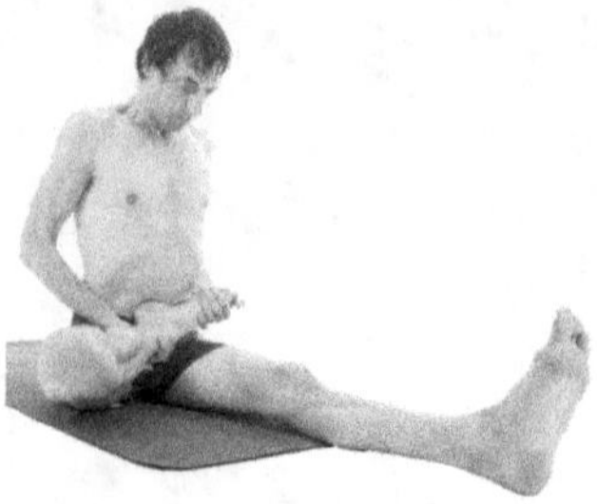

Right leg to Half Lotus; bind right foot with right hand.

— Use the Flip Move to bring your right foot to Half Lotus:

1) Take your extended right leg out to the right.
2) Turn your right thigh out and externally rotate your femur in the hip socket.
3) Dexterously flip your right foot towards you, aiming to position the foot up on top of your left thigh.
4) Catch hold of your right foot with your hands and finish drawing the heel up towards your navel to achieve Half Lotus.

Vinyāsa Meta View
Use the Flip Move to gesture intelligently rather than being passive with your leg or overusing your arms to do the work of taking Half Lotus.

Inhale

Right arm behind back, catch left foot, and strike Setup.

— Swing your right arm behind your back and use your right hand to bind the right foot.

— Then, reach forward with your left hand to grip your outer left foot.

— Stop at halfway and summon these actions:

- Root your limbs.
- Lift up your chest.
- Lengthen your spine.
- Suck up your navel and maximize your readiness for action.

FULL VINYĀSA

SAMASTHITI
1 EKAM / INHALE — ŪRDHVA HASTĀSANA
2 DVE / EXHALE — UTTĀNĀSANA
3 TRĪṆI / INHALE — ARDHA UTTĀNĀSANA
4 CATVĀRI / EXHALE — CATURAṄGA DAṆḌĀSANA
5 PAÑCA / INHALE — ŪRDHVA MUKHA ŚVĀNĀSANA
6 ṢAṬ / EXHALE — ADHO MUKHA ŚVĀNĀSANA

8 AṢṬAU
8TH POSITION, EXHALE

Exhale, 5 to 8 Breaths

Fold forward with a swoop, first side.

— Decisively sweep your torso down to your extended leg.

— Come to the end point of your movement and strike your position.

— As you stay, use your internal focus to increase the weight of your legs, arms, pelvis, torso, and head.

— Emulate the earth with your body and create great steadiness. Using your will to increase your weight is a special power known by yogīs as Garimā Siddhi.

State of the Āsana

ARDHA BADDHA PADMA PASCHIMOTTĀNĀSANA

Right Side — 5 to 8 Breaths
Dṛṣṭi: Pādayorāgrai *(Foot)*

9 NAVA
9TH POSITION, INHALE

Inhale

Sweep head and torso up to Setup position.

— Lift up your head and torso to a halfway point while holding on to your feet with your hands.

— Pause briefly and with split-second timing, ground your legs, lift up your spine, and perform Uḍḍīyāna Bandha.

— Animating your body in the Setup is a good way to charge your Nāḍīs with Prāṇa and cause Śakti to flow in Suṣumṇā.

Exhale

Crouch!

— Sit up and lean back. Keep your hips down as you bend your knees and cross your ankles with your feet up off the floor.

— Plant your hands on the ground in front of your hips, flush the air out of your lungs with skillful force, and get ready for the sudden lift-up move.

10 DAŚA
10TH POSITION, INHALE

Inhale

Lift up!

— Strike down with your hands and lift up your seat and feet evenly. Then, swiftly suck your feet back and lean forward with your head and chest.

ARDHA BADDHA PADMA PASCHIMOTTĀNĀSANA

(Half Bound Lotus Western Stretching Pose)

11 EKĀDAŚA

11TH POSITION, EXHALE

Exhale

Jump back.

— Bend your elbows, dive your chest towards the ground, and pivot on your arms.

— Project your upper body forward and swing your legs back.

Exhale (continued)

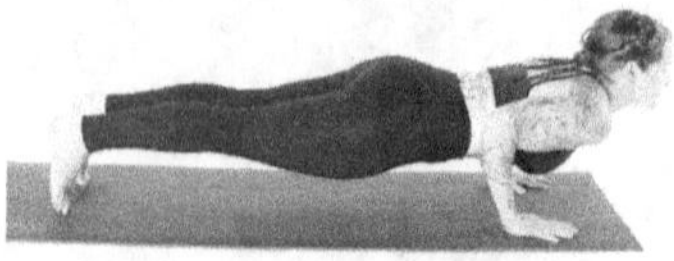

Caturaṅga Daṇḍāsana.

— Strike Four-Limbed Staff Pose. Stop with precision.

— Stay long enough to enjoy this most excellent destination.

— Befriend the horizontal stick shape.

12 DVĀDAŚA

12TH POSITION, INHALE

Inhale

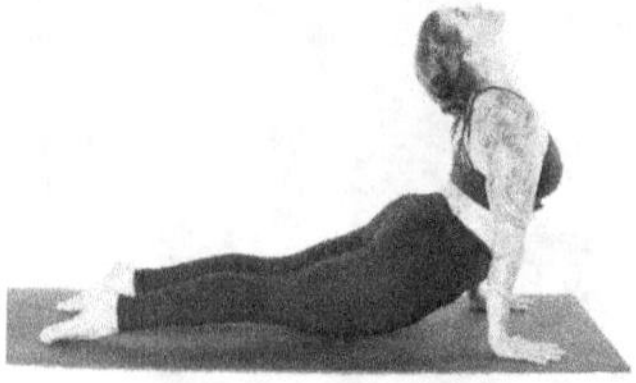

Ūrdhva Mukha Śvānāsana.

— Lift your head and circle your spine up to the peak of the position in a single move.

— Fix your legs and arms in an adamant position and project your chest forward to a perfect location betwen your tall, sturdy arm pillars.

13 TRAYODAŚA

13TH POSITION, EXHALE

Exhale

Adho Mukha Śvānāsana.

— Swing your hips back with plenty of force, and at the same time, expel the air from your lungs with gusto.

— Pretend that your exhale is a strong, benevolent wind that blows your hips back with effortless power.

14 CATURDAŚA

14TH POSITION, INHALE

Exhale (continued)

Crouch.

— Lower your hips towards the earth and brace your arms.

— Build up energy as if pulling back a slingshot.

— Steer the force of your exhalation down your spine to the power center at your base.

Inhale

Spring!

— Direct all the force that you built up in your crouch into a forward leap.

— Shoot your feet between your arms to a point well in front of your hands.

— Bring wise economy to your move. Aim to go from point A to point B in a direct line. Avoid jumping up, stalling, or otherwise interrupting the pure forward trajectory of your leap.

Free Breathing

Left leg to Half Lotus; bind left foot with left hand.

— Use the Flip Move steps to bring your left foot to Half Lotus:

1) Move your fully extended left leg out to the left.
2) Turn your left thigh out and externally rotate your left femur in the hip socket.
3) With a frog-like leg movement, flip your left foot up to a point on top of your right thigh.
4) To finish your move, catch your left foot with your hands and draw your heel up towards your navel.

Inhale

Left hand grips left foot; strike Setup position.

— Swing your left arm behind your back and use your left hand to bind the left foot.

— Reach forward with your right hand and grip your right foot. Pause at halfway and activate your body.

— Root your thighs, lift up your chest, elongate your spine, suck up your navel, and prepare for a mighty downward swoop.

ARDHA BADDHA PADMA PASCHIMOTTĀNĀSANA

(Half Bound Lotus Western Stretching Pose)

15 PAÑCADAŚA

15TH POSITION, EXHALE

Exhale, 5 to 8 Breaths

Fold forward; take second side.

— Zoom your torso down to your extended leg with a gesture.

— Be strategic about the move that takes you into your forward bend; deliberately use momentum to galvanize your body's forces and achieve a more vivacious pose.

— Anticipate the end of your movement and define the distinct stopping point.

— Experience the ebb and flow rhythm of your breath. Send waves of Prāṇa flowing throughout your entire body that are generated by your skillful breathing.

— Delight in creating not just stillness but dynamic stillness.

State of the Āsana

ARDHA BADDHA PADMA PASCHIMOTTĀNĀSANA

Left Side — 5 to 8 Breaths
Dṛṣṭi: Pādayorāgrai *(Foot)*

16 ṢOḌAŚA

16TH POSITION, INHALE

Inhale

Head up and return to Setup.

— Lift your chest, retain the grip on your right foot, and create a swift pause.

— Stamp down your legs, fill up your lungs, expand your chest abundantly, and pull up energy from the root of your spine.

Exhale

Crouch!

— Sit up, lean back, bend your knees, and lift up your feet.

— Coil your body into a compact shape.

— Become spring-loaded, ready to stamp down and lift up.

17 SAPTADAŚA

17TH POSITION, INHALE

Inhale

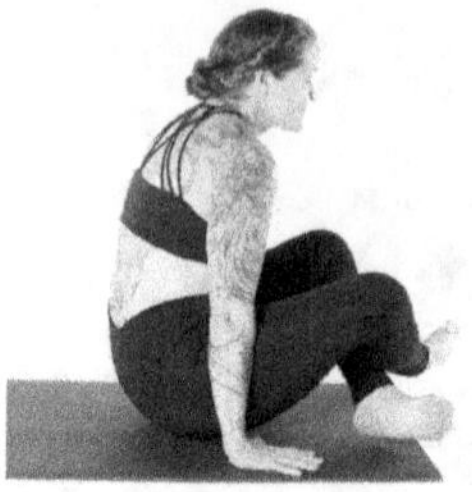

Lift up with a sudden strike!

— Stamp your hands down firmly to clear your hips and feet just off the ground.

— Swiftly suck your feet back and lean forward with your upper body.

18 AṢṬADAŚA
18TH POSITION, EXHALE

Exhale

Jump back.

— Bend your elbows; pivot on your arms with your body in a compact shape.

— Shoot your legs back and keep bending your elbows as you lower your upper body into place.

Exhale (continued)

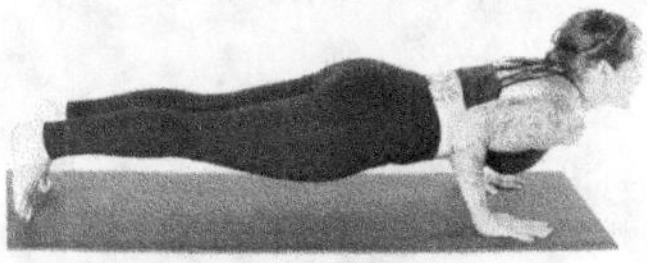

Caturaṅga Daṇḍāsana.

— Stop with precision, strengthen your limbs, and transform your head, torso, pelvis, and legs into an unbreakable stick.

— Ground your four limbs and achieve a worthy Daṇḍa.

— Create a whole world in a moment of clear stillness.

19 EKONAVIṂŚATI
19TH POSITION, INHALE

Inhale

Root arms and legs; arch spine.

— Just before you come up, hunker back in Caturaṅga and generate a slight amount of backward momentum by rooting into your legs.

— Then, lift up your head and spine with a great thrust of power while continuing to root back stubbornly through your legs.

— To finish your move, expand your chest with gusto and press your arms straight.

20 VIṂŚATI
20TH POSITION, EXHALE

Exhale

Downward Facing Dog.

— Propel your hips back with a force that is both strong and benevolent.

— Keep your legs and arms fully extended as you sweep back with speedy skill.

— Arrive in Down Dog awake to your inner world. Come to a complete standstill. In the briefest pause, stop time and contemplate the source of all light, the Self-Luminous Being who dwells in the Lotus of your Heart *(Anāhata Chakra).*

FULL VINYĀSA

21 EKAVIṂŚATI / INHALE — ARDHA UTTĀNĀSANA

22 DVĀVIṂŚATI / EXHALE — UTTĀNĀSANA

SAMASTHITI

TRIAṄGA MUKHAIKAPĀDA PASCHIMOTTĀNĀSANA

(Three Limbs Face One Leg Western Stretching Pose)

7 SAPTA

7TH POSITION, INHALE

Exhale

Bring hips low to the ground.

— Crouch low and love the Earth.

Vinyāsa Meta View

To embody the Earth element in a pose is to become deeply rooted in your stance, to generate great stopping power with any part of your body that you choose, to resist movement at will, and to create adamant stability of body and mind in the State of the Āsana. Other Earth qualities include: constancy, loyalty, generosity, and trustworthiness.

Inhale

Spring to Daṇḍāsana.

— Leap forward, like a sprinter launching out of the starting blocks.

— Drive your legs straight through to Daṇḍāsana.

Free Breathing, Inhale

Right leg to Ardha Vīrāsana; strike Setup at halfway.

— Fold back your right leg and snug your shin up to your thigh.

— Separate your knees and make your thighs parallel.

— Evenly root both sitting bones, shift forward, and stamp down your thighs.

— Reach forward with your arms, catch your wrist around the ball of your left foot, and make a clean stop at the end point of the 7th Vinyāsa Position.

— To finalize your Setup, pull back towards you through your arms as you root your extended leg in place. Lift up your spine, pull up your navel, and awaken Kuṇḍalinī Śakti who sleeps at your base.

Earth Element

8 AṢṬAU

8TH POSITION, EXHALE

Exhale, 5 to 8 Breaths

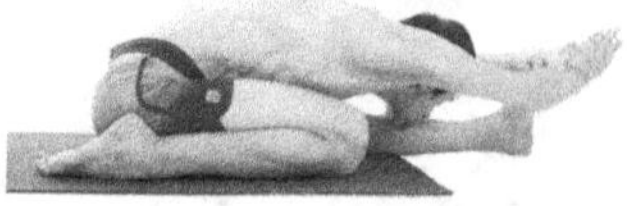

Ground thighs and swoop head down to extended leg.

— To maximize your forward fold, project your spine up, out, forward, and then lower your head to your shin.

Vinyāsa Meta View

It is common to think that the goal of a forward bend is only to try to get your forehead down towards your legs as soon and as much as possible. But placing too much focus on getting your head down can cause physical injury, disturb your mind, and also distract you from contemplating how to best create essential, satisfying spinal length. When going into a forward bend, it is helpful to imagine that you reach through the spine and pass through three different spinal trajectories (UP, OUTWARD, and FORWARD) before finally bringing your torso down towards your legs. This image reminds you that forward bending is equal parts reaching out into space with your spine and releasing your spine downwards towards your legs.

State of the Āsana

TRIAṄGA MUKHAIKAPĀDA PASCHIMOTTĀNĀSANA

Right Side — 5 to 8 Breaths
Dṛṣṭi: Pādayorāgrai *(Foot)*

FULL VINYĀSA

SAMASTHITI
1 EKAM / INHALE — ŪRDHVA HASTĀSANA
2 DVE / EXHALE — UTTĀNĀSANA
3 TRĪṆI / INHALE — ARDHA UTTĀNĀSANA
4 CATVĀRI / EXHALE — CATURAṄGA DAṆḌĀSANA
5 PAÑCA / INHALE — ŪRDHVA MUKHA ŚVĀNĀSANA
6 ṢAṬ / EXHALE — ADHO MUKHA ŚVĀNĀSANA

9 NAVA

9TH POSITION, INHALE

Inhale

Return to Setup and pause.

— Lift your chest, stamp down your legs, extend your arms, and retain the connection between your hands and straight leg.

— Stop cleanly at halfway, fill up your lungs to the brim, and infuse your entire body with Prāṇa.

Exhale

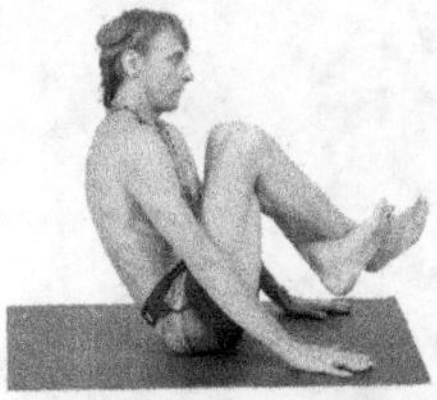

Prepare to lift up.

— Sit up, lean back, and bend your knees. Lift up your feet, coil your body into a compact shape, and plant your hands on the ground in front of your hips.

— Use your crouching position to build up tremendous energy in anticipation of your lift-up move.

10 DAŚA

10TH POSITION, INHALE

Inhale

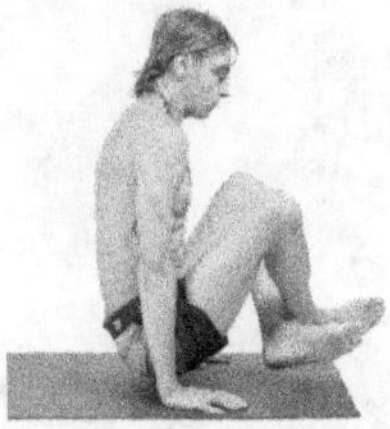

Lift up!

— Strike down suddenly and swiftly clear your body off the ground.

— Deliberately create a burst of power and hoist up your body, like a weight lifter doing a clean-and-jerk move.

11 EKĀDAŚA

11TH POSITION, EXHALE

Exhale

Jump back.

— Bend your elbows, pivot on your arms with your body in a compact shape, and lean forward.

— Make a controlled nose-dive as you drive your legs back.

— Stop in place as you finish extending your legs and plant your feet on the ground.

TRIAṄGA MUKHAIKAPĀDA PASCHIMOTTĀNĀSANA

(Three Limbs Face One Leg Western Stretching Pose)

Exhale (continued)

Strike destination and finish breathing out.

— Make a clean stop in Four-Limbed Staff Pose and discover Nirodha *(Cessation)*, yoga's greatest technique.

12 DVĀDAŚA

12TH POSITION, INHALE

Inhale

Lift up head and extend arms with a press move.

— Arch your spine on the way up to the peak and perfectly time your inhalation with your gesture.

— Arrive at your destination and clearly define your body's position in space.

— Swiftly add refinements such as:

- Press down evenly with your hands.
- Lengthen your arms.
- Lift your head and raise your spine up off of your shoulder girdle.
- Make your legs adamant by sending a sweep of energy flowing back through the bones from hips to toes.

Vinyāsa Meta View
With each transition, know the end point of your movement. Be clear about the shape you aim to strike, then stop at your destination with supreme confidence at the right moment. Use your strategic movements and your decisive stops to join in yoga's great game of citta vṛtti nirodha.

13 TRAYODAŚA

13TH POSITION, EXHALE

Exhale

Strike Downward Dog.

— Swing your hips back with authority and generate a powerful exhalation.

— Make this transition an exercise in Prāṇāyāma *(Breath Control)* and strike your pose in a luminous state of no-mind.

14 CATURDAŚA

14TH POSITION, INHALE

Exhale (continued)

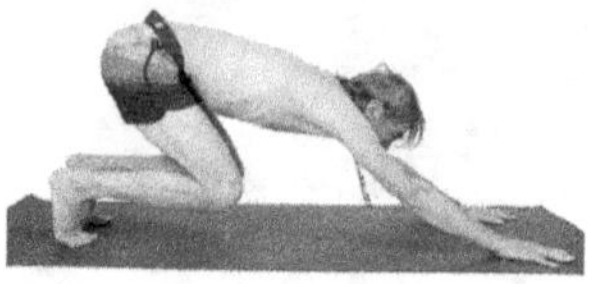

Crouch.

— Stamp the ground with your hands, bend your knees, and thrust back with your hips.

— Pause, build up energy, hunker back, and anticipate a great forward leap.

— Delight in the action that comes before the action.

Inhale

Spring!

— Jump forward with speedy skill.

— Lead with your feet, suck your thighs towards your chest in a pike move, and zoom to Daṇḍāsana.

Free Breathing, Inhale

Bring left leg into Half Hero Pose; strike Setup position.

— Fold your left leg back, snug your shin up to your thigh, and root down your hips.

— Separate your knees and pin down your thighs.

— Reach your arms forward and grip your left wrist with your right hand around the ball of your right foot.

— Pause and galvanize your forces in anticipation of your forward bend.

15 PAÑCADAŚA

15TH POSITION, EXHALE

Exhale, 5 to 8 Breaths

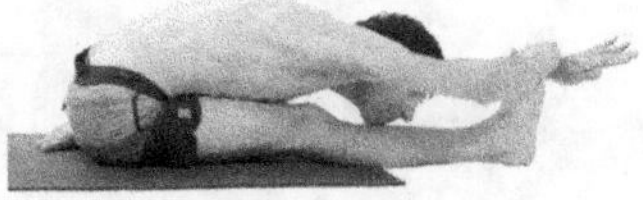

Fold forward and bring head or chin to shin.

— Project your spine forward.

— Swoop your torso down to your extended leg.

— Lower your head to your shin.

— Find your body's innate attraction to the ground and express the element of Earth.

— Marvel as you are irresistibly drawn down into a deep, earth-connected pose, like iron rushing to a powerful magnet.

State of the Āsana

TRIAṄGA MUKHAIKAPĀDA PASCHIMOTTĀNĀSANA

Left Side — 5 to 8 Breaths
Dṛṣṭi: Pādayorāgrai *(Foot)*

16 ṢOḌAŚA

16TH POSITION, INHALE

Inhale

Return to the Setup position.

— Lift up your chest, extend your arms, draw in a great breath, and pause.

— Kick away through your extended leg, pull back with your arms, and galvanize your center.

TRIAṄGA MUKHAIKAPĀDA PASCHIMOTTĀNĀSANA

(Three Limbs Face One Leg Western Stretching Pose)

Exhale

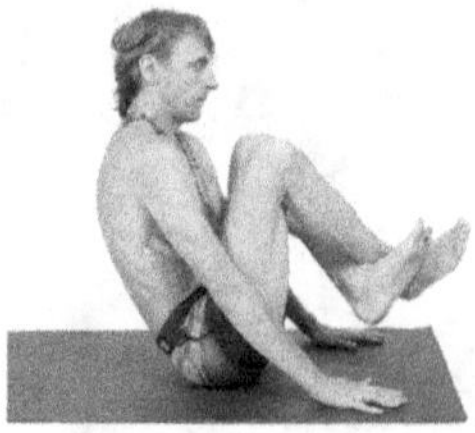

Crouch!

— Sit up, coil your body into a soul-stirring crouch, and exhale to the base of your spine.

— Build up energy as an art form unto itself.

17 SAPTADAŚA

17TH POSITION, INHALE

Inhale

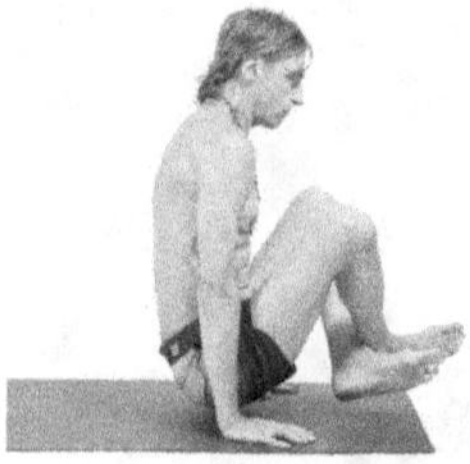

Stamp hands and clear seat up off ground.

— Lift up using timing and rhythm as your allies.

— Strike down with your hands, lift up, and suck your feet back.

Exhale

Jump back.

— Bend your elbows, lean forward, and pivot on your arms.

— Project your chest forward and drive your legs back.

18 AṢṬADAŚA

18TH POSITION, EXHALE

Exhale (continued)

Strike a pure line from head to feet.

— Land Caturaṅga Daṇḍāsana in a gesture of prostration, a prayer performed with your whole body.

19 EKONAVIṂŚATI
19TH POSITION, INHALE

Inhale

Move to Up Dog with breath.

— Come to Up Dog with a sure move, stabilize your limbs, and agreeably arch your spine.

— To enhance your backbend, project your chest forward in contrast to rooting back through your legs and circling your head back with a mighty spiral gesture.

20 VIṂŚATI
20TH POSITION, EXHALE

Exhale

Pull back to Down Dog.

— Swing to Downward Dog Pose, body and breath moving as one.

— Make your limbs, senses, and mind steady.

— Retreat into the solitude of your own body.

— Give thanks as you meditate on the presence of The Divine, The Pure, The Blissful Eternal One dwelling in the Lotus of your Heart.

FULL VINYĀSA

21 EKAVIṂŚATI / INHALE — ARDHA UTTĀNĀSANA
22 DVĀVIṂŚATI / EXHALE — UTTĀNĀSANA
SAMASTHITI

JĀNU ŚĪRṢĀSANA A (Head to Knee Pose A)

7 SAPTA
7TH POSITION, INHALE

Exhale

Crouch; energize limbs.

— Lower your hips into a poised squat and build up energy in your body, like a pitcher winds up to throw a baseball.

Inhale

Spring to Daṇḍāsana.

— Jump forward exuberantly and swing your legs through to Daṇḍāsana with a lively forward throw of your feet.

Free Breathing, Inhale

Root legs and arms, lift chest, and strike Setup!

— Take your right knee back to 90° and rotate your torso to the left.

— Reach forward with your arms and use your left hand to catch your right wrist around your left foot.

— Hold steady at the end point of the 7th Vinyāsa Position.

— In the tiny pause, lift up your head and chest, stamp down your legs, and pull back towards you with your arms.

Vinyāsa Meta View
Playing with opposing forces allows you to discover the subtle energetic technique of Mudrā that serves to help you create internal awareness, the hallmark of meditation. An example of opposing forces in this pose is to fix your extended leg in position as you pull back towards you with your arms.

8 AṢṬAU
8TH POSITION, EXHALE

Exhale, 5 to 8 Breaths

Transition into State of the Āsana.

— Be awake to the act of folding forward and use your movement to achieve a dynamic destination.

— Tap into the primal rhythm of your breath to participate more fully in your forward bend.

State of the Āsana

JĀNU ŚĪRṢĀSANA A

Right Side — 5 to 8 Breaths
Dṛṣṭi: Pādayorāgrai *(Foot)*

FULL VINYĀSA

SAMASTHITI
1 EKAM / INHALE — ŪRDHVA HASTĀSANA
2 DVE / EXHALE — UTTĀNĀSANA
3 TRĪṆI / INHALE — ARDHA UTTĀNĀSANA
4 CATVĀRI / EXHALE — CATURAṄGA DAṆḌĀSANA
5 PAÑCA / INHALE — ŪRDHVA MUKHA ŚVĀNĀSANA
6 ṢAṬ / EXHALE — ADHO MUKHA ŚVĀNĀSANA

9 NAVA
9TH POSITION, INHALE

Inhale

Exhale

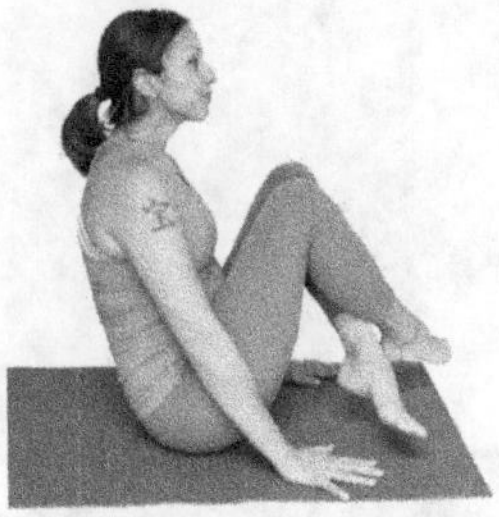

Return to Setup.

— Lift up your head and torso and pause at the halfway point.

— With speedy poise, anchor your thighs and pull up from the root of your spine.

— Drop all false imaginings and pierce through to Now in a glorious moment of illumination.

Crouch!

— Sit up, lean back, and bend your knees. Lift up your feet, plant your hands on the ground in front of your hips, and pause.

— Charge your limbs and build up to a threshold of power; store up enough force within your body to propel a formidable jump-back move!

10 DAŚA
10TH POSITION, INHALE

Inhale

Spring!

— Stamp your hands down swiftly; lift up decisively and clear your body off the ground.

— Suck your feet back and begin to lean forward with your upper body.

11 EKĀDAŚA
11TH POSITION, EXHALE

Exhale

Jump Back.

— Bend your elbows, pivot in place, balance on your arms in midair as you lean forward and shoot your legs back.

— Continue to shift your chest forward and bend the elbows until your upper arm bones are parallel to the ground.

JĀNU ŚĪRṢĀSANA A (Head to Knee Pose A)

Exhale (continued)

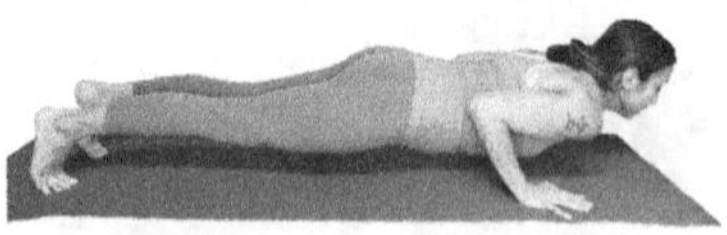

Caturaṅga Daṇḍāsana; exhale thoroughly.

— Come to the end of your movement and find stillness.

— Subtly activate the different parts of your body in a coordinated effort: suck in your elbows, brace your arms, charge your legs with vitality, and stabilize your three main body masses.

— To build strength, stay in place and hover just above the ground for as many as five breaths at a time.

12 DVĀDAŚA

12TH POSITION, INHALE

Inhale

Upward Facing Dog; inhale thoroughly.

— Rear up from the ground swiftly like a cobra preparing to strike.

— In a single, economical move: lift up your head, arch your spine, straighten your arms, and root your legs.

— As you spring to the destination, go the same speed from start to finish.

13 TRAYODAŚA

13TH POSITION, EXHALE

Exhale

Swing hips back and arrive in Downward Dog.

— Put your body in motion playfully to create the Yantra lovingly known as Adho Mukha Śvānāsana.

14 CATURDAŚA

14TH POSITION, INHALE

Exhale (continued)

Crouch and anticipate action.

— Lower your body toward the earth, squeeze every bit of air out of your lungs, and prepare for a bold strike.

Inhale

Spring forward.

— Launch your body forward all at once, drive your extended legs through, and sit down with your hips just behind your hands.

Free Breathing, Inhale

Head up and lengthen spine; strike Setup.

— Bend your left knee and bring your left foot back towards your pelvis. Angle your left thigh out to 90° and rotate your torso to the right.

— Reach forward with your arms and use the right hand to catch the left wrist around your right foot.

— Pause in order to animate your Setup position. Lengthen your extended leg, brace your arms, lift up your chest, and suck up your belly.

— *Pro tip:* to maintain a continuity of awareness throughout your practice, focus on striking the Setup position time and again. Gaining skill in Vinyāsa teaches the yogī how to be in a perpetual state of meditation— equally "with-it" in movement or stillness.

15 PAÑCADAŚA

15TH POSITION, EXHALE

Exhale, 5 to 8 Breaths

Bend forward to a realized form.

— Spring your torso down towards your extended leg as you skillfully sweep the air out of your lungs.

— Anchor your legs in the act of folding forward.

— Come to a natural stopping place and release unnecessary tension throughout your body.

— Drop the weight of your limbs and merge with the Earth, Pṛthivī. Allow your pose to express the element of Earth and learn such qualities as steadfastness, stability, trustworthiness, patience, receptivity, generosity, and vitality.

State of the Āsana

JĀNU ŚĪRṢĀSANA A

Left Side — 5 to 8 Breaths
Dṛṣṭi: Pādayorāgrai *(Foot)*

16 ṢOḌAŚA

16TH POSITION, INHALE

Inhale

Head up, brace limbs, and honor the Setup position.

— Lift up your chest, extend your arms, and hold on to your foot with your hands in a play of forces.

— Pull up your navel strongly, awaken the energy plexus at the base of your spine known as Root Support *(Mūlādhāra)*, and send energy up the Central Channel.

JĀNU ŚĪRṢĀSANA A (Head to Knee Pose A)

Exhale

Prepare to strike.

— Sit up with speed.

— Lean back, bend your knees, lift your feet, and coil your body into a crouch.

— Make your arms ready, galvanize your center, and become spring-loaded.

17 SAPTADAŚA
17TH POSITION, INHALE

Inhale

Lift up.

— All of a sudden, strike down with your hands and clear your feet and hips off the ground.

— Suck your feet under you and begin to lean forward with your upper body.

18 AṢṬADAŚA
18TH POSITION, EXHALE

Exhale

Jump back!

— Swing your feet back, project your upper body forward, bend your elbows, and pivot on your arms.

— Stay forward as you lower your chest and head into position and drive your legs directly backwards.

Exhale (continued)

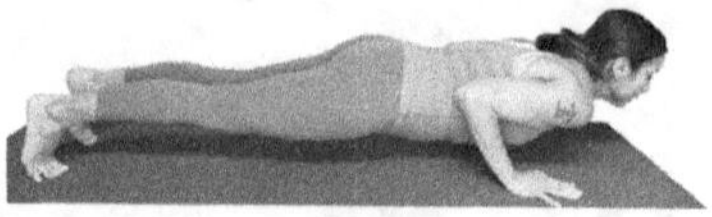

Strike Four-Limbed Staff Pose all at once.

— Make a clean stop in your Horizontal Staff Pose. Stamp down your hands, strengthen your arms, powerfully extend your legs, and plant your toes on the ground.

— Hold absolutely steady for a few seconds or more.

19 EKONAVIṂŚATI

19TH POSITION, INHALE

Inhale

Arch spine while straightening arms.

— Push your toes back and anchor your legs as you lift up your head and press your arms straight.

— Aim to arrive in your position having already established your backbend.

— As you inhale, draw the air into your lungs against resistance from your constricted throat; this will help you expand your chest magnificently.

Vinyāsa Meta View
Use the technique of Ujjāyī breathing to draw large quantities of Prāṇa, Vital Force, into your body. With practice, you can breathe like the great Yogī, Agastya, who sucked up all the waters of the cosmos in a single draw to rescue the world from a group of crafty demons who had figured out how to replenish their powers by hiding in the waters at night after the day's battle.

20 VIṂŚATI

20TH POSITION, EXHALE

Exhale

Thrust hips back and strike Down Dog.

— Sweep your hips back with prodigious force.

— Perform the purifying actions of emptying your lungs thoroughly and wringing out your internal organs. As the great sage Krishnamacharya stated in *The Yogarahasya of Nāthamuni*, "Those illnesses that cannot be cured by other methods can be cured by the steady practice of Yogāsanas."

FULL VINYĀSA

21 EKAVIṂŚATI / INHALE — ARDHA UTTĀNĀSANA

22 DVĀVIṂŚATI / EXHALE — UTTĀNĀSANA

SAMASTHITI

JĀNU ŚĪRṢĀSANA B (Head to Knee Pose B)

7 SAPTA
7TH POSITION, INHALE

Exhale

Bend knees; come into a powerful crouch.

— Lower your hips and get ready to spring, like a sprinter in the blocks on high alert, awaiting the start gun and aiming for gold.

Inhale

Leap forward!

— Spring forward with a mighty, nimble leap and zip your legs through to Daṇḍāsana in a flash.

Free Breathing, Inhale

Sit on right heel; strike Setup position.

— Bring your right foot back to your pelvis and angle your right knee out to 90°.

— Go up on your fingertips, lift your hips, and sit your pelvic floor down on your right heel.

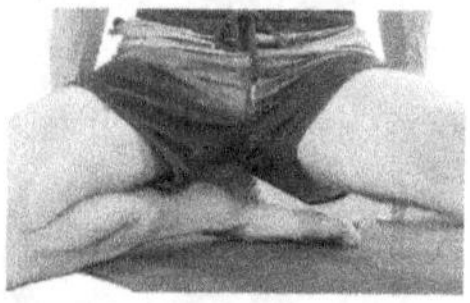

— Reach forward with your arms; use your left hand to catch your right wrist around your left foot.

— Root your straight leg and pull back through your extended arms.

— Lift up your chest, hollow your belly, and pull up from the base of your spine.

Vinyāsa Meta View
This Setup position is a powerful Śakti-raising Prāṇāyāma technique called Mahā Mudrā (Great Seal). Performing Mahā Mudrā involves sitting on the heel, retaining the breath after exhaling, locking Mūla, Uḍḍīyāna, and Jālandhara Bandhas, and causing awakened Life Force to flow freely up Suṣumṇā. When you do Jānu Śīrṣāsana B, be inspired by Mahā Mudrā, even though typically you'll do a less extreme version of the technique.

8 AṢṬAU
8TH POSITION, EXHALE

Exhale, 5 to 8 Breaths

Transition into State of the Āsana.

— In the act of folding forward: elongate, prostrate, and offer the weight of your body to the Earth Goddess, Pṛthivī, the inexhaustible Source of Abundance.

State of the Āsana

JĀNU ŚĪRṢĀSANA B

Right Side — 5 to 8 Breaths
Dṛṣṭi: Pādayorāgrai *(Foot)*

FULL VINYĀSA

SAMASTHITI
1 EKAM / INHALE — ŪRDHVA HASTĀSANA
2 DVE / EXHALE — UTTĀNĀSANA
3 TRĪṆI / INHALE — ARDHA UTTĀNĀSANA
4 CATVĀRI / EXHALE — CATURAṄGA DAṆḌĀSANA
5 PAÑCA / INHALE — ŪRDHVA MUKHA ŚVĀNĀSANA
6 ṢAṬ / EXHALE — ADHO MUKHA ŚVĀNĀSANA

9 NAVA
9TH POSITION, INHALE

Inhale

Pause at halfway point; strike Setup.

— Lift up your head and chest; extend your arms in contrast to grounding your legs and anchoring your pelvis.

— Galvanize your center, fly your belly up, and awaken Kuṇḍalinī Śakti at your base.

Exhale

Crouch.

— Sit up; lean back. Bend your knees, lift up your feet, coil your spine into flexion, galvanize your forces, and anticipate the speedy lift-up move.

10 DAŚA
10TH POSITION, INHALE

Inhale

Lift up your feet and seat.

— Strike down with your hands and lift up with sudden force.

— Swiftly suck your legs back and lean forward.

11 EKĀDAŚA
11TH POSITION, EXHALE

Exhale

Jump back!

— Bend your elbows, pivot on your arms, and lower your body down towards the ground.

— Project your chest forward and drive your legs back.

JĀNU ŚĪRṢĀSANA B (Head to Knee Pose B)

Exhale (continued)

Stop clearly in Four-Limbed Staff Pose.

— Strike your pose with supreme confidence and instantly achieve the magical shape.

— Be strong, bow down, and kiss the earth with tender lips of devotion.

Vinyāsa Meta View

This main line of Caturaṅga Daṇḍāsana is called the daṇḍa, meaning staff or stick, and gives the pose its name. In the photo above, the model wisely stops short of the full Caturaṅga Daṇḍāsana because she is working on an appropriate step in order to build the strength to both come down low and preserve the integrity of the line formed by her head, torso, pelvis, and legs.

As a rule, in Caturaṅga Daṇḍāsana, it is better to bend your elbows less and keep your three main body masses aligned than to come down low and lose the integrity of your daṇḍa. In other words, repeatedly stopping in a suitable position rather than repeating a faulty position is the best way to protect your body from harm and gain the arm, upper body, and core strength that are required to lower all the way down into the pose with a sound daṇḍa.

12 DVĀDAŚA

12TH POSITION, INHALE

Inhale

Upward Facing Dog.

— Lift your head, extend your arms, and arch your spine in a single move.

— Strengthen your arms and legs; win the bracing power to support the arcing flight of your spine.

13 TRAYODAŚA

13TH POSITION, EXHALE

Exhale

Propel your hips back to Down Dog.

— Upon arrival, pause and elongate your spine along a diagonal line that passes through the core of your body from your tail to head. This center line is called Suṣumṇā Nāḍī *(Most Glorious Prāṇic Channel).*

— A skillful yogī who breathes up and down the length of the Main Nāḍī becomes charged with vitality and lights up the inner world.

14 CATURDAŚA

14TH POSITION, INHALE

Exhale (continued)

Crouch before the Spring!

— Hunker down in earnest and send the contraction force of your out-breath *(Apāna Vāyu)* down the length of your spine.

Vinyāsa Meta View

When you inhale and inflate your lungs, you expand your ribs and chest. When you exhale and deflate your lungs, you contract or narrow your ribs and chest. These two opposing patterns of expansion (inhalation) and contraction (exhalation) manifest to create every breath you take. Like a great piston within the center of your torso, your diaphragm drives this principal, unceasing rhythm. Synchronizing your breath with your Vinyāsas is an essential tool for learning to actively participate in and draw forth this great ebb and flow rhythm. By design, the movements that make up the Vinyāsas of Ashtanga perfectly mirror the breath, alternating between expansion and contraction movements. Using the Vinyāsas to tap into your breath's rhythm will teach you to breathe with skill and authority.

Inhale

Jump through, straight legs; sit down.

— Leap forward in a beeline to Daṇḍāsana.

Free Breathing, Inhale

Sit on left heel; strike Setup at halfway.

— Bring your left foot back towards your pelvis and angle your left knee out to 90°.

— Go up on your fingertips, lift your hips, and sit your pelvic floor down on top of your left heel.

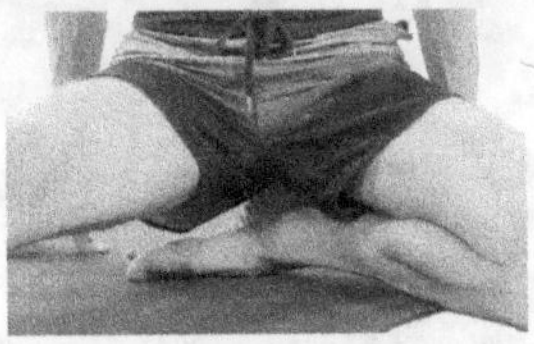

— Reach your arms forward and catch your left wrist around your right foot.

— Pause and conjure an image of Mahā Mudrā, the Great Seal, to help you animate your Setup position.

— Brace your arms as you lift up your head, chest, and navel.

— Pull up from your pelvic floor. Send powerful, vital energy up the Middle Channel and set your inner cosmos ablaze.

15 PAÑCADAŚA

15TH POSITION, EXHALE

Exhale, 5 to 8 Breaths

Sweep torso down to extended leg.

— Project your spine forward as you come down and touch your chin to your right shin.

— Use your focused mind to increase the weight of your body and add great grounding power to your pose.

— Merge with the earth as your means of achieving Samādhi: adamantine steadiness of body, breath, and mind.

State of the Āsana

JĀNU ŚĪRṢĀSANA B

Left Side — 5 to 8 Breaths
Dṛṣṭi: Pādayorāgrai *(Foot)*

16 ṢOḌAŚA

16TH POSITION, INHALE

Inhale

Return to Setup and stop in place.

— Lift up your head and torso, firmly grip your foot, and pause.

— Make your spine tall by grounding your extended leg and pulling back with your arms. Then, draw up from the root of your pelvis and send electrified Energy traveling up the Main Nāḍī.

Vinyāsa Meta View

Highlight the special Bandha feature of this Setup position. The contact between your heel and the pelvic floor can help you learn to catch Mūla Bandha. Use your heel to exert pressure upon your pelvic floor and pull up from the root of your spine. This is a great way to send Śakti flying up the Middle Channel and infuse your whole body with vitality.

JĀNU ŚĪRṢĀSANA B (Head to Knee Pose B)

Exhale

Pause and prepare to lift up.

— Sit up, lean back, bend your knees, and lift your feet off the ground.

— Plant your hands in front of your hips and extend your arms.

— Slightly round your back and galvanize your center.

— Learn to take control over the rhythm of your movements and be ready to lift up with split-second timing.

17 SAPTADAŚA

17TH POSITION, INHALE

Inhale

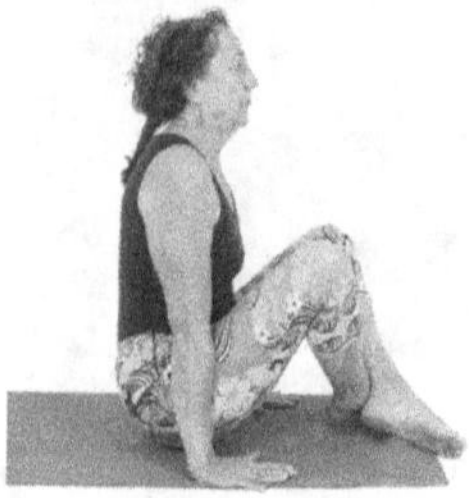

Root down and lift up.

— Strike down with your hands and lift up mightily; clear your hips and feet off the ground.

— Then, swiftly whip your feet back under you and begin to lean forward with your upper body.

18 AṢṬADAŚA

18TH POSITION, EXHALE

Exhale

Upper body forward, lower body back.

— Bend your elbows and lean forward as you pivot on your arms in a compact shape.

— Extend your legs and drive back through your feet.

Exhale (continued)

Root limbs and charge up center in Caturaṅga Daṇḍāsana.

— Strike your pose with integrity by applying stopping power to your limbs and shoring up the daṇḍa that is composed of your three main sections (head, torso, pelvis). In this way, rivet yourself here now.

Vinyāsa Meta View
One skilled in Haṭha Yoga knows this secret Mantra:

Steady body, steady mind.
Steady body, steady mind.

19 EKONAVIṂŚATI

19TH POSITION, INHALE

Inhale

Spring to Upward Dog and breathe in deeply.

— Perform these actions in rhythmic succession: lift up your head, coil your spine, extend your arms, and root back with your legs.

— Come to a clean stopping place and situate your spine precisely in the middle of your two vertical arm pillars.

— When you are skilled in Haṭha Yoga, your arms and legs work together in tandem to become a powerful, stabilizing force for your backbend.

20 VIṂŚATI

20TH POSITION, EXHALE

Exhale

Move to Down Dog with rhythm and breath.

— Swing your hips back and roll over your feet with a bold thrust of power.

— Time your move with flushing the air out of your lungs.

FULL VINYĀSA

21 EKAVIṂŚATI / INHALE — ARDHA UTTĀNĀSANA

22 DVĀVIṂŚATI / EXHALE — UTTĀNĀSANA

SAMASTHITI

JĀNU ŚĪRṢĀSANA C (Head to Knee Pose C)

7 SAPTA
7TH POSITION, INHALE

Exhale

Crouch as a prayer.

— Lower your God-given hips toward the Holy Ground. Stamp the Sacred Earth with the pair of hands that Heaven fashioned especially for you.

— Sweep your exhalation down the length of your one-of-a-kind spine.

— Look and listen inward with the eyes and ears that the Divine Friend gifted to you so that you can perceive the parade of wondrous happenings that are continually taking place within the far interior realms of your Grace-filled body.

Inhale

Spring to Daṇḍāsana.

— Leap forward with surprising suddenness and thrilling swiftness. Don't hesitate! Strike your target!

Free Breathing, Inhale

Right foot to pelvis, toes to side, reach forward to Setup.

— Bring your right foot back to your pelvis and place your toes on the ground facing to the side.

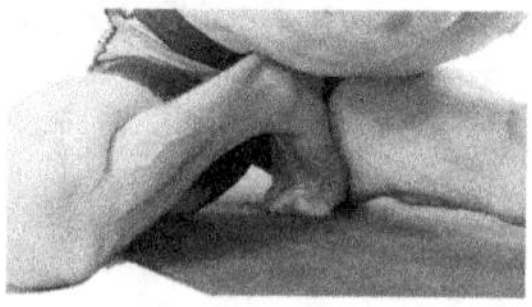

— Vertically align the heel over the toes and and bring your right knee down to a 45° angle.

— Reach forward; use your left hand to catch your right wrist around your left foot.

— Lean slightly to the right and actively ground your right toes.

— Lift your chest and pull back towards you with your arms.

8 AṢṬAU
8TH POSITION, EXHALE

Exhale, 5 to 8 Breaths

Dive down skillfully; strike destination.

— Swoop your torso down to your extended leg and bring your chin or forehead to your shin with a rhythmic move.

— Squeeze the air out of your lungs and press your right heel up into your belly.

State of the Āsana

JĀNU ŚĪRṢĀSANA C

Right Side — 5 to 8 Breaths
Dṛṣṭi: Pādayorāgrai *(Foot)*

Vinyāsa Meta View

Your circulatory system has a network of arteries to carry life-giving blood to all parts of you. Similarly, there is a network of subtle channels within you that serves to carry healing Life Force (Prāṇa or Śakti) to all parts of you. Through repeating Vinyāsas, learn to direct the flow of this energy, gather together awakened forces from all your peripheral channels, and direct the flow of healing energy into the famous Middle Channel called Suṣumṇā (Most Glorious). As the Haṭha Yoga Pradīpikā, Chapter III on Mudrās, states:

"The yogī who has been able to move the Śakti (Energy) within his body deserves success. It is useless to say more, suffice to say he conquers death playfully."

FULL VINYĀSA

SAMASTHITI
1 EKAM / INHALE — ŪRDHVA HASTĀSANA
2 DVE / EXHALE — UTTĀNĀSANA
3 TRĪṆI / INHALE — ARDHA UTTĀNĀSANA
4 CATVĀRI / EXHALE — CATURAṄGA DAṆḌĀSANA
5 PAÑCA / INHALE — ŪRDHVA MUKHA ŚVĀNĀSANA
6 ṢAṬ / EXHALE — ADHO MUKHA ŚVĀNĀSANA

9 NAVA
9TH POSITION, INHALE

Inhale

Return to Setup position and hold.

— Lift your chest and navel, extend your arms, and continue to grip your left foot.

— Stay put for a moment. Use this auspicious position to pull up from the root and light up your whole body with Śakti.

Exhale

Pause and get ready for action.

— Sit up and lean back; bend your knees and lift up your feet.

— Coil your body into a crouch and build up energy for a sudden strike.

Vinyāsa Meta View
Wholeheartedly dedicate yourself to the Crouch that comes before the Spring! Before each jump back, coil your body into a compact shape, store up force within your arms and legs, and skillfully squeeze the air out of your lungs. Apply yourself to the small tasks, like being faithful to the Crouch and Spring in every move, and soon you'll be ready for the Great Vow (Mahāvrata) of the yogī that consists of practicing the Yamas (Restraints, First Limb of the Eightfold Path of Yoga) for life.

10 DAŚA
10TH POSITION, INHALE

Inhale

Clear feet and seat off the ground with a power lift.

— Stamp down your hands and lift up your hips.

11 EKĀDAŚA
11TH POSITION, EXHALE

Exhale

Project head forward and swing feet back.

— Bend your elbows, pivot on your arms, nosedive your upper body in a controlled face-plant, and drive your legs back.

JĀNU ŚĪRṢĀSANA C (Head to Knee Pose C)

Exhale (continued)

Four-Limbed Staff Pose.

— Stop in the great strength-builder pose.

— Make your head, torso, pelvis, and legs straight and strong like a stick, and gain a steady mind.

12 DVĀDAŚA

12TH POSITION, INHALE

Inhale

Inhale up to the peak and coil spine.

— Come to Upward Dog with a circular movement of your head, leading with your nose. A wise yogī knows that the nose knows.

— Draw your upper spine into a coil within your chest cavity.

— Fully extend your legs and hover your stable hips and thighs just above the ground.

13 TRAYODAŚA

13TH POSITION, EXHALE

Exhale

Sweep hips back to Down Dog.

— Propel hips back with a targeted burst of power and roll directly over the tops of your feet.

— Upon arrival in Downward Dog Pose, root down through your hands, strengthen your arms, and stabilize your shoulders.

— Project your pelvis up and back, transfer your weight into your legs, and press your thighbones back strongly.

— Lastly, without allowing your limbs to budge, subtly dip your spine down toward the ground and back toward your legs.

14 CATURDAŚA

14TH POSITION, INHALE

Exhale (continued)

Crouch low and target jump-through move.

— Tuck your tail, lower your hips, and hunker back into a poised squat.

— Strike the ground with your hands and stabilize your arms.

— Come down into a dynamic position, breathe out thoroughly, and awaken the powerful Contraction Force of Apāna Vāyu within you.

Vinyāsa Meta View
Apāna Vāyu is an internal manifestation of Prāṇa or Life Force that governs the downward and outward flow of energy inside the body. When you breathe out, Apāna Vāyu is expressed as a contraction force that moves down the length of your spine. By crouching well and exhaling skillfully, a yogī aims to befriend and harness this force and win a great ally on the path of Yoga.

Inhale

Spring forward and pike legs.

— Jump through with a mighty forward leap so that your legs straighten with surprising forcefulness and your feet come to the ground well out in front of your hands.

Free Breathing, Inhale

Left foot to pelvis, toes to side; come forward to Setup.

— Bring your left foot back to your pelvis; place the toes on the ground facing to the side.

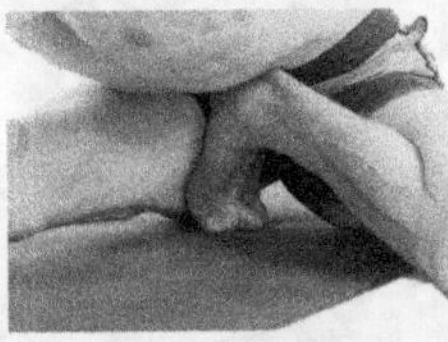

— Line up your heel vertically over your big toe. Angle your left knee in 45° and root the thigh. Actively press your left toes into the ground.

— Come halfway forward, use your right hand to catch your left wrist around your right foot, and lean to the left.

— To honor the Setup, shift your weight forward into your legs, lift your chest, and elongate your spine.

15 PAÑCADAŚA

15TH POSITION, EXHALE

Exhale, 5 to 8 Breaths

Reach torso up, out, forward, and down into State of Āsana.

— Bend forward with a move that invigorates your entire body en masse.

— Root your legs, elongate your spine, pull back with your arms, and sweep your head down to your shin.

— As you come to a standstill, allow your body to become more weighted by going with the downward pull of gravity.

— Work to flatten your torso onto your extended leg and allow your left heel to press up into your abdomen, an action that triggers Uḍḍīyāna Bandha.

State of the Āsana

JĀNU ŚĪRṢĀSANA C

Left Side — 5 to 8 Breaths
Dṛṣṭi: Pādayorāgrai *(Foot)*

16 ṢOḌAŚA

16TH POSITION, INHALE

Inhale

Head up, grip feet, stop, and focus well.

— Lift up your head and chest, extend your arms, and increase your grip on the foot of the extended leg.

— Pause as you inflate your lungs to full capacity and awaken the flow of Śakti within the Middle Nāḍī.

JĀNU ŚĪRṢĀSANA C (Head to Knee Pose C)

Exhale

Charge up limbs and rev up for the lift-up move.

— Perform the below actions in rapid succession in conjunction with flushing the air out of your lungs:

- Sit up and lean back.
- Bend your knees and lift up your feet.
- Ready your arms for a decisive strike.

17 SAPTADAŚA

17TH POSITION, INHALE

Inhale

Stamp ground with hands; lift up hips and feet.

— Lift up Pratibhā! Press the floor with your hands and clear your seat off the ground with the speed of a lightning strike!

— Suck your feet under you as you lean forward with your upper body.

18 AṢṬADAŚA

18TH POSITION, EXHALE

Exhale

Bend elbows with control and shoot feet back.

— Commit to bending your elbows and pivoting on your arms.

— Simultaneously plunge your upper body towards the earth and drive your feet straight back.

Exhale (continued)

Stop; make body as straight and strong as a stick.

— To complete your move, keep lowering your body towards the ground while anticipating the perfect instant to stop your momentum and strike the shape of an unbreakable staff.

— Stop your whole body in place. Hover just above the earth and defy gravity. Halt time and experience the "golden eternity." In the words of Jack Kerouac, "Everything is ecstasy, inside. We just don't know it because of our thinking-minds... stop breathing for 3 seconds, listen to the silence inside the illusion of the world... It is all one vast awakened thing. I call it the golden eternity. It is perfect."

19 EKONAVIṂŚATI

19TH POSITION, INHALE

Inhale

Lift up head and open chest with a mighty inhale.

— With a swift, sure spring, circle your head all the way up to the peak, ground your extended arms, and center your spine between your arm pillars.

20 VIṂŚATI

20TH POSITION, EXHALE

Exhale

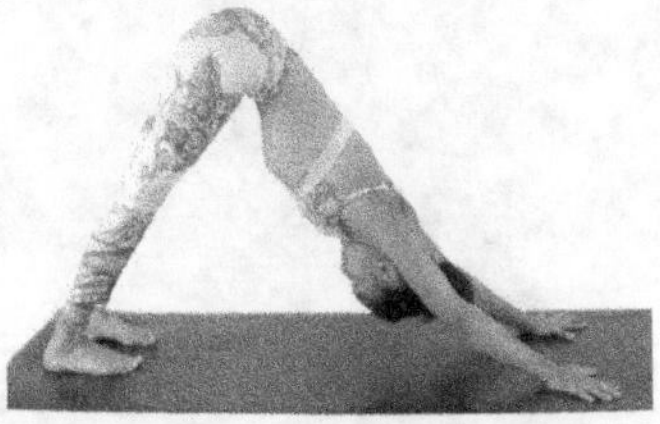

Press hands down, swing hips back, strike Down Dog.

— Cast your hips back skillfully to the beloved form.

— Upon arrival, stop in place for a few beats. Electrify your skeleton and allow awakened energy to flow freely within your Nāḍīs.

— Lengthen your spine and make your abdomen fly up into the shape of a greyhound dog's belly.

FULL VINYĀSA

21 EKAVIṂŚATI / INHALE — ARDHA UTTĀNĀSANA

22 DVĀVIṂŚATI / EXHALE — UTTĀNĀSANA

SAMASTHITI

MARĪCHYĀSANA A (Great Sage Pose A)

7 SAPTA
7TH POSITION, INHALE

Exhale

Crouch low and patiently store up force.

— Lower your hips towards the ground with the agility of a frog.

— Press your hands down firmly and project your pelvis back.

— Intentionally put forces in play within your body that prepare you for a mighty forward leap.

Inhale

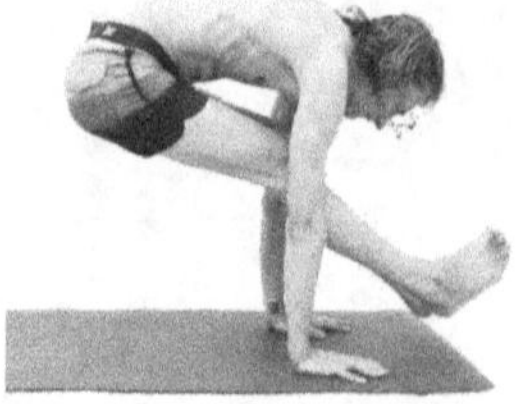

Spring to Daṇḍāsana.

— Shoot your legs forward to Daṇḍāsana, straight as an arrow.

Vinyāsa Meta View

Visualize a dragster racing down the track with total commitment and pure speed. As you jump, stabilize your hips to better control the strong action of throwing your feet and legs forward, like a parachute released from the back of a dragster to slow it down.

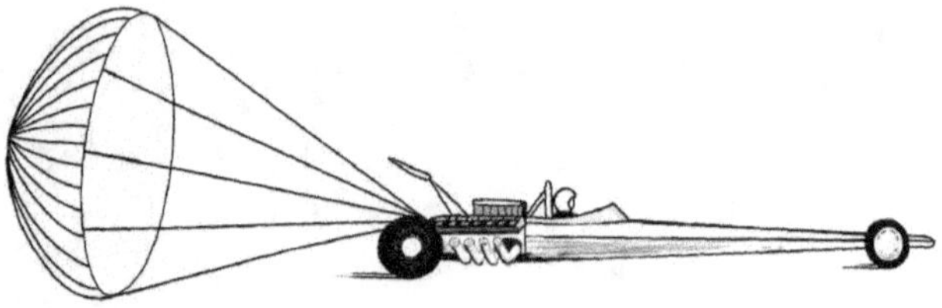

Inhale (continued)

Plant right foot in front of hip; wrap arms behind back.

— Bring your right foot back to your right hip; shift forward. Lean to the left, lift your right sitting bone, and take your right arm around your right shin.

— Internally rotate your shoulders as you reach your left arm behind you; use your right hand to catch your left wrist. Both palms face out.

— Bend forward to a halfway point, add grounding power to your legs, and stabilize your pelvis.

— To fully embody your Setup position, perform the following actions:

- Weight your legs more than your pelvis.
- Stamp down your right foot.
- Ground your left thigh.
- Endlessly lengthen your left leg.
- Use your arms to lasso your squatting leg.
- Squeeze your leg with your arms to create a Mudrā *(Energetic Seal)*.
- Lift your head, open your chest, and strongly pull up your navel.
- Coaxingly lengthen your spine from head to tail and make ready for action.

8 AṢṬAU
8TH POSITION, EXHALE

Exhale, 5 to 8 Breaths

Stamp squatting foot, ground straight leg, and bow forward.

— Elongate your spine as you dive your torso down towards your extended leg.

— Sweep your lungs empty by contracting the intercostal and abdominal muscles within your torso.

State of the Āsana

MARĪCHYĀSANA A

Right Side — 5 to 8 Breaths
Dṛṣṭi: Pādayorāgrai *(Foot)*

FULL VINYĀSA

SAMASTHITI
1 EKAM / INHALE — ŪRDHVA HASTĀSANA
2 DVE / EXHALE — UTTĀNĀSANA
3 TRĪṆI / INHALE — ARDHA UTTĀNĀSANA
4 CATVĀRI / EXHALE — CATURAṄGA DAṆḌĀSANA
5 PAÑCA / INHALE — ŪRDHVA MUKHA ŚVĀNĀSANA
6 ṢAṬ / EXHALE — ADHO MUKHA ŚVĀNĀSANA

9 NAVA
9TH POSITION, INHALE

Inhale

Come up halfway and define the Setup position anew.

— Lift up your head and chest as you tighten the circle of your arms around your squatting leg and knowingly catch the secret Mudrās *(Energetic Seals)* hidden in the form.

— Use the Ujjāyī Breathing technique to fill up your lungs smoothly and expand your chest.

Vinyāsa Meta View
By doing the basic, monotonous Haṭha work of faithfully honoring your entrance into and exit from each pose, you'll pierce through the veil of illusion (Māyā) and know firsthand the hidden Spiritual Dimension that has highest value in this world.

Exhale

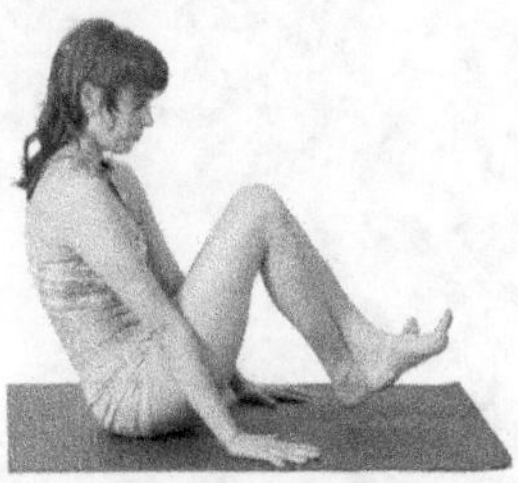

Prepare a mighty strike-and-lift move.

— Sit up, lean back, and bend your knees. Lift up your feet, round your back, and make a fierce crouch.

— Swiftly pause, build up energy, tap the limitless power of your center, and perfectly picture your jump-back move.

10 DAŚA
10TH POSITION, INHALE

Inhale

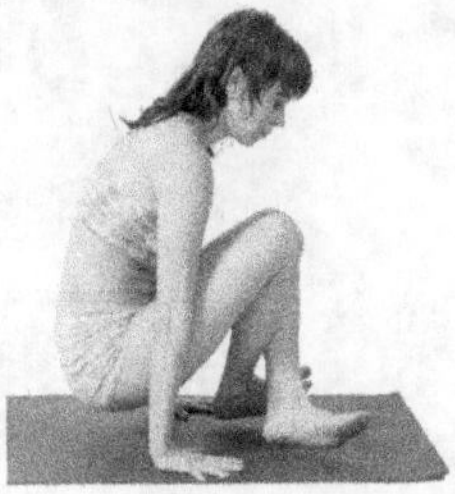

Lift up with strategic suddenness.

— Stamp down and lift up with rapid-fire speed and make the element of surprise your ally.

— Suck your feet back and lean forward with your upper body.

11 EKĀDAŚA
11TH POSITION, EXHALE

Exhale

Dive upper body forward and jump back.

— Bend your elbows decisively and pivot on your arms. Shoot your legs back with determination.

MARĪCHYĀSANA A (Great Sage Pose A)

Exhale (continued)

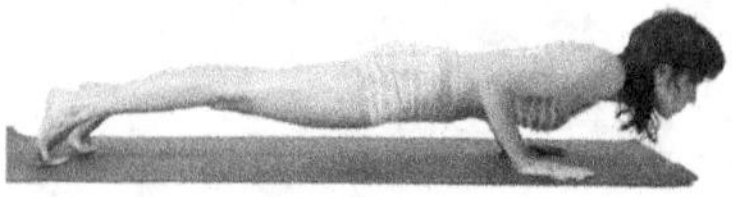

Caturaṅga Daṇḍāsana.

— Strike your pose with dispatch. Stamp down your hands and brace your arms.

— Integrate the position of your legs, pelvis, torso, and head by aligning them along a single horizontal axis.

— A yogī who remains truly motionless for two seconds in this Yantra *(Magical Shape)* knows the infinite power of Tapas.

12 DVĀDAŚA

12TH POSITION, INHALE

Inhale

Ūrdhva Mukha Śvānāsana.

— Lift up your head in a great circle as you extend your arms and puff your chest expansively. Visualize a spinnaker sail at the bow of a sailboat filled with wind.

13 TRAYODAŚA

13TH POSITION, EXHALE

Exhale

Adho Mukha Śvānāsana.

— Sweep your hips back in time with driving the air from your lungs; perform these actions benevolently, without harshness, and delight in taking command of your body and breath.

Vinyāsa Meta View
Know and worship the deities of:

Earth
Water
Fire
Air
Space

Inside your own body!

Perceiving the Five Elements as Deities to worship is a less known definition of the word Dhāraṇā, the Sixth Limb of Yoga. In the Yoga-Taraṅgiṇī (a commentary on the Gorakṣa-Śataka) Verse 2.53 states:

"Holding the Five Elements within the heart, each one separately with complete immobility of the mind, is called Dhāraṇā."

14 CATURDAŚA

14TH POSITION, INHALE

Exhale (continued)

Skillfully exhale.

— As a lover of action, give over to your Crouch. Invest in preparing for action before acting.

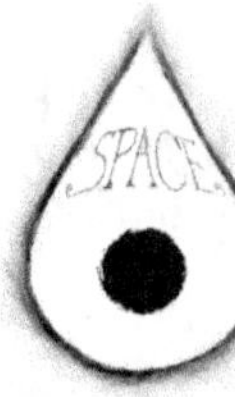

Inhale

Spring!

— Leap forward and put your backbone into it.

— Come directly to Daṇḍāsana.

Inhale (continued)

Squat on left leg; catch wrist behind back.

— Bring your left foot back to your outer left hip as if you are squatting.

— Shift your body forward, lift your left sitting bone, and add grounding power to your legs.

— Take your left arm around your shin and swing your right arm behind your back. Use your left hand to catch your right wrist. Internally rotate your arms so both palms face out.

— Come halfway forward and stop in position. Lighten your seat, anchor your legs, and snug your arms up to your squatting leg.

— Project your spine outward into the space above your extended leg. Take your time with this gesture; know that the effort to achieve maximum spinal length before you fold forward protects your back and helps you extract the healing medicine from your shape.

15 PAÑCADAŚA

15TH POSITION, EXHALE

Exhale, 5 to 8 Breaths

Come down with a swift move to the destination.

— Swoop your torso down to your extended leg.

— Become expert in going from the Setup position into the State of the Āsana with a gesture, a strategic, confident move.

— As you come to your stopping place, remain forward. Stamp down your left foot, ground your right thigh, and add weight to your torso and head.

State of the Āsana

MARĪCHYĀSANA A

Left Side — 5 to 8 Breaths
Dṛṣṭi: Pādayorāgrai *(Foot)*

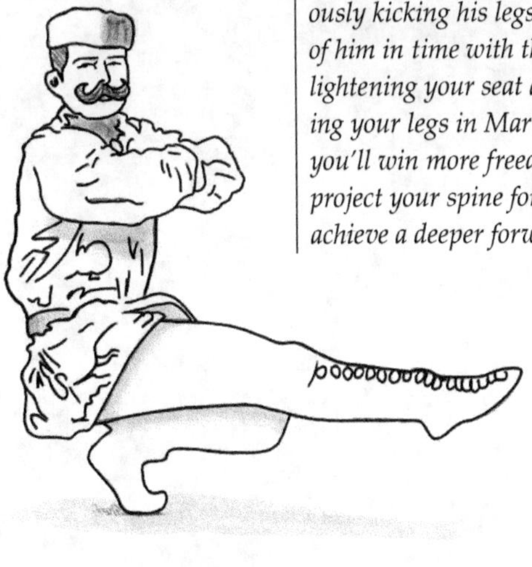

16 ṢOḌAŚA

16TH POSITION, INHALE

Inhale

Return to Setup position.

— Lift your head, come up halfway, and stop.

— Before you release and sit up, make your mind razor-sharp by performing the following actions:

- Anchor your legs.
- Brace your arms.
- Pull up your belly.
- Open your chest.

— Know this Setup position as a great ally of the yogī.

Vinyāsa Meta View

When doing the Marīchyāsana poses (A, B, C, D) remember to place more of the weight in your legs rather than sitting back on your pelvis. Visualize a Russian folk dancer in a low squat with hips just off the ground, dexterously kicking his legs out in front of him in time with the music. By lightening your seat and grounding your legs in Marīchyāsana, you'll win more freedom to project your spine forward and achieve a deeper forward bend.

MARĪCHYĀSANA A (Great Sage Pose A)

Exhale

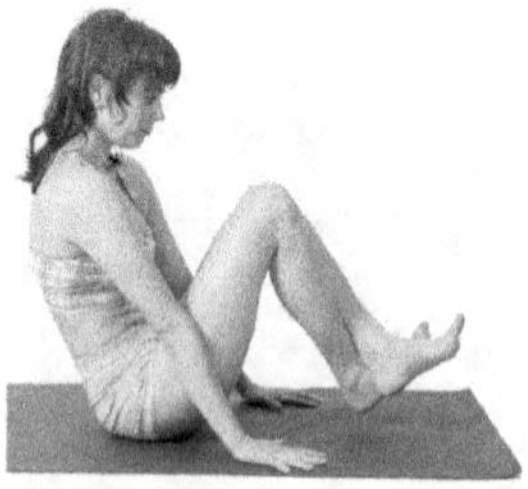

Coil body into a ready crouch.

— Perform these actions in rapid succession:

- Sit up; lean back.
- Bend your knees; lift up your feet.
- Flex your spine; exhale forcefully.
- Build up to a mighty spring.

17 SAPTADAŚA

17TH POSITION, INHALE

Inhale

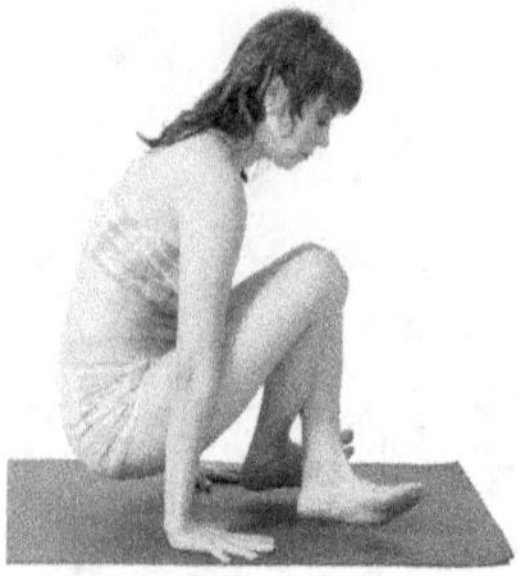

Lift up—purely up!

— With a burst of power, stamp down your hands and lift up your hips and feet.

— Sweep your feet back under you and begin to lean your upper body forward.

Vinyāsa Meta View

O Yogī, know the supreme value of the pure lift-up move! Take to the monotonous work and summon great force each time you strike down and lift up. Earnest repetition will reward you with the strength to slay demons.

18 AṢṬADAŚA

18TH POSITION, EXHALE

Exhale

Lean forward and kick feet back.

— Bend your elbows and pivot on your arms with your body in a compact shape. Keep your hips down and your legs tucked up under you.

— Project your head forward as you continue to lower your chest towards the ground.

— Drive your legs straight back and stop all movement with speedy precision.

Exhale (continued)

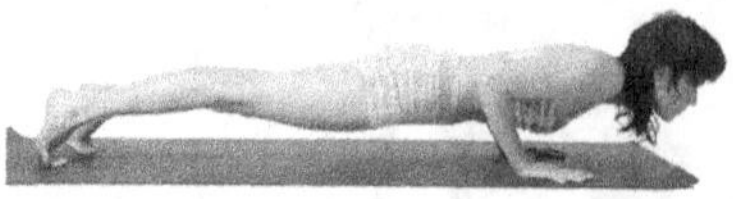

Strike Four-Limbed Staff Pose with great stopping power.

— Strike your pose instantly. Anchor your limbs and achieve a light, strong daṇḍa.

— Pause well and greet the earth with a bow.

19 EKONAVIMŚATI

19TH POSITION, INHALE

Inhale

Rise up and gracefully arch spine.

— Lift your head all the way up to its desired destination in a single sweep. At the same time, press your arms straight and expand your chest greatly.

— To complete your move, anchor your feet, ground your thighs, and send an energetic force driving back through your legs from hips to toes.

20 VIMŚATI

20TH POSITION, EXHALE

Exhale

Project hips back and come to Downward Dog.

— Sweep your body back to Downward Dog Pose as an intentional device to exhale more thoroughly.

Vinyāsa Meta View

By making it a practice to connect your movement with your breath, seek to participate more actively in filling up or emptying your lungs. In other words, each little Vinyāsa move is actually a Prāṇāyāma exercise in disguise.

FULL VINYĀSA

21 EKAVIMŚATI / INHALE — ARDHA UTTĀNĀSANA

22 DVĀVIMŚATI / EXHALE — UTTĀNĀSANA

SAMASTHITI

MARĪCHYĀSANA B (Great Sage Pose B)

7 SAPTA
7TH POSITION, INHALE

Exhale

Squat down low.

— Rally all of your forces and visualize a great forward leap. Take pleasure in hunkering back, storing up force in your legs, and skillfully expelling the air from your lungs.

Inhale

Launch feet forward.

— Catapult your whole body forward all at once. Seek to act without any doubt; eliminate subtle fear of falling. Hold nothing back as you zip your legs through and sit down in Daṇḍāsana.

Inhale (continued)

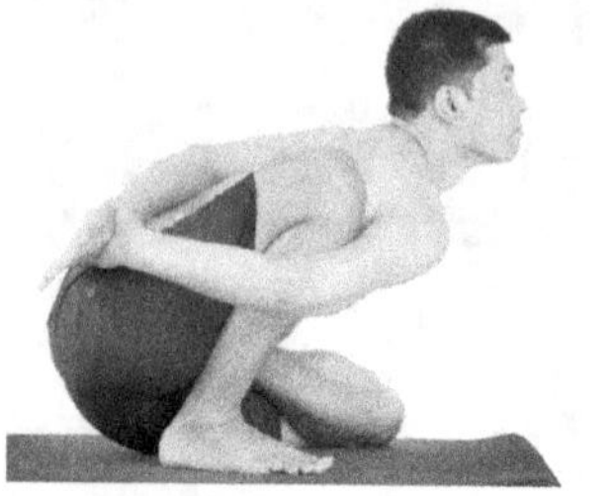

Left leg to Half Lotus, right leg squat, arms behind back.

— To take Half Lotus:

- Turn your left thigh out.
- Bend your left knee.
- Bring your left foot to the right inner groin crease.

— Bring your right foot back to a squat.

— Shift forward and lift your right sitting bone.

— Wrap your right arm around your right shin and swing your left arm behind you.

— Use your right hand to catch your left wrist.

— Come halfway forward and stop in place to formalize your Setup position.

— Go through this maestro's checklist for galvanizing your body's forces:

- ☐ Take deep interest in my Setup.
- ☐ Stamp down my squatting foot.
- ☐ Ground my Lotus thigh.
- ☐ Roll back my shoulders.
- ☐ Snug my arms to my leg.
- ☐ Lift up my spine.
- ☐ Open my chest.
- ☐ Wake up the energy at my root.
- ☐ Bring myself to a scintillating readiness for action.

8 AṢṬAU
8TH POSITION, EXHALE

Exhale, 5 to 8 Breaths

Fold forward into State of the Āsana.

— Project your head and torso down towards the ground while remaining centered in the middle between your legs. Make a swift move with a swift mind.

— Finish off your transition with these flourishes:

- Stamp down with your squatting foot.
- Anchor your left thigh.
- Bow down low to the beloved earth.

State of the Āsana

MARĪCHYĀSANA B

Right Side — 5 to 8 Breaths
Dṛṣṭi: Nasagrai *(Nose)*

FULL VINYĀSA

SAMASTHITI
1 EKAM / INHALE — ŪRDHVA HASTĀSANA
2 DVE / EXHALE — UTTĀNĀSANA
3 TRĪṆI / INHALE — ARDHA UTTĀNĀSANA
4 CATVĀRI / EXHALE — CATURAṄGA DAṆḌĀSANA
5 PAÑCA / INHALE — ŪRDHVA MUKHA ŚVĀNĀSANA
6 ṢAṬ / EXHALE — ADHO MUKHA ŚVĀNĀSANA

9 NAVA

9TH POSITION, INHALE

Inhale

Lift up to the halfway point; re-establish Setup position.

— Root your legs brilliantly and lift your chest against resistance from your arms that are lassoed around your squatting leg. Pause, and enjoy the lucidity that comes from using these various Mudrās to rivet your body in place.

Vinyāsa Meta View
For every famous Mudrā such as Uḍḍīyāna Bandha, there are scores of lesser known yet equally important Mudrās that offer you excellent ways of sealing energy within your body. Marīchyāsana B and D both have multiple interlocking Mudrās including: taking Half Lotus, wrapping your arms around your squatting leg, and binding your hands together behind your back. Learning to view these basic actions as opportunities to harness the Life Force that is circulating throughout your body is a great way to express your Āsana potently, create Absorption (Samādhi), and extract more knowledge out of your experience.

Exhale

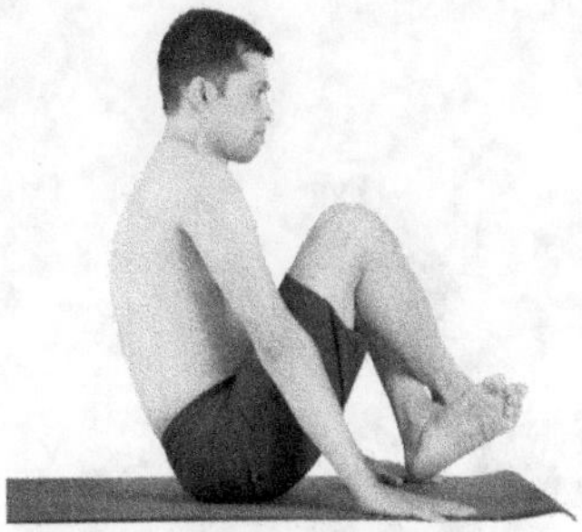

Crouch; galvanize center.

— Sit up, lean back, and bend your knees. Lift up your feet, plant your hands on the ground in front of your hips, and coil your torso into a ready crouch.

10 DAŚA

10TH POSITION, INHALE

Inhale

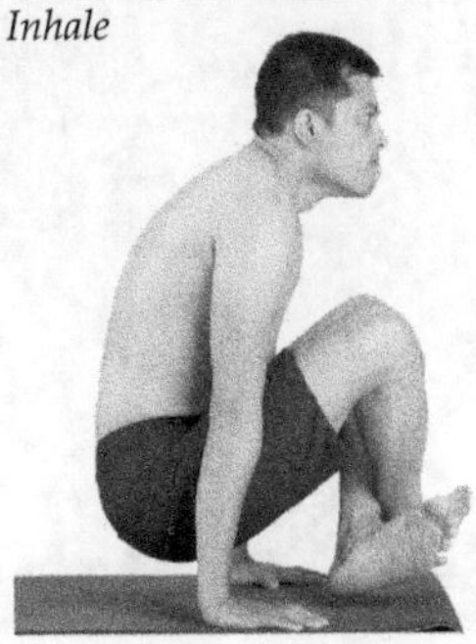

Lift up!

— Press your hands down with a sudden, decisive strike and lift up your hips and feet.

— Whip your feet back under you as you lean forward with your upper body.

11 EKĀDAŚA

11TH POSITION, EXHALE

Exhale

Project upper body forward and lower body back.

— Bend your elbows and lower your upper body towards the ground as you pivot on your arms.

— Keep your legs suspended in the air underneath your torso during this rhythmic process.

MARĪCHYĀSANA B (Great Sage Pose B)

Exhale (continued)

Jump back and strike Four-Limbed Staff Pose.

— When your feet come to the ground behind you, strike a statuesque pose in an instant and enjoy perfect stillness for any amount of time.

12 DVĀDAŚA
12TH POSITION, INHALE

Inhale

Inhale, rise up, and expand chest.

— To enhance this transition, pretend you are a cobra rearing up from the earth all at once to meet danger.

— Lift up your head and spine with command.

— Press your arms straight with a mighty surge of power.

— Coil your upper spine into a tight spiral, expand your chest greatly.

— Hunker down with your stubborn, earth-loving legs.

Vinyāsa Meta View
Through your skillful action, transform a mere body position into a Sacred Yantra and honor the snake, a primal symbol of creativity. The image of the snake is a wonderful reminder that every creative form that manifests in this world spins out in circular movements and spiral patterns of energy.

13 TRAYODAŚA
13TH POSITION, EXHALE

Exhale

Swing body back to Down Dog with an exhale.

— Take to the rhythmic aspect of this transition; use momentum to thrust your hips back. Create enough force to carry you all the way to your position in a single sweep.

— Arrive with your body full of natural dynamism and agreeably arrange your skeleton without ado.

14 CATURDAŚA
14TH POSITION, INHALE

Exhale (continued)

Crouch!

— Get on the hunt for Daṇḍāsana. Sweep your lungs empty, fully animate your entire being, and take to crouching with the exuberance of an animal at play.

15 PAÑCADAŚA
15TH POSITION, EXHALE

16 ṢOḌAŚA
16TH POSITION, INHALE

Inhale

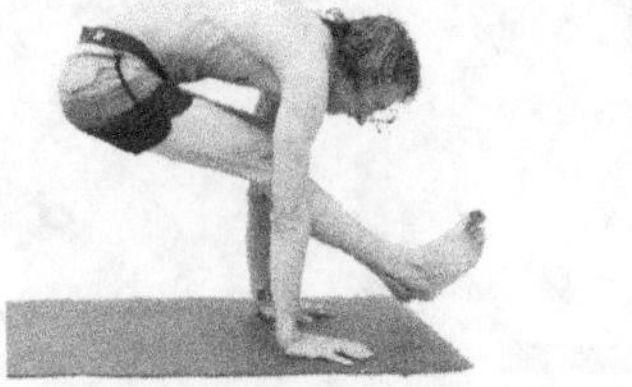

Jump forward without reserve and strike destination.

— Wholly commit to your leap; use enough force to project your legs forward into the space beyond your hands.

Inhale (continued)

Strike a smart Setup position.

— To gain Half Lotus:

- Turn your right thigh out.
- Bend your right knee.
- Bring your right foot back to the inner groin crease of your left leg.

— With your right foot in Half Lotus, bring your left foot back to your outer left hip. Form a squat and lift your left sitting bone.

— Wrap your left arm around your left shin and swing your right arm behind you.

— Use your left hand to catch your right wrist, both palms facing out.

— Bend forward and stop cleanly in place at a halfway point. Use the following physical actions to awaken the subtle energy *(Śakti)* that sleeps at the base of your pelvis: plant your squatting foot, ground your legs, brace your arms, lift up your head, and lengthen your spine from tail to head.

Exhale, 5 to 8 Breaths

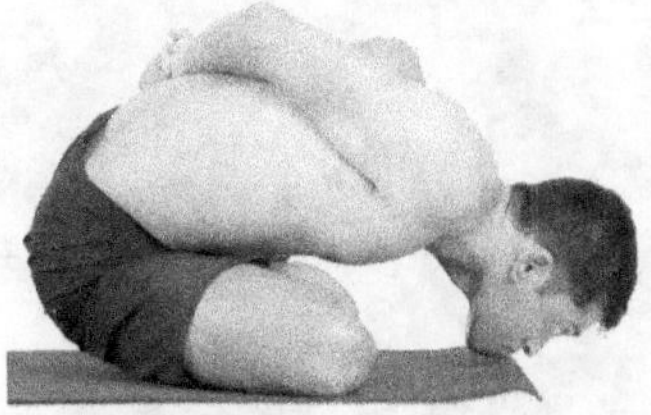

Bend forward with a distinct move.

— Swoop your torso down and swoosh the air out of your lungs.

— Perfect the gesture of folding forward by simultaneously activating this pair of opposites: extend outward into space and release down to the earth.

State of the Āsana

MARĪCHYĀSANA B

Left Side — 5 to 8 Breaths
Dṛṣṭi: Nasagrai *(Nose)*

Inhale

Achieve the Setup position anew; inhale.

— Lift up your head and chest and stop at the halfway point. Brace your arms and ground your legs. Empty your palate in a flash and light up your body with intelligence.

Vinyāsa Meta View

Student: "What does empty your palate mean?"

Teacher: "Research."

MARĪCHYĀSANA B (Great Sage Pose B)

Exhale

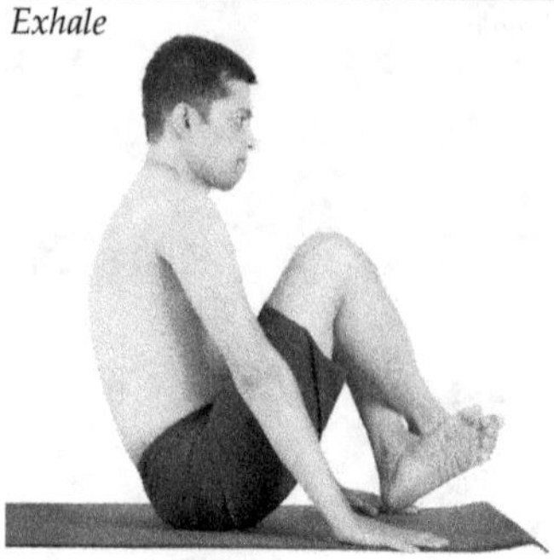

Crouch! Prepare for sudden action.

— Sit up and lean back. Bend your knees, lift up your feet, and round your back.

— Skillfully flush the air out of your lungs to access your core strength and get ready for the power lift.

17 SAPTADAŚA

17TH POSITION, INHALE

Inhale

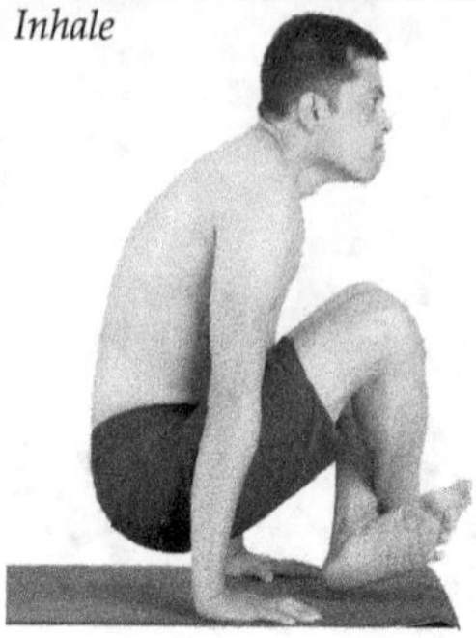

Lift up.

— Perform a strike-and-lift move with a determined one-two punch: strike down with your hands and lift up your hips and feet.

— Immediately whip your feet back under you and begin to lean forward with your head and chest.

18 AṢṬADAŚA

18TH POSITION, EXHALE

Exhale

Lean forward; thrust back legs.

—Bend your elbows; continue leaning forward as you pivot on your arms with your legs suspended in the air under your torso.

— Swing your feet back and straighten your legs as you lower your head and chest towards the ground.

Exhale (continued)

Come to Caturaṅga and stop all movement.

— Arrive with your head, torso, pelvis, and legs in a perfectly straight, single Yantra line.

19 EKONAVIṂŚATI

19TH POSITION, INHALE

Inhale

Open chest and root back legs.

— Use timing and momentum to press your arms straight and coil your spine into a mighty arch within your torso.

— Reach back through your legs in resistance to projecting your spine forward.

20 VIṂŚATI

20TH POSITION, EXHALE

Exhale

Zoom back to the inverted V shape.

— Boldly thrust back with your hips. Take athletic control over your movement and involve your entire body in the transition to Down Dog.

— Lose your inhibition, let fly a full-on move, and trust your ability to apply force.

Vinyāsa Meta View
The Vinyāsa way involves turning practice into a laboratory for studying yourself in action. This includes learning to take bold risks. Bringing power, dynamism, and certainty to your transitions is important for learning to trust yourself and knowing that you can wield power with skill, intelligence, and kindness.

FULL VINYĀSA

21 EKAVIṂŚATI / INHALE — ARDHA UTTĀNĀSANA

22 DVĀVIṂŚATI / EXHALE — UTTĀNĀSANA

SAMASTHITI

MARĪCHYĀSANA C (Great Sage Pose C)

7 SAPTA
7TH POSITION, INHALE

Exhale

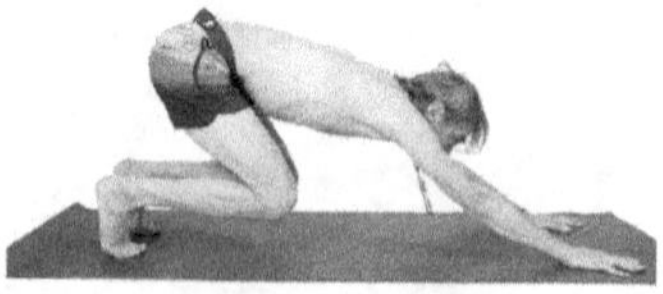

Lower hips into a Crouch.

— Hunker back through your hips, stamp the ground firmly with your hands, strengthen your arms, and store up force in your legs.

— Visualize a great leap.

Inhale

Jump legs forward of arms.

— Leap forward with gusto.

— Send your legs ahead of your arms in a direct line to Daṇḍāsana, just like an arrow going straight to the target when launched from the bow of a skilled archer.

5 to 8 Breaths

Plant right foot in a squat, twist, and clasp hands.

— From Daṇḍāsana, bring your right foot back into a squat, lean your torso to the left, and lift your right hip slightly up off the ground.

— Shift more of your weight into your legs rather than your pelvis.

— Stamp your squatting foot down and anchor your extended leg; lift your spine and rotate to the right.

— Wrap your left arm around your right knee, swing your right arm behind you, and use your right hand to grip your left wrist.

— Root your limbs and rotate your torso evenly from the base of your spine up through the crown of your head.

State of the Āsana

MARĪCHYĀSANA C

Right Side — 5 to 8 Breaths
Dṛṣṭi: Pārśva *(Side)*

8 AṢṬAU
8TH POSITION, EXHALE

Exhale

Face front, make a compact shape, and galvanize center.

— Release your twist, face forward, and make a crouch.

— Lean back, bend your knees, and lift up your feet.

— Slightly round your spine and plant your hands on the ground in front of your hips.

— Forcefully expel the air out of your lungs and build up energy for a spring.

FULL VINYĀSA

SAMASTHITI
1 EKAM / INHALE — ŪRDHVA HASTĀSANA
2 DVE / EXHALE — UTTĀNĀSANA
3 TRĪṆI / INHALE — ARDHA UTTĀNĀSANA
4 CATVĀRI / EXHALE — CATURAṄGA DAṆḌĀSANA
5 PAÑCA / INHALE — ŪRDHVA MUKHA ŚVĀNĀSANA
6 ṢAṬ / EXHALE — ADHO MUKHA ŚVĀNĀSANA

Inhale

Lift up with a power strike!

— Swiftly stamp your hands down; lift up your pelvis and feet.

— Suck your feet under you without touching them to the ground and lean forward.

9 NAVA

9TH POSITION, EXHALE

Exhale

Commit forward and jump back.

— Bend your elbows and pivot on your arms. Swing your legs back keeping your feet off the ground as you lower your head and chest into the desired Caturaṅga position.

Exhale (continued)

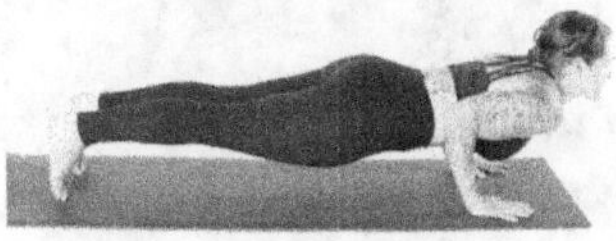

Land in horizontal staff pose.

— When your movement brings you into position, stop with precision and hold steady for a beat or two.

— The connoisseur of yoga knows the Horizontal Staff Pose is a great giver of strength.

10 DAŚA

10TH POSITION, INHALE

Inhale

Spring to Up Dog without delay.

— Lift up your head in a perfect circle.

— Straighten your arms with a strong, slow-motion press move.

— Expand your chest regally and invest your legs with prodigious stopping power.

MARĪCHYĀSANA C (Great Sage Pose C)

11 EKĀDAŚA
11TH POSITION, EXHALE

Exhale

Exhale. Flow back to Adho Mukha Śvānāsana.

— Sweep your hips back maintaining the same speed from start to finish.

— Put on your psychic brakes and stop all at once when you hit the position.

12 DVĀDAŚA
12TH POSITION, INHALE

Exhale (continued)

Crouch and target your leap.

— Bend your knees, lower your hips, and store up force in your legs.

Inhale

Jump through, straight legs; sit down.

— Leap forward feetfirst and fully extend your legs like an eagle coming in for a landing talons first.

— Stabilize your hips as you shoot your legs forward, like an eagle spreading its wings to apply the brakes and snare its prey with deadly accuracy.

5 to 8 Breaths

Root legs, rotate spine, and clasp hands.

— Bring your left foot back to a squat, lean to the right, and allow your left sitting bone to lift up off the ground.

— Shift your weight forward, lighten your pelvis, anchor your squatting foot, and ground your extended leg.

— Lift up your torso and rotate your spine to the left.

— Wrap your right arm around your outer left knee. Reach back with your left arm and use your left hand to catch your right wrist behind you with your palms facing out.

— Tighten the lasso of your arms around your leg, lift up your chest, and twist in earnest.

— Cast a steady gaze all the way around to the side.

— Enjoy.

State of the Āsana

MARĪCHYĀSANA C

Left Side — 5 to 8 Breaths
Dṛṣṭi: Pārśva *(Side)*

13 TRAYODAŚA

13TH POSITION, EXHALE

Exhale

Face forward and coil into a poised crouch.

— Release your twist; face forward. Bend your knees, lift up your feet, plant your hands on the ground in front of your hips, and round your spine into flexion.

— Build up energy and strategize your destination before launching into action, as if pulling back a bow and taking aim before shooting an arrow.

Inhale

Lift up with surprising suddenness.

— Strike the ground with your hands and lift up your hips and feet with a burst of power.

— Whip your feet back under you and lean forward with your head and chest.

14 CATURDAŚA

14TH POSITION, EXHALE

Exhale

Lean forward, bend elbows, and send feet back.

— Bend your elbows; pivot on your arms. Swing your legs back between the arms with your feet up off the ground.

— Boldly lower your head and chest towards the earth and extend your legs.

Exhale (continued)

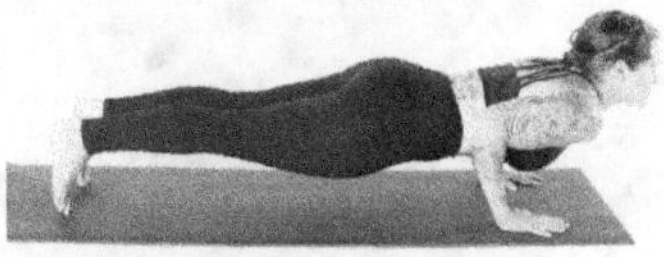

Four-Limbed Staff Pose.

— Control the end of your transition; stop all movement as soon as your head, torso, pelvis, and legs horizontally align.

— Command your center and make one pure Yantra line.

— Enjoy the spectacular view that is gifted to one who attains even a moment of absolute stillness.

MARĪCHYĀSANA C (Great Sage Pose C)

15 PAÑCADAŚA
15TH POSITION, INHALE

Inhale

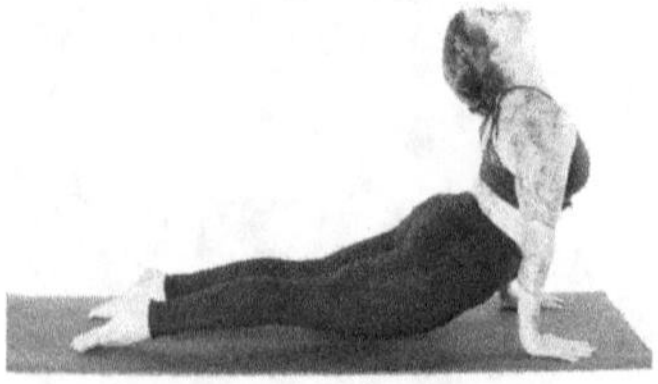

Lift spine up with applied strategy.

— Circle your head up to the end point, arch your spine, press your arms straight, and stubbornly root your legs. Repeatedly perform the actions in rapid-fire succession and you're sure to get the knack for this tricky transition.

16 ṢOḌAŚA
16TH POSITION, EXHALE

Exhale

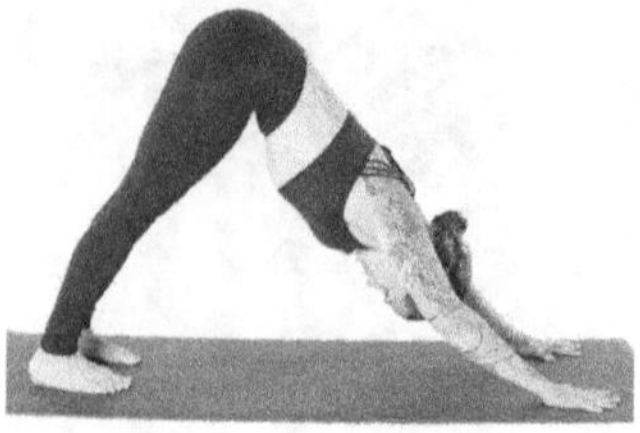

Adho Mukha Śvānāsana.

— Sweep the air out of your lungs as you thrust your hips back. Define your backward-driving move to Down Dog and strike the pose in a flash of illumination.

FULL VINYĀSA

17 SAPTADAŚA / INHALE — ARDHA UTTĀNĀSANA
18 AṢṬADAŚA / EXHALE — UTTĀNĀSANA
SAMASTHITI

MARĪCHYĀSANA D (Great Sage Pose D)

7 SAPTA
7TH POSITION, INHALE

Exhale

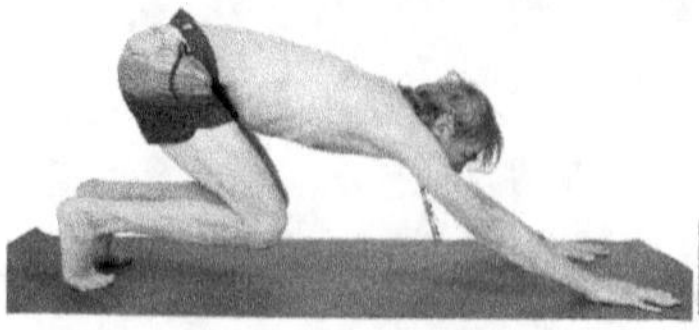

Crouch as if pulling back a slingshot.

— Use rhythm to bend your knees into a low crouch.

— Flush the air out of your lungs, energize your center, and become ready to leap forward.

Inhale

Launch a distinct move and jump through feetfirst.

— Shoot your legs forward as if launching yourself out of a catapult. Project your feet into the space well in front of your hands.

5 to 8 Breaths

Bring right foot back to a squat; twist to right.

— To take Half Lotus:

- Turn your left thigh out.
- Bend your left knee.
- Bring your left foot back to the inner groin crease of your right leg.

— Bring your right foot back into a squat and shift forward. Allow your right sitting bone to lift and stamp the ground with your weighted legs.

— Turn to the right, wrap your left arm around your right knee. Reach your left arm behind your back and use your left hand to catch your right wrist.

— Rotate your torso to the right; discerningly twist from the base of your spine up the axis to the root of your palate.

— Gaze to the side circularly.

State of the Āsana

MARĪCHYĀSANA D

Right Side — 5 to 8 Breaths
Dṛṣṭi: Pārśva *(Side)*

8 AṢṬAU
8TH POSITION, EXHALE

Exhale

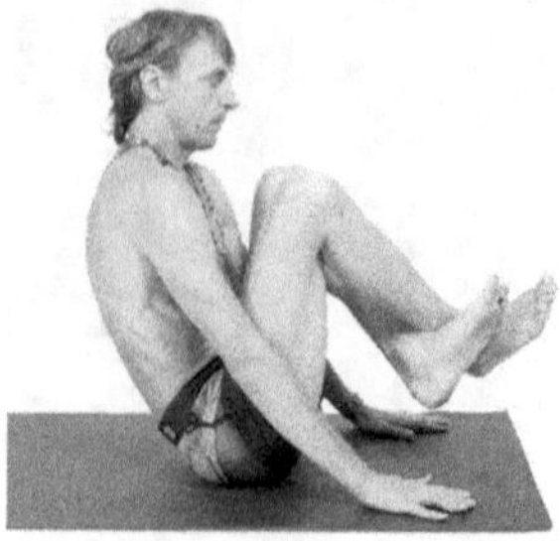

Face front, release Half Lotus, and make a ready Crouch.

— Release, face forward, and crouch. Make your body compact like a coiled spring.

— Charge your arms with force and anticipate the strike-and-lift move.

FULL VINYĀSA

SAMASTHITI
1 EKAM / INHALE — ŪRDHVA HASTĀSANA
2 DVE / EXHALE — UTTĀNĀSANA
3 TRĪṆI / INHALE — ARDHA UTTĀNĀSANA
4 CATVĀRI / EXHALE — CATURAṄGA DAṆḌĀSANA
5 PAÑCA / INHALE — ŪRDHVA MUKHA ŚVĀNĀSANA
6 ṢAṬ / EXHALE — ADHO MUKHA ŚVĀNĀSANA

Inhale

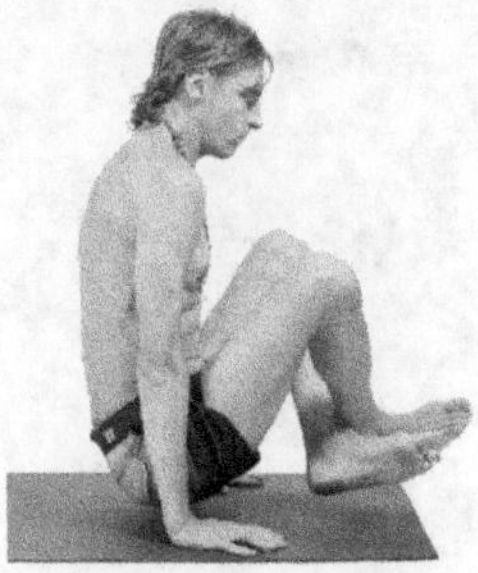

Sweep body up off the ground.

— Strike down with your hands and lift up your seat and feet.

— Whip your feet back under you and begin to lean forward with your head and chest.

9 NAVA
9TH POSITION, EXHALE

Exhale

Lean forward and swing legs back.

— Continue to lean forward, bend your elbows, and allow your compact body to turn in place as you pivot on your arms.

— Project your chest forward and drive your legs back, seeking the strength to lower your body into position with control.

Exhale (continued)

Stop decisively at the destination.

— Meet the challenge of stopping all movement at precisely the right moment and gain the superpower known as Nirodha Siddhi, the power to stop all activity at will.

10 DAŚA
10TH POSITION, INHALE

Inhale

Lift head with a circular motion to Up Dog.

— Synchronize your breath with your movement; mark the beginning, middle, and end of coming to Up Dog:

- Start inhaling when you go into action.
- Continue to inhale as you move through the arc of your gesture.
- Finish inhaling as you come to the end of your movement and strike your position.

MARĪCHYĀSANA D (Great Sage Pose D)

11 EKĀDAŚA
11TH POSITION, EXHALE

Exhale

Stop in Downward Dog.

— Swing your hips back with speedy skill and arrive in the shape of an inverted V.

— In a brief pause, become still. Steady your limbs, lengthen your breath, and quest inward to find your intrinsic essence as a Seer to the world.

12 DVĀDAŚA
12TH POSITION, INHALE

Exhale (continued)

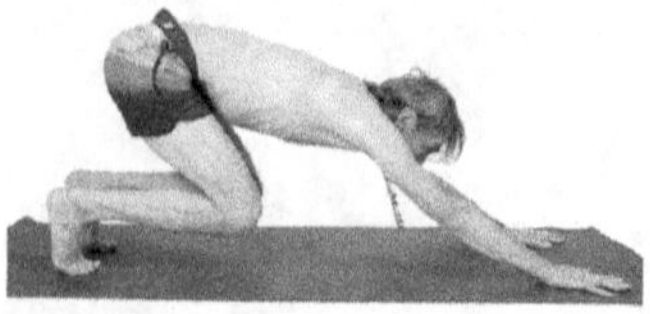

Crouch skillfully.

— Get low, summon frog leap power, empty your lungs, focus your mind, and prepare to strike.

Inhale

Spring forward.

— Shoot your legs forward with lightning speed.

5 to 8 Breaths

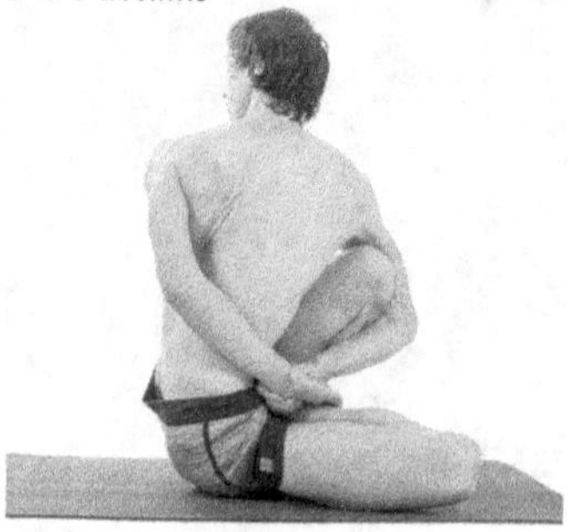

Right leg into Half Lotus; turn to the left.

— Externally rotate your right thigh. Bring your right foot to your left inner groin crease and into Half Lotus.

— Bring your left foot into a squat; allow your left sitting bone to lift up. Sit forward and ground your legs.

— Lift up your torso and rotate your spine to the left. Wrap your right arm around your left knee. Reach your right arm back and use your right hand to catch your left wrist.

— See the action of rotating your spine as a device to cleanse your visceral organs and wake up the whole system of Nāḍīs *(Energy Channels)* throughout your body.

Vinyāsa Meta View

"To twist is to purify."

Repeat this excellent Āsana Mantra whenever you twist. Take command of your spinal column. Rotate up from the base of your pelvis to the crown of your head. Gently squeeze and flush your internal organs and stimulate the workings of your digestive system.

State of the Āsana

MARĪCHYĀSANA D

Left Side — 5 to 8 Breaths
Dṛṣṭi: Pārśva *(Side)*

13 TRAYODAŚA

13TH POSITION, EXHALE

Exhale

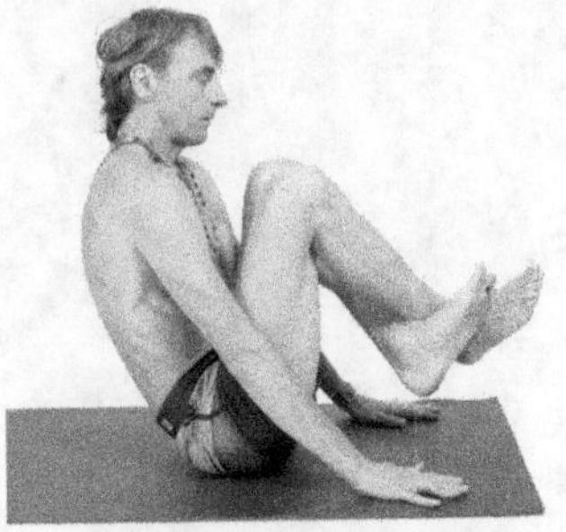

Face forward, charge limbs, and galvanize center.

— Release your twist and coil your body into a poised crouch; charge up your arms and legs.

— Be clear about working to build up energy before you launch into action.

Inhale

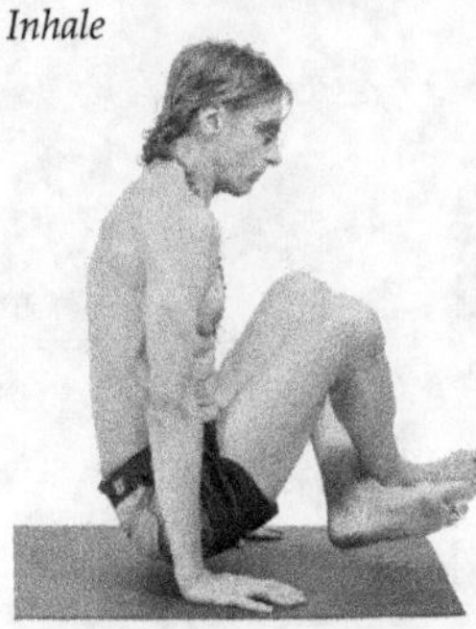

Lift up with a burst of power.

— With precise timing, strike down with your hands and lift up your seat and feet.

— Suck your legs under you and fight to keep your feet in the air while leaning forward with your head and chest.

14 CATURDAŚA

14TH POSITION, EXHALE

Exhale

Project head forward and drive legs back.

— Bend your elbows and pivot on your strong arms.

— Cause your compact body to turn in midair as you cantilever your chest forward, drive your legs back, and lower yourself into a noble position.

Exhale (continued)

Move and stop with equal skill; strike the form.

— Use mind control to stop all movement at the precise moment that your head, torso, pelvis, and legs arrive in the secret, potent stick shape prized by yogīs.

MARĪCHYĀSANA D (Great Sage Pose D)

15 PAÑCADAŚA

15TH POSITION, INHALE

Inhale

Lift head and raise spine up.

— Straightening your arms with a press move as you stubbornly root your legs and create maximum expansion across your chest.

— Enjoy your movement into Ūrdhva Mukha Śvānāsana as a surefire way to enjoy the pose.

16 ṢOḌAŚA

16TH POSITION, EXHALE

Exhale

Glide hips back to Adho Mukha Śvānāsana.

— Go from Up Dog to Down Dog by lifting up your hips and sweeping them back without doubt or interruption.

— Find rhythm and economy in your move; keep your arms and legs fully extended from start to finish.

— When your limbs are long and strong they make good levers that lend power to your move.

Vinyāsa Meta View
Know the end point of every transition as a pose called Nirodhāsana (Cessation Pose).

FULL VINYĀSA

17 SAPTADAŚA / INHALE — ARDHA UTTĀNĀSANA
18 AṢṬADAŚA / EXHALE — UTTĀNĀSANA
SAMASTHITI

NĀVĀSANA (Boat Pose)

7 SAPTA

7TH POSITION, INHALE

Exhale

Crouch and build up for a mighty leap.

— Bend your knees, shift your hips back, and get low to the ground.

— Savor the feeling of storing up force within your body and targeting your strike.

Inhale

Launch forward directly to Nāvāsana.

— Leap forward and immediately swing your legs up to your target of Boat Pose.

5 to 8 Breaths

Sit forward, lean upper body back, extend legs and arms.

— Swiftly lean your upper body back, lift up your feet to eye level, and fully extend your legs.

— Reach forward through your arms from shoulders to fingers.

— Kick out through your feet and project your legs forward with a mighty gesture of extension.

— Use the forward-driving force that is passing through your legs to shift onto the back edges of your sitting bones and off of your tailbone.

State of the Āsana

NĀVĀSANA

5 to 8 Breaths or more

Dṛṣṭi: Pādayorāgrai *(Feet)*

Exhale

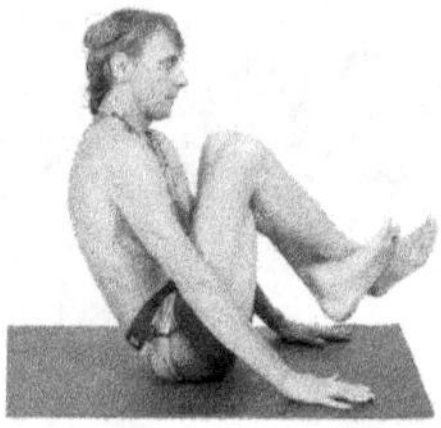

Coil body into a compact shape and gather force.

— Bend your knees; cross your ankles in front of you. Plant your hands on the ground in front of your hips. Stop for a quick second and build up energy for a power lift.

FULL VINYĀSA

SAMASTHITI

1 EKAM / INHALE — ŪRDHVA HASTĀSANA

2 DVE / EXHALE — UTTĀNĀSANA

3 TRĪṆI / INHALE — ARDHA UTTĀNĀSANA

4 CATVĀRI / EXHALE — CATURAṄGA DAṆḌĀSANA

5 PAÑCA / INHALE — ŪRDHVA MUKHA ŚVĀNĀSANA

6 ṢAṬ / EXHALE — ADHO MUKHA ŚVĀNĀSANA

8 AṢṬAU
8TH POSITION, INHALE

Inhale

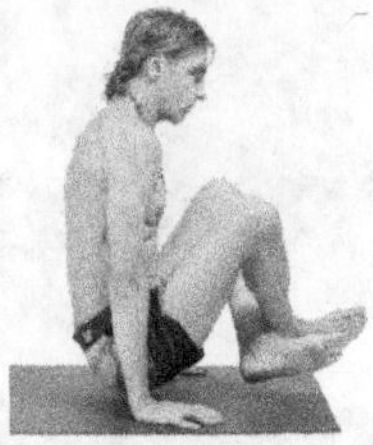

Plant hands, strengthen arms, and lift up cleanly.

— Stamp down your hands and swiftly lift up your seat.

7 SAPTA
7TH POSITION, INHALE

Free Breathing, 5 to 8 Breaths

Return to Boat Pose and hold.

— Sit down and return to Nāvāsana for another round.

— Repeat Boat Pose for a total of five times or more, lifting up in the interval between each stay in the pose.

Vinyāsa Meta View
Hail Nāvāsana! Take to the Great Belly Strengthener! The singular importance of the humble and easy-to-hate Boat Pose cannot be overstated!

State of the Āsana

NĀVĀSANA

5 to 8 Breaths or more
Dṛṣṭi: Pādayorāgrai *(Feet)*

Exhale

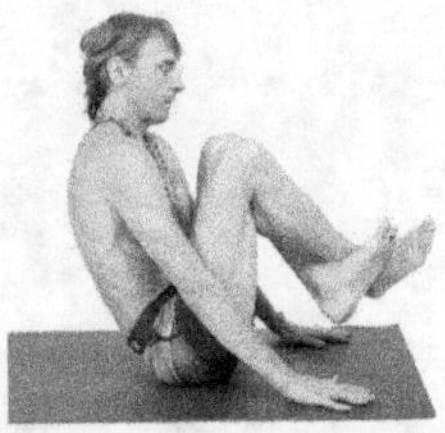

Cross ankles, root limbs, and gather force.

— After you repeat Nāvāsana for the last time, coil your body into a crouch and prepare to jump back.

— Plant your hands on the ground in front of your hips and build up energy for a power lift.

8 AṢṬAU
8TH POSITION, INHALE

Inhale

Lift up—purely up!

— Stamp the earth with your hands and swiftly lift up your feet and knees.

NĀVĀSANA (Boat Pose)

9 NAVA
9TH POSITION, EXHALE

Exhale

Jump back.

— Lean forward, bend your elbows, and pivot on your arms. Continue to lower your head and chest down towards the ground as you propel your legs back.

Exhale (continued)

Four-Limbed Staff Pose.

— Find a clear stopping place and halt all movement instantly.

— In the momentary pause, swiftly strengthen your arms and legs, and also firm your buttocks and abdomen. In short, activate the "Big Four" muscle groups (quads, hamstrings, glutes, abdomen) that surround your center.

— Holding steady and galvanizing your body's forces strengthen your body and will.

10 DAŚA
10TH POSITION, INHALE

Inhale

Upward Dog.

— Come to Upward Dog with rhythm.

— Lift up your head in a great arcing circle.

— Pull up from the root of your spine and open your chest.

11 EKĀDAŚA
11TH POSITION, EXHALE

Exhale

Downward Dog.

— Sweep your hips back as you flush the air out of your lungs. Come to Downward Dog with marvelous dynamism.

FULL VINYĀSA

12 DVĀDAŚA / INHALE — ARDHA UTTĀNĀSANA
13 TRAYODAŚA / EXHALE — UTTĀNĀSANA
SAMASTHITI

BHUJAPĪḌĀSANA (Arm Pressure Pose)

7 SAPTA
7TH POSITION, INHALE

Exhale

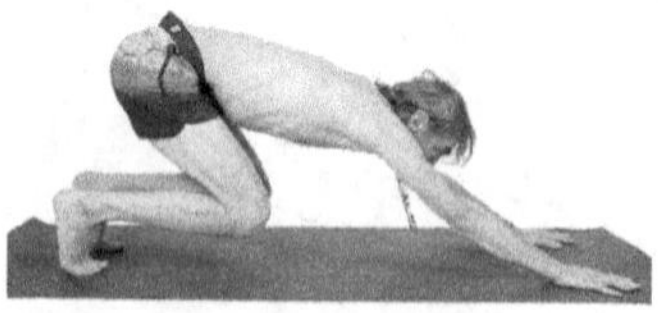

Crouch low and store up force.

— Strengthen your arms, bend your knees, hunker back, and build up energy in your legs.

Inhale

Jump legs onto arms and balance; strike Setup position.

— With great dynamism, throw your feet forward, land your thighs on top of your arms up towards your shoulders, and boldly wrap your legs around your arms.

— Cross your ankles in front of you with a dexterous flip of your feet.

— Strike an upright position on the edge of imbalance and animate your whole body with these actions:

- Stamp down your hands.
- Lengthen and strengthen your arms.
- Make your hips heavy and lift up your feet.
- Squeeze your arms with your legs and snug your crossed ankles up to each other.

Vinyāsa Meta View
An alternative way to go from Down Dog to the Setup position is to jump your feet to the ground outside your hands, then lift your legs and kick forward through your feet.

8 AṢṬAU
8TH POSITION, EXHALE

Exhale, 5 to 8 Breaths

Bend forward with arm strength.

— Bend your elbows with a press move, shift your center of gravity back and keep weight in your arms.

— As you come down, point your toes with your ankles crossed and suck your feet up under you.

— Lower your chin or head to the ground with control.

— Upon arrival, rely on the strength of your arms and your skill in balance to hold steady in position.

— Avoid leaning forward and placing excessive weight on your head.

State of the Āsana
BHUJAPĪḌĀSANA
5 to 8 Breaths or more
Dṛṣṭi: Nasagrai *(Nose)*

9 NAVA
9TH POSITION, INHALE

Inhale

Maintain crossed ankles and lift up to the Setup position.

— Stamp your hands down with a burst of power, sweep your head up off the ground with authority, and press your arms straight.

— Lift up your feet in front of you with your ankles crossed, squeeze your arms with your legs, and strike the Setup position anew.

— The wise yogī perceives the upright Setup position as a rare meditation seat, and therefore he frequently stops there, calmly balancing and growing strong.

FULL VINYĀSA

SAMASTHITI
1 EKAM / INHALE — ŪRDHVA HASTĀSANA
2 DVE / EXHALE — UTTĀNĀSANA
3 TRĪṆI / INHALE — ARDHA UTTĀNĀSANA
4 CATVĀRI / EXHALE — CATURAṄGA DAṆḌĀSANA
5 PAÑCA / INHALE — ŪRDHVA MUKHA ŚVĀNĀSANA
6 ṢAṬ / EXHALE — ADHO MUKHA ŚVĀNĀSANA

Inhale (continued), Exhale

Kick forward through feet and straighten legs.

— Uncross your ankles, sink your hips down, and shoot your legs forward with a mighty gesture of extension into Tittibhāsana *(Firefly Pose).*

— Pause, balance on your arms with full confidence, and get ready for action.

10 DAŚA

10TH POSITION, INHALE

Inhale

Sweep feet and shins back; balance on arms.

— Hinge at your knees, and with a powerful throw, swing your feet and shins back to Bakāsana *(Crow Pose).*

— In a swift pause, stamp down your hands, thrust down through your arms, and suck up your feet, shins, and thighs.

— Dome your upper back, tuck your tail, and make ready to jump back.

11 EKĀDAŚA

11TH POSITION, EXHALE

Exhale

Jump back.

— From Bakāsana, keep your chest forward, bend your elbows, and nimbly shoot your legs back.

Exhale (continued)

Stop in Four-Limbed Staff Pose!

— Stop in place with precision and instantly organize the subtle particulars of your horizontal Stick Shape:

- Brace your arms and lift your chest.
- Tuck your tail and pull up your navel.
- Fully extend your legs and stamp the earth with your feet.

— Stay and enjoy the glory of Caturaṅga!

BHUJAPĪDĀSANA (Arm Pressure Pose)

12 DVĀDAŚA
12TH POSITION, INHALE

Inhale

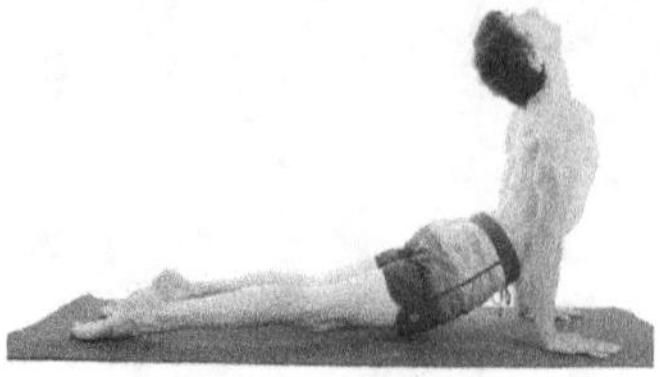

Come to Upward Dog with skillful economy.

— Lift up your head and spine, press your arms straight, open your chest, and anchor your legs.

13 TRAYODAŚA
13TH POSITION, EXHALE

Exhale

Pull back smoothly and strike Down Dog.

— Stamp down your hands, drive your hips back, empty your lungs, and come to Downward Dog without delay.

— Pause and renew your position.

— Direct your breath up and down the Central Axis. Hollow your belly when you empty your lungs and broaden your palate as you fill up your lungs.

Vinyāsa Meta View
By following your breath to either end of the Central Axis and visualizing energy traveling along your spinal column, cause a cessation of discursive thought and enter a state of yoga, union between the individual self and the Universal Self.

FULL VINYĀSA

14 CATURDAŚA / INHALE — ARDHA UTTĀNĀSANA
15 PAÑCADAŚA / EXHALE — UTTĀNĀSANA
SAMASTHITI

KŪRMĀSANA / SUPTA KŪRMĀSANA (Tortoise Pose / Lying Down Tortoise Pose)

7 SAPTA
7TH POSITION, INHALE

Exhale

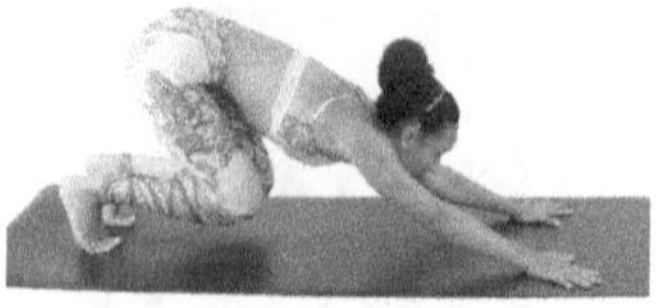

Crouch.

— Lower your hips and mind into a deep, Bhakti-drenched crouch.

— Prepare a mighty jump to Kūrmāsana.

Inhale

Spring! Jump legs onto arms.

— With a poised leap, throw your feet forward, land your legs on top of your upper arms, and extend your legs with your feet up off the ground.

Vinyāsa Meta View

An alternative way to go from your crouch to the Firefly Setup position is to jump your feet to the ground outside your hands, then lift your legs, and kick forward through your feet.

Exhale, 5 to 8 Breaths

Bend elbows and lower body to ground.

— Bend your elbows with a controlled press move.

— Do your best to confine your movement to hinging at your elbows. Lower your body as a unit, like a hovercraft landing.

— Continue to extend your legs as you come down.

— Touch your hips, head, and feet down to the ground with your legs separated to the width of your mat.

— Straighten your legs by pushing forward through your heels.

— Lengthen your arms by walking your hands out to the sides away from each other.

— Work to subtly lengthen your legs, arms, and spine. Then, strike an immovable spot and hold steady.

State of the Āsana

KŪRMĀSANA

5 to 8 Breaths or more
Dṛṣṭi: Broomadhya
(Eyebrow Center)

8 AṢṬAU
8TH POSITION, EXHALE

Exhale

Sit up, take legs behind head, and balance.

— Press yourself upright. Put your left leg behind your head followed by the right leg. Snug your ankles up to each other, balance, and make ready to lower yourself to the ground.

Vinyāsa Meta View

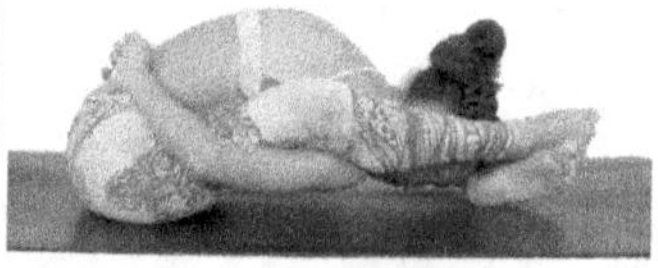

Alternate way to take pose.

From Kūrmāsana, stay where you are and perform the following actions in order:

— Bend your elbows and walk your hands onto your back towards each other.

— Bend your knees and walk your feet towards each other.

— Cross one ankle over the other in front of your head.

— Clasp your fingers behind your back.

Performing these actions in this order can improve your chances of being able to cross your ankles in front of you and clasp your fingers behind your back, but feel free to experiment with the order of positioning your arms and legs as suits you.

FULL VINYĀSA

SAMASTHITI
1 EKAM / INHALE — ŪRDHVA HASTĀSANA
2 DVE / EXHALE — UTTĀNĀSANA
3 TRĪṆI / INHALE — ARDHA UTTĀNĀSANA
4 CATVĀRI / EXHALE — CATURAṄGA DAṆḌĀSANA
5 PAÑCA / INHALE — ŪRDHVA MUKHA ŚVĀNĀSANA
6 ṢAṬ / EXHALE — ADHO MUKHA ŚVĀNĀSANA

Free Breathing

Walk hands forward and lower head to the ground.

— From the upright position, keeping your legs crossed behind your head, walk your hands forward and lower yourself into Supta Kūrmāsana.

5 to 8 Breaths

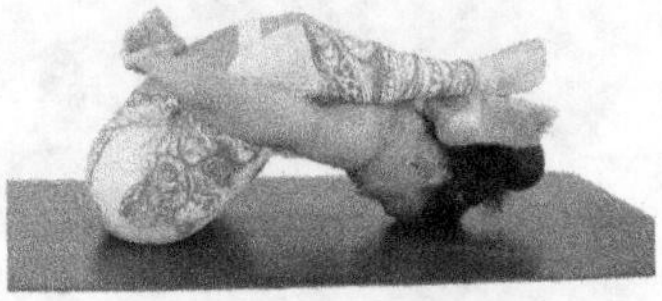

Forehead to ground, grip hands behind back, hold steady.

— Clasp your fingers behind your back.

— Stabilize your legs and arms and ground your hips and head.

— Come to stillness. Withdraw your senses and mind inward, like a tortoise withdrawing its limbs into its shell. Internalize your awareness and take refuge inside your own body.

State of the Āsana

SUPTA KŪRMĀSANA

5 to 8 Breaths or more
Dṛṣṭi: Broomadhya
(Eyebrow Center)

9 NAVA

9TH POSITION, INHALE

Free Breathing

Push down with hands and come upright.

— Release your clasped fingers and walk your hands forward to a point under your shoulders.

— Press down with your hands, extend your arms, and come upright with your feet crossed behind your head.

— Pause and get ready to lift up.

Inhale

Root hands and lift up; clear seat off ground and hold.

— Press down with your hands and clear your hips off the ground with a percussive burst of power.

— Pause and appreciate the rare predicament of balancing on your arms with your legs crossed behind your head.

KŪRMĀSANA / SUPTA KŪRMĀSANA (Tortoise Pose / Lying Down Tortoise Pose)

10 DAŚA
10TH POSITION, EXHALE

Inhale, Exhale

Kick forward through legs and stamp hands.

— Uncross your ankles. Sink your hips, extend your legs with a mighty forward kick, and momentarily strike Tittibhāsana *(Firefly Pose).*

11 EKĀDAŚA
11TH POSITION, INHALE

Inhale

Hinge at knees, swing feet back, and balance on arms.

— Flex your knee joints, swing your feet back, and lodge your knees on the backs of your upper arms into Bakāsana *(Crow Pose).*

— Economize this transition. Confine your movement to swinging your feet and shins back while keeping the rest of your body stationary.

12 DVĀDAŚA
12TH POSITION, EXHALE

Exhale

Jump back!

— In Bakāsana, shift forward to the edge of imbalance and bend your elbows with a controlled press move.

— Drive your legs back and lower your body towards the ground evenly.

Exhale (continued)

Caturaṅga Daṇḍāsana.

— Stop in place and achieve the magical shape of a Horizontal Stick *(Daṇḍa).* Integrate your head, torso, and pelvis with great precision.

— Though difficult to achieve, singling out each try and making a full stop in the horizontal Staff Pose can bring you all the way to Samādhi *(Absorption).*

13 TRAYODAŚA

13TH POSITION, INHALE

Inhale

Arch spine by circling up to the position.

— Lift up your head and press your arms straight.

— Expand your chest and reach back stubbornly with your legs.

— As you come up to your stopping place, situate your spine in the middle between your adamant arms, neither ahead of nor behind your foundation.

14 CATURDAŚA

14TH POSITION, EXHALE

Exhale

Thrust back with force to an awakened Down Dog.

— Keep your arms and legs extended as you propel yourself all the way to Downward Dog Pose in a single, uninterrupted move.

Vinyāsa Meta View
Through skillful, conscious repetition, perfect all of your transitions.

FULL VINYĀSA

15 PAÑCADAŚA / INHALE — ARDHA UTTĀNĀSANA
16 ṢOḌAŚA / EXHALE — UTTĀNĀSANA
SAMASTHITI

GARBHA PIṆḌĀSANA / KUKKUṬĀSANA (Embryo in the Womb Pose / Rooster Pose)

7 SAPTA
7TH POSITION, INHALE

Exhale

Express a magnificent crouch and exhale.

— Get ready to spring!

Inhale

Jump forward daringly!

— Strap on your helmet and jump through feetfirst with thrilling speed and power, like a circus performer being shot out of a cannon.

Exhale

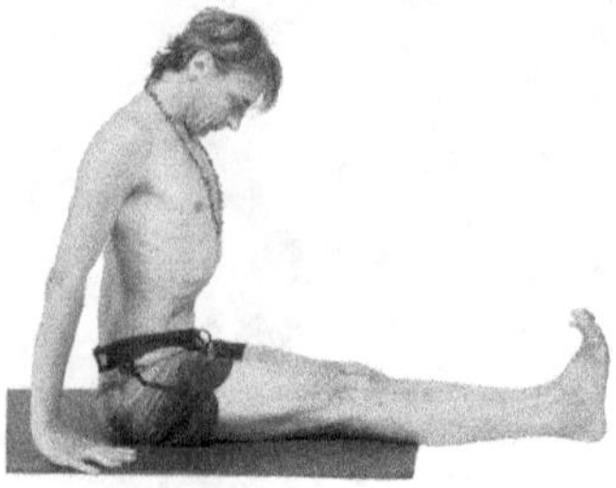

Strike Daṇḍāsana.

— Pause momentarily and transform your body into the auspicious form of a staff.

8 AṢṬAU
8TH POSITION, EXHALE

Free Breathing, 5 to 8 Breaths

Take Lotus, slot arms through legs, and balance.

— Cross your legs into Full Lotus with your right leg first. Use your left hand to lift your left shin.

— Slot your right hand, palm facing down, through the gap between your right shin and thigh.

— Slot your left hand, palm facing down, through the gap between your left shin and thigh.

— Externally rotate your arms so your palms face up. Work your arms through to a point on the upper arm above the elbow.

— Cup your chin with your hands and balance.

— Push your head down into your hands and brace your arms to create a Mudrā *(Energetic Seal)* that stabilizes your pose and helps you remain upright.

State of the Āsana

GARBHA PIṆḌĀSANA

5 to 8 Breaths or more
Dṛṣṭi: Nasagrai *(Nose)*

FULL VINYĀSA

SAMASTHITI
1 EKAM / INHALE — ŪRDHVA HASTĀSANA
2 DVE / EXHALE — UTTĀNĀSANA
3 TRĪṆI / INHALE — ARDHA UTTĀNĀSANA
4 CATVĀRI / EXHALE — CATURAṄGA DAṆḌĀSANA
5 PAÑCA / INHALE — ŪRDHVA MUKHA ŚVĀNĀSANA
6 ṢAṬ / EXHALE — ADHO MUKHA ŚVĀNĀSANA

9 NAVA
9TH POSITION, EXHALE

Exhale Back, Inhale Up

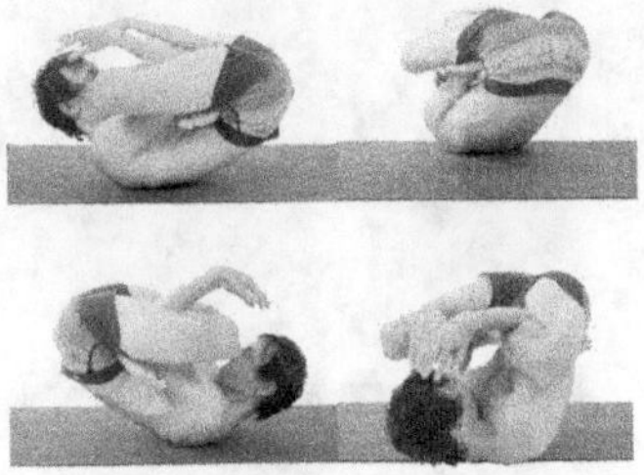

Roll back and forth in a circle with rhythm.

— Maintain your round, compact shape and roll across your spine from tail to head and from head to tail.

— Exhale back and inhale forward.

— As you swing back and forth, move in a circle. Create small turns as you roll; keep going around until you complete a full circle.

Inhale, 5 to 8 Breaths

Come upright, suck legs up arms, and balance.

— On your final roll, generate enough momentum to swing yourself all the way upright and balance on your arms.

— Shift forward, stamp down through your hands, and extend your arms.

— Draw your legs up along your forearms towards your elbows.

— Hold steady on the edge of imbalance and create a state of Nirodha *(Cessation)* in this dynamic version of Padmāsana, the quintessential meditation seat.

Vinyāsa Meta View
Every transition into a pose offers you a unique way to gain skill in risk-taking. Repeatedly test the hypothesis that you find the greatest stability when you go out on the edge of imbalance—a great paradox indeed!

State of the Āsana
KUKKUṬĀSANA
5 to 8 Breaths or more
Dṛṣṭi: Nasagrai *(Nose)*

Exhale

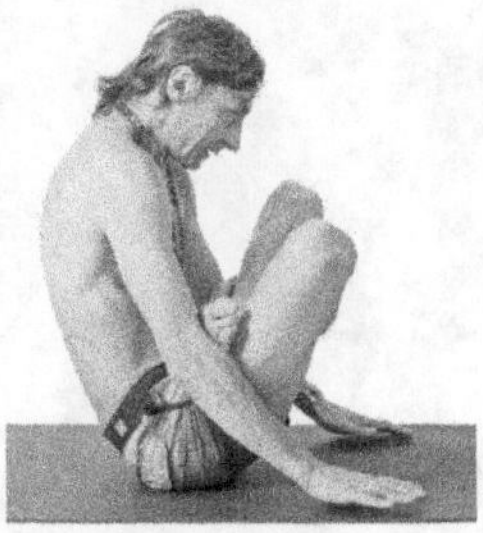

Come down and prepare a strike-and-lift move.

— Lower your hips to the ground and withdraw your arms from your folded legs.

— Retain your Lotus, lean back, and lift your knees.

— Plant your hands on the ground in front of your hips and coil your body into a compact shape.

— Store up force and make ready for your jump-back move.

10 DAŚA
10TH POSITION, INHALE

Inhale

Press down, spring, and clear seat off the ground cleanly.

— Stamp the ground with your hands and lift up your hips.

GARBHA PIṆḌĀSANA / KUKKUṬĀSANA (Embryo in the Womb Pose / Rooster Pose)

11 EKĀDAŚA
11TH POSITION, EXHALE

Exhale

Jump back.

— Bend your elbows, lean forward, and pivot on your arms.

— Lower your head and chest towards the ground and release your Lotus as you kick your legs back.

Exhale (continued)

Strike Four-Limbed Staff Pose.

— Arrive in Caturaṅga Daṇḍāsana and create a clear stopping point.

— Brace your arms and strengthen your legs.

— Engage your belly and tone your buttocks.

— Lengthen your tail and pull up your navel.

— Swiftly scan the awakened line of your core and enjoy your wild, meticulous form.

12 DVĀDAŚA
12TH POSITION, INHALE

Inhale

Ūrdhva Mukha Śvānāsana.

— Synchronize your breath with your movement. Start inhaling when you go into action.

— Continue to inhale as you move through the arc of your gesture.

— Finish inhaling as you come to the end of your movement and strike your position.

— When your breath and movement are joined together, each supporting and strengthening the other, the resulting pose is a form to behold.

13 TRAYODAŚA
13TH POSITION, EXHALE

Exhale

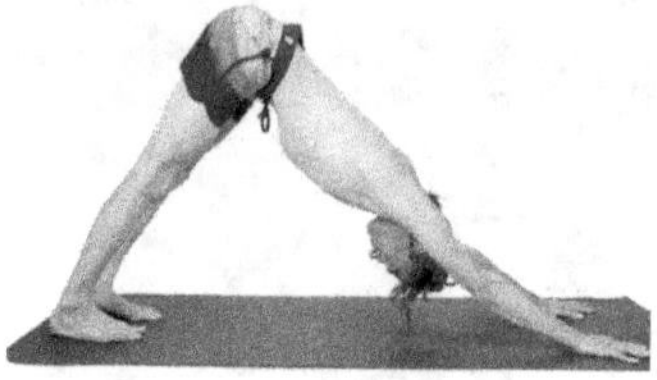

Pull back to Adho Mukha Śvānāsana with an exhale.

— Sweep your hips back and flush the air from your lungs.

— Roll over the tops of your feet and strike the A-frame shape.

— Pause, stamp your hands down, brace your arms, press your thighs back, and lengthen your spine from tail to head.

Vinyāsa Meta View
O Yogī, Vinyāsa teaches you that a confident transition leads to a fully realized form. Repeat your transitions with the specific goal to eliminate doubt from your actions and grow skillful in all your doings.

FULL VINYĀSA

14 CATURDAŚA / INHALE — ARDHA UTTĀNĀSANA
15 PAÑCADAŚA / EXHALE — UTTĀNĀSANA
SAMASTHITI

BADDHA KOṆĀSANA A - B (Bound Angle Pose A - B)

7 SAPTA
7TH POSITION, INHALE

Exhale

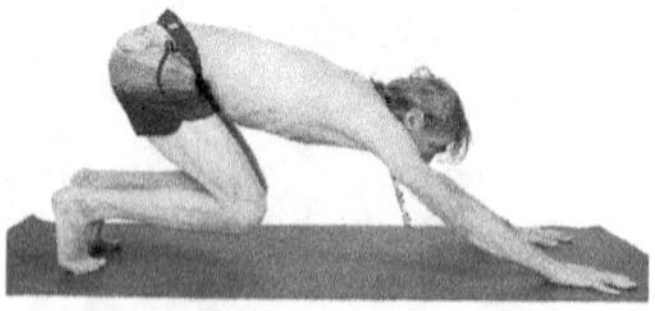

Crouch generously and hunker back.

— Strengthen your arms and store up force in your body. Delight in the move that sets up the move.

Inhale

Spring!

— Spring forward with gentle power and arrive in Daṇḍāsana with a light touch.

Free Breathing

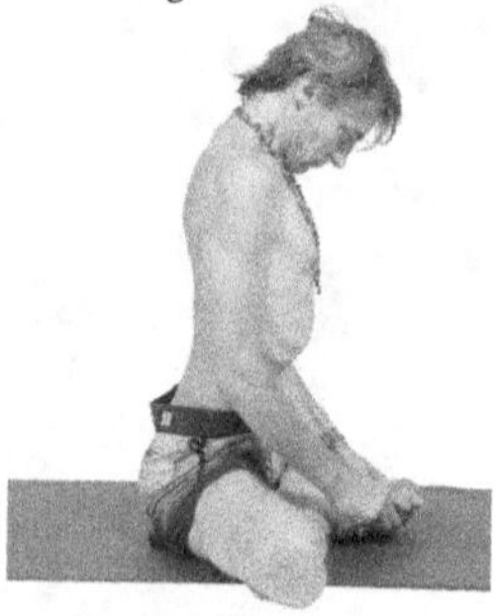

Honor the upright Setup, a hall of fame Āsana.

— Bring your heels back to your pelvis and open your thighs out to the sides. Lower your knees to the ground on either side of you.

— Press your heels together. Shift forward and vertically stack your head, spine, and pelvis.

— Level your pelvis, stamp your thighs down firmly, and lengthen your femur bones from hips to knees.

— Pull up your belly and raise up Śakti from the Root Support.

— Lower your gaze, bow your head, and make your chest bright like a sun. Spread rays of light outward from your Heart Center and illuminate the four directions of space.

Vinyāsa Meta View
O Yogī! Don't be in a rush to fold forward. Hear this list of reasons to stay in the upright version of this legendary Āsana:

- *It's a classic meditation seat specially designed for exploring breath control and stillness.*
- *It's a refuge offering protection from the heat of Tapas generated by devotion to Sādhanā.*
- *It helps you prepare for your inevitable reckoning with Yama, God of Death and King of Dharma (Sacred Duty).*

Inhale

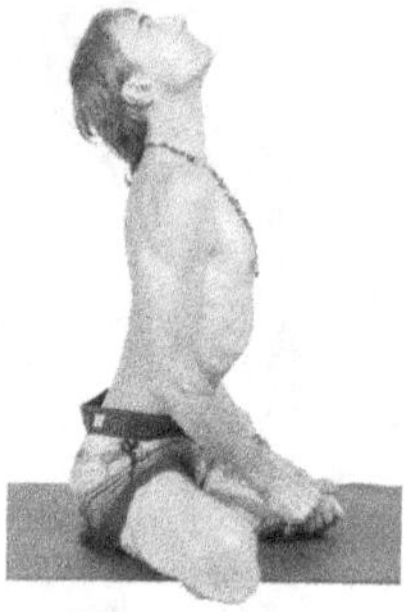

Open feet with hands, lift chest, and prepare to fold.

— Look up, take your head back, and open your chest.

— Lift up from the root of your spine and stamp down your thighs.

— Build up to a pinnacle of galvanized energy within your body.

FULL VINYĀSA

SAMASTHITI
1 EKAM / INHALE — ŪRDHVA HASTĀSANA
2 DVE / EXHALE — UTTĀNĀSANA
3 TRĪṆI / INHALE — ARDHA UTTĀNĀSANA
4 CATVĀRI / EXHALE — CATURAṄGA DAṆḌĀSANA
5 PAÑCA / INHALE — ŪRDHVA MUKHA ŚVĀNĀSANA
6 ṢAṬ / EXHALE — ADHO MUKHA ŚVĀNĀSANA

8 AṢṬAU

8TH POSITION, EXHALE

Exhale, 5 to 8 Breaths

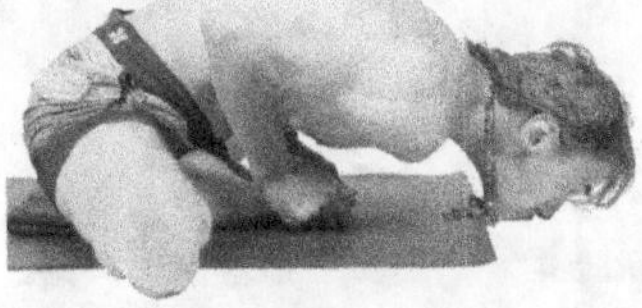

Bend forward with a gesture.

— Project your spine forward away from your rooted legs as you swoop down with a vigorous move.

— To complete your gesture, aim to touch your chin or head to the ground as far forward as possible while continuing to anchor your legs and seat.

Vinyāsa Meta View

In this position, utilize the contact that exists between your pelvic floor and the ground to "trigger" Mūla Bandha (Perineal Lock). To trigger means to contract your pelvic floor, pull up energy from the root of your spine, and cause Śakti to flow up the great Central Nāḍī with surprising speed and power.

State of the Āsana

BADDHA KOṆĀSANA A

5 to 8 Breaths or more
Dṛṣṭi: Nasagrai *(Nose)*

9 NAVA

9TH POSITION, INHALE

Inhale

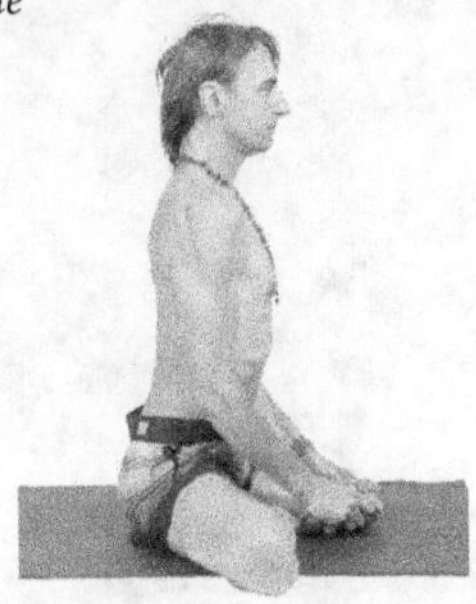

Sweep body up to Setup position.

— Return to an upright position and galvanize your forces for another forward fold.

Exhale, 5 to 8 Breaths

Bend forward with a round back.

— In a single move, swoop down, flex your spine, and bring your head to your feet.

— Upon arrival, stamp down your thighs and actively press your forehead onto your feet.

— Internalize the sound of your breath, withdraw your senses, and travel into the vast space of your Heart Center.

State of the Āsana

BADDHA KOṆĀSANA B

5 to 8 Breaths
Dṛṣṭi: Nasagrai *(Nose)*

10 DAŚA

10TH POSITION, INHALE

Inhale

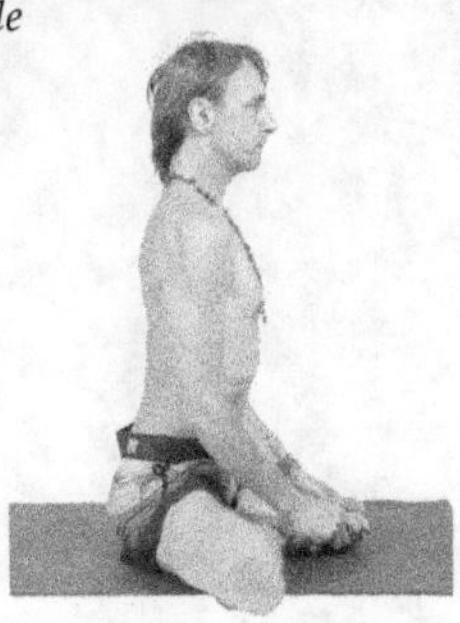

Come up to vertical and strike Setup position.

— Come upright with a confident move and pull your breath in against resistance from your narrowed throat.

— Pause and instantly strike this powerful meditation form.

— Invite your entire body to participate in the great act of sitting.

— Sharpen your mind with internal focus and transform the core of your body into a Pillar of Light.

— Know this: your inner world is an oasis that you can depend upon always, a place of your very own to rest, revitalize, and enjoy solitude.

BADDHA KOṆĀSANA A - B (Bound Angle Pose A - B)

Exhale

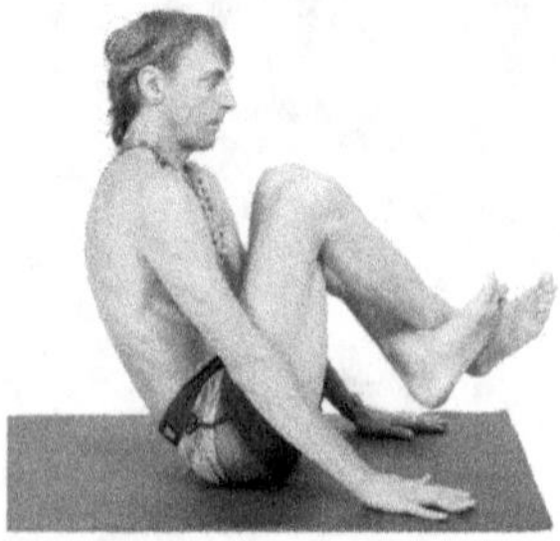

Cross ankles, place hands in front of hips, and prepare.

— Fashion your pliable body into a poised animal crouch.

— Summon your strength for a power-lift move.

11 EKĀDAŚA

11TH POSITION, INHALE

Inhale

Lift up seat and feet equally.

— With suddenness, strike down through your hands and lift your seat and feet up off the ground.

— Whip your feet back and commit your head and chest forward.

12 DVĀDAŚA

12TH POSITION, EXHALE

Exhale

Bend elbows, lean forward, and pivot on arms.

— Execute a controlled nosedive and drive your legs back.

Exhale (continued)

Caturaṅga Daṇḍāsana.

— Stop your body's motion when your head, torso, pelvis, and legs achieve the shape of a Horizontal Stick.

— Hover just above the earth and develop skill in performing subtle actions such as:

- Tuck your tail, lift your navel, and stabilize your pelvis at neutral.
- Suck your front lower ribs up toward your spine and widen your mid-back.
- Stabilize your rib cage and achieve a neutral spinal position.

13 TRAYODAŚA

13TH POSITION, INHALE

Inhale

Lift up into the serpentine form.

— Lift up your head and arch your spine as you press your arms straight.

— Fill up your lungs to the very top of your chest.

— Cause Life Force to rise up your spine as you draw in your breath.

— Expand your chest greatly. Visualize beams of brilliant light radiating out from your Heart Center and spreading in all directions like the life-affirming rays of the sun.

— Let the light penetrate your thick body, illuminating the vast, interior mystical spaces that are hidden deep within your legs, arms, pelvis, torso, and head.

— The attempt alone to do this work, never mind success, wins you power to proclaim the goodness of life.

14 CATURDAŚA

14TH POSITION, EXHALE

Exhale

Come to Down Dog as a method to exhale thoroughly.

— Propel your hips back as your means of zooming the air out of your lungs.

— Perform your movement and your exhalation with equal speed and power.

— Use dynamic movement to strike a dynamic form.

FULL VINYĀSA

15 PAÑCADAŚA / INHALE — ARDHA UTTĀNĀSANA

16 ṢOḌAŚA / EXHALE — UTTĀNĀSANA

SAMASTHITI

UPAVIṢṬHA KOṆĀSANA A - B (Seated Angle Pose A - B)

7 SAPTA
7TH POSITION, INHALE

Exhale

Sweep down and prepare to leap.

— Crouch like a huntress on the hunt.

Inhale

Spring forward and focus on the destination.

— Create a piked position as you jump through to Daṇḍāsana. Leap forward feetfirst, keep your legs extended, and suck your thighs up toward your chest.

Free Breathing, Inhale

Skillfully adopt the wide-legged Setup position.

— Separate your legs to 120°. Reach forward and grip your outer feet with your hands.

— Stamp the earth with your thighs and lengthen your legs from hips to toes.

— Pull back toward you with your arms in resistance to the forward-driving force of your legs.

— Lift your chest, pull up your navel, and project your spine forward.

— If you ground your limbs and lengthen your spine as a contemplation of the infinite, then you will cause Kuṇḍalinī to awaken at your base and rocket up the Middle Channel with marvelous speed.

8 AṢṬAU
8TH POSITION, EXHALE

Exhale, 5 to 8 Breaths

Fold forward into State of the Āsana.

— On the way down into your fold, anchor your legs, brace your arms, and lengthen your spine.

— Swoop down into your pose with a decisive gesture.

Vinyāsa Meta View
Devote yourself to a deep study of the connection between your transition and the resulting pose. Soon you'll discover how often you move into your pose doubtfully or with haphazard stops along the way. With each transition, seek to create an instance of pure action, to go from point A to point B in a single, daring move, and strike your pose with command. Every earnest attempt to connect your transition to the pose is sure to help you extract the gold of yoga knowledge from the mother lode of Vinyāsa. And one more thing, don't forget to enjoy yourself while doing it!

State of the Āsana

UPAVIṢṬHA KOṆĀSANA A

5 to 8 Breaths or more
Dṛṣṭi: Broomadhya
(Eyebrow Center)

FULL VINYĀSA

SAMASTHITI
1 EKAM / INHALE — ŪRDHVA HASTĀSANA
2 DVE / EXHALE — UTTĀNĀSANA
3 TRĪṆI / INHALE — ARDHA UTTĀNĀSANA
4 CATVĀRI / EXHALE — CATURAṄGA DAṆḌĀSANA
5 PAÑCA / INHALE — ŪRDHVA MUKHA ŚVĀNĀSANA
6 ṢAṬ / EXHALE — ADHO MUKHA ŚVĀNĀSANA

9 NAVA
9TH POSITION, INHALE

Inhale, 5 to 8 Breaths

Lift up, catch feet with hands, extend legs, and lean back.

— Swiftly come upright retaining your wide-legged stance.

— Lean your upper body back and swing your legs up off the ground with a move.

— Shift forward onto your sitting bones and create stability on the edge of imbalance.

— Think of your pelvis as an anchor, the weighted fulcrum from which to stabilize your pose.

— Grip your outer feet firmly with your hands. Kick forward through your legs with stupendous force as you pull back through your fully extended arms with an equal counterforce.

— Take your head back, look up towards the sky, and open your chest as you balance with skillful nonchalance.

State of the Āsana

UPAVIṢṬHA KOṆĀSANA B

5 to 8 Breaths or more
Dṛṣṭi: Ūrdhva *(Upward)*

Exhale

Gather force and crouch.

— To exit, release the grip on your feet and plant your hands on the ground in front of your hips.

— Coil your body into a compact shape and get ready for action.

10 DAŚA
10TH POSITION, INHALE

Inhale

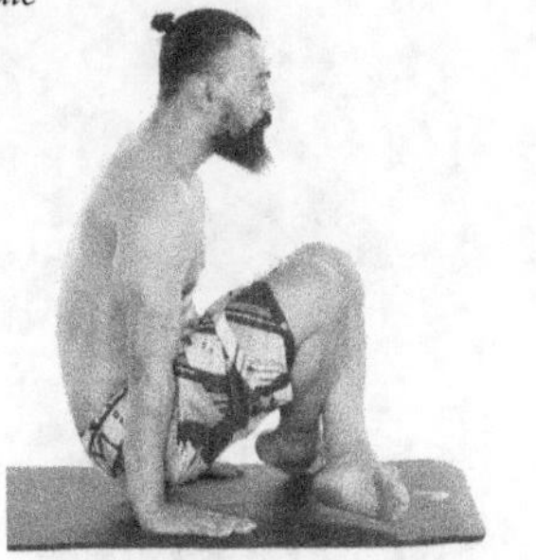

Perform a mighty lift-up move.

— Strike the ground powerfully with your hands and clear your seat off the ground with decisive force, like the clean-and-jerk move of a weight lifter.

— With rhythm, swiftly whip your feet back and under you (without touching them to the ground) and commit your upper body forward.

11 EKĀDAŚA
11TH POSITION, EXHALE

Exhale

Lean forward and kick feet back.

— Bend your elbows; pivot on your arms. Lower your head and chest towards the ground as you shoot your legs back.

UPAVIṢṬHA KOṆĀSANA A - B (Seated Angle Pose A - B)

Exhale (continued)

Strike the rousing shape of a Horizontal Stick.

— Arrive and instantly strengthen your arms, root your legs, stabilize your backbone, and SHAZAM! Behold the glorious world that opens within you.

12 DVĀDAŚA

12TH POSITION, INHALE

Inhale

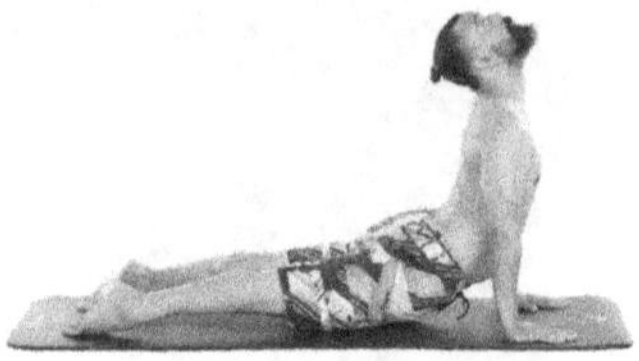

Upward Facing Dog.

— Use rhythm and timing to orchestrate your move to Upward Facing Dog and transform the following actions into a dance:

- Lift your head.
- Extend your arms.
- Arch your spine.
- Anchor your legs.

13 TRAYODAŚA

13TH POSITION, EXHALE

Exhale

Thrust hips back and strike Downward Facing Dog.

— Come to your position and arrange your bones in accordance with the potent geometry of the triangular, A-frame shape:

- Your long, grounded legs form one line of the A-frame and your sturdy backbone and powerfully braced arms form the other.
- Your pelvis, perfectly tilted to neutral on the diagonal, forms the well-angled, pointy apex of the triangle.

— Draw upon the power of the triangle to connect with the ground beneath you. Utilize the sacred geometry of each Haṭha Yoga form to steady your wily mind.

FULL VINYĀSA

14 CATURDAŚA / INHALE — ARDHA UTTĀNĀSANA

15 PAÑCADAŚA / EXHALE — UTTĀNĀSANA

SAMASTHITI

SUPTA KOṆĀSANA (Lying Down Angle Pose)

7 SAPTA
7TH POSITION, INHALE

Exhale

Crouch.

— Get low to the ground, hunker back in earnest, and patiently envision your target.

Inhale

Jump forward with a clear sense of direction.

— Leap forward feetfirst to Daṇḍāsana.

— Apply yourself well to playing the game of Crouch and Spring.

Exhale

Lie down in Supta Samasthiti.

— Lower your head and torso to the ground; engage your belly and core muscles to control your descent.

— The plane of the ground beneath you provides a precise, straight line that you can use to organize your body along the central axis and awaken your core.

8 AṢṬAU
8TH POSITION, INHALE

Inhale, 5 to 8 Breaths

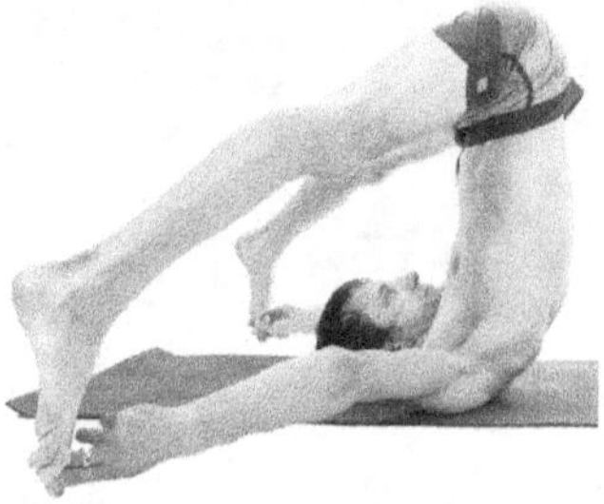

Swing legs and arms overhead; grip toes in a wide stance.

— Dynamically hoist your legs and arms overhead as if doing a backward somersault, but stop in place when your hips are vertical over your shoulders.

— Bring your feet to the ground behind you in a wide stance.

— Firmly grip your big toes with your fingers; extend your legs and arms.

— Lift your pelvis, press up through your inner thighs, and make your spine maximally tall.

Vinyāsa Meta View
Make a clear connection between the rhythm of your movement and the pose that you strike. With every transition, put opposing forces in play within your body that help you arrive in a fully awakened form. For this pose, an example of opposing forces is reaching back behind you with your legs as you brace your arms to resist the action of your legs. Then, utilize this pair of opposites to help you execute the rolling move when you exit the pose.

State of the Āsana

SUPTA KOṆĀSANA

5 to 8 Breaths or more
Dṛṣṭi: Ūrdhva *(Upward)*

FULL VINYĀSA

SAMASTHITI
1 EKAM / INHALE — ŪRDHVA HASTĀSANA
2 DVE / EXHALE — UTTĀNĀSANA
3 TRĪṆI / INHALE — ARDHA UTTĀNĀSANA
4 CATVĀRI / EXHALE — CATURAṄGA DAṆḌĀSANA
5 PAÑCA / INHALE — ŪRDHVA MUKHA ŚVĀNĀSANA
6 ṢAṬ / EXHALE — ADHO MUKHA ŚVĀNĀSANA

9 NAVA

9TH POSITION, EXHALE

Exhale

Crouch and prepare to roll.

— Make a figurative crouch in the upside-down position.

— Shift back into your legs; grip your toes firmly. Brace your arms, build up energy, and get ready to roll forward with great dynamism.

Inhale

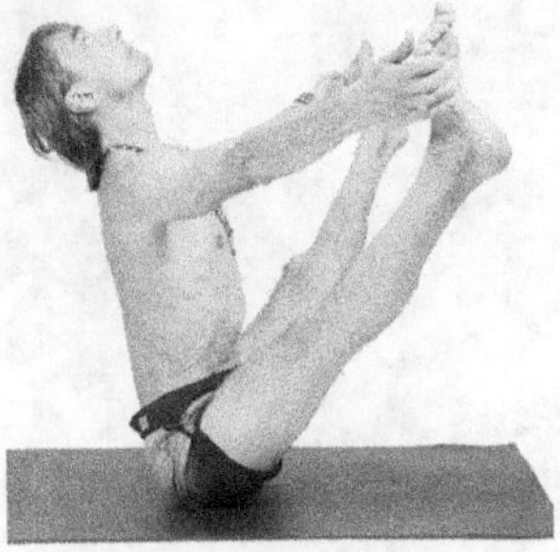

Spring; propel legs forward.

— Swing your legs forward with a combination of gusto and control. Generate enough momentum to roll across your spine and up to a balance point.

— Pause briefly; then continue forward past the balance point and control your descent to Upaviṣṭha Koṇāsana.

Exhale

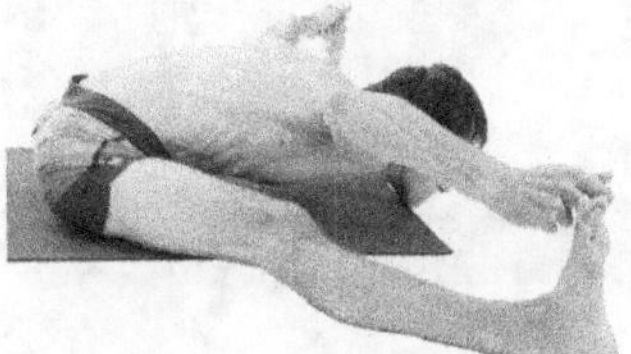

Extend legs, brace arms, and touch calves down lightly.

— To come down into position safely and slow down your forward momentum, lean your upper body back and pull back with your extended arms.

— Keep your legs extended and touch your calves down to the ground before your heels.

— As soon as your legs touch down, lower your head and torso to the ground and strike Upaviṣṭha Koṇāsana.

10 DAŚA

10TH POSITION, INHALE

Inhale

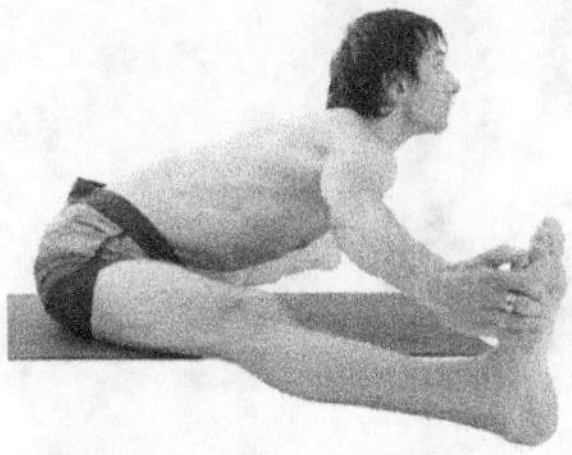

Lift up to Setup position at halfway point.

— Root your legs, lift up your chest, extend your arms, and grip your feet with your hands.

— Lengthen your spine and pull up your belly.

— Fill up your lungs mightily by pulling in the air against resistance from your narrowed throat.

SUPTA KOṆĀSANA (Lying Down Angle Pose)

Exhale

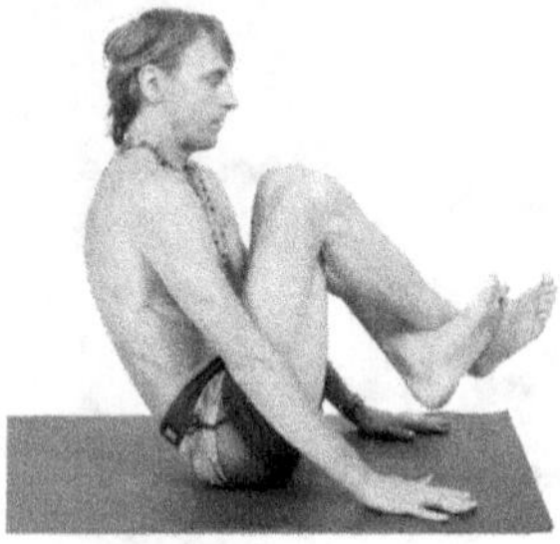

Withdraw inwards and make a crouch.

— Sit up, lean back, and bend your knees.

— Lift up your feet and plant your hands on the ground in front of your hips.

— Pause and build up energy. Discover the power of committing your resources to your Setup.

11 EKĀDAŚA

11TH POSITION, INHALE

Inhale

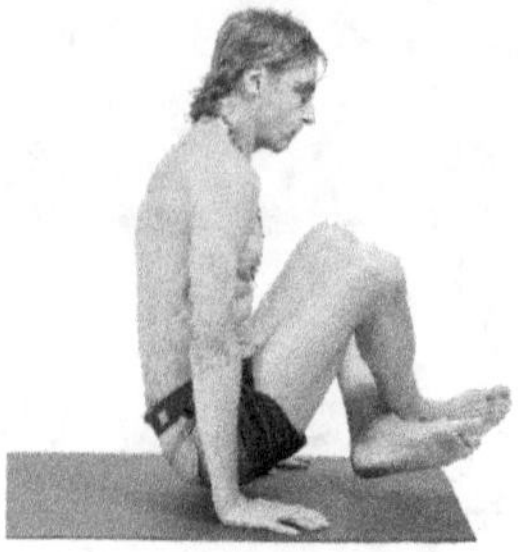

Lift up in a burst of power!

— Strike down firmly with your hands and lift your seat and feet up off the ground.

— Suck your feet back and begin to lean forward with your upper body.

12 DVĀDAŚA

12TH POSITION, EXHALE

Exhale

Jump back.

— Bend your elbows and pivot on your arms. Lower your upper body towards the ground and shoot your legs back.

Exhale (continued)

Stop in the Magical Stick Position.

— Four-Limbed Staff Pose is a perfect destination to drink from the oasis of Nirodha.

13 TRAYODAŚA

13TH POSITION. INHALE

Inhale

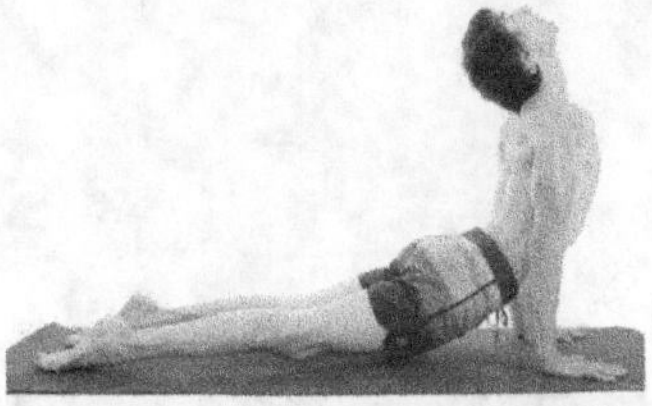

Come to Up Dog by joining breath with movement.

— Upon arrival: strengthen your arms, lift your head and spine up off your shoulder girdle, and cast your gaze circularly up, over, and back.

— Stubbornly anchor your legs in contrast to projecting your chest forward.

14 CATURDAŚA

14TH POSITION. EXHALE

Exhale

Slingshot hips back to Adho Mukha Śvānāsana.

— Thrust back, masterfully expel the air from your lungs, and arrive in Downward Dog with a flourish.

Vinyāsa Meta View

Learn to distinguish between the movement and the sudden stopping place at the end of the movement.

FULL VINYĀSA

15 PAÑCADAŚA / INHALE — ARDHA UTTĀNĀSANA

16 ṢOḌAŚA / EXHALE — UTTĀNĀSANA

SAMASTHITI

SUPTA PĀDĀṄGUṢṬHĀSANA (Lying Down Hand to Big Toe Posture)

7 SAPTA
7TH POSITION, INHALE

Exhale

Crouch skillfully.

— Brace your arms, bend your knees, and lower your hips towards the ground.

— Find a force-gathering, center-galvanizing, momentum-generating rhythm.

— Wake up your whole body by your efforts and you'll be rewarded with a yogī's superpower known as Darduri Siddhi—Frog Leap Power!

Inhale

Jump through—straight legs—sit down!

— Put your body in motion all at once. Leap in a purely forward direction and target your destination with both abandon and precision.

— Spring forward expressing the dignity of the yoga.

Vinyāsa Meta View
Make your practice a "rite of ferocious love." Draw forth the intrinsic beauty that is hidden in each gesture and form. With your noble efforts, express the "dignity of the yoga," words inspired by a song from a Baul poet who said: "The rites of ferocious love rest in the essence of supreme beauty and the dignity of the yoga, as the connoisseur knows."

Exhale

Come to Supta Samasthiti.

— Lay your head and torso back by controlling your center.

— The ground beneath you is a horizontal plane, a useful reference point for striking your form.

— Gather all your separate parts together and express the pure somatic geometry of a single line.

— Bring adamantine firmness to your body along the horizontal axis and transform your core into a Pillar of Fire, an energetically awake Daṇḍa, a Magical Staff.

— Enter a state of no-mind, fondly known by yogīs as becoming void-minded, and meet the numinous Self who cannot be known by your ego or your thinking mind.

8 AṢṬAU
8TH POSITION, INHALE

Inhale

Swing right leg up; grip big toe.

— Lift your right leg and catch your right big toe with your fingers.

— Kick up through your right leg with a mighty force and brace your arm with an equal counterforce.

— Lengthen and ground your left leg. Extend your left arm and press down on your left thigh with your left hand.

Vinyāsa Meta View
The Setup position that you strike before each pose is usually some version of the half-piked Daṇḍāsana shape. Sure, it does come in slightly different disguises depending upon whether you are standing, sitting, lying down, or inverting, but the same basic shape remains constant. Repeatedly drawing upon your knowledge of Daṇḍāsana when you set up your poses, can teach you to perceive the deep, profound commonalities shared by all transitions and poses. This knowledge will economize your efforts and help you pierce through to the pith or intrinsic essence of each transition or pose instead of getting caught up overvaluing the external or superficial details. Eventually, by steeping yourself in Vinyāsa, you'll see only one Setup position (Crouch), one transition (Spring), and one pose (Destination) in the midst of any and all diversity.

FULL VINYĀSA
SAMASTHITI
1 EKAM / INHALE — ŪRDHVA HASTĀSANA
2 DVE / EXHALE — UTTĀNĀSANA
3 TRĪṆI / INHALE — ARDHA UTTĀNĀSANA
4 CATVĀRI / EXHALE — CATURAṄGA DAṆḌĀSANA
5 PAÑCA / INHALE — ŪRDHVA MUKHA ŚVĀNĀSANA
6 ṢAṬ / EXHALE — ADHO MUKHA ŚVĀNĀSANA

9 NAVA
9TH POSITION, EXHALE

Exhale, 5 to 8 Breaths

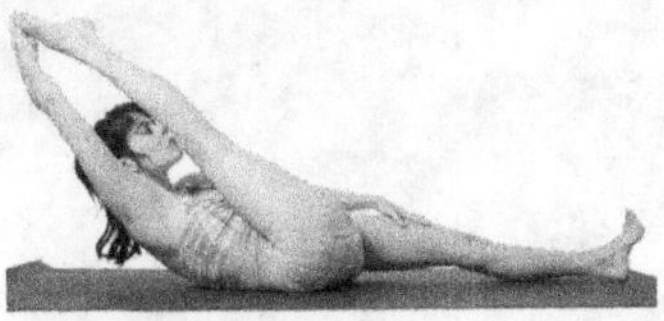

Lift head up to meet shin.

— Lift up your torso and pull down with your right arm while engaging your abdomen.

— Touch your head to your leg and hold steady.

— Ground your left leg, extend your left arm, and stamp your left hand down on your left thigh.

State of the Āsana

SUPTA PĀDĀṄGUṢṬHĀSANA

Right Side — 5 to 8 Breaths
Dṛṣṭi: Pādayorāgrai *(Foot)*

10 DAŚA
10TH POSITION, INHALE

Inhale

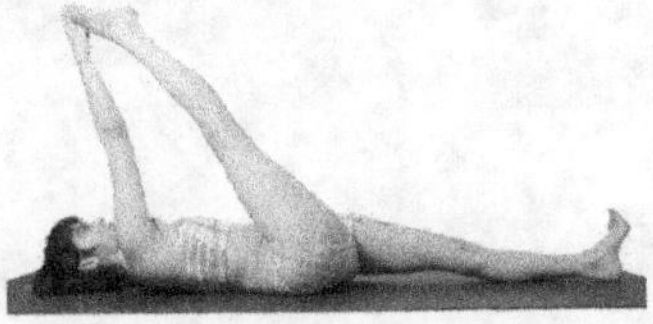

Return to the all-important root pose.

— Lower your head to the ground. Firmly grip your big toe with your fingers, brilliantly extend your limbs, and pause to celebrate the Setup position.

11 EKĀDAŚA
11TH POSITION, EXHALE

Exhale, 5 to 8 Breaths

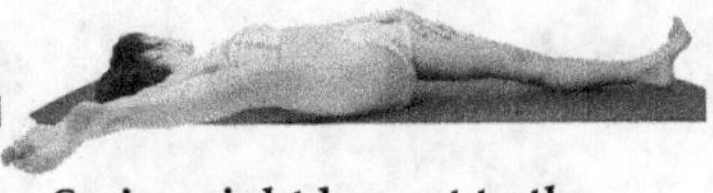

Swing right leg out to the right with a throw.

— Sweep your right leg out to the side, expel the air from your lungs, and touch your right foot to the ground.

— Take control over the movement of your right leg; actively circle the leg to its destination in the side plane and brace your right arm.

— Turn your head and cast your gaze to the left.

— Anchor your left thigh and keep the whole left side of your body pinned down to the ground in an effort to stabilize your transition and your pose.

State of the Āsana

SUPTA PĀDĀṄGUṢṬHĀSANA

Right Side — 5 to 8 Breaths
Dṛṣṭi: Pārśva *(Side)*

12 DVĀDAŚA
12TH POSITION, INHALE

Inhale

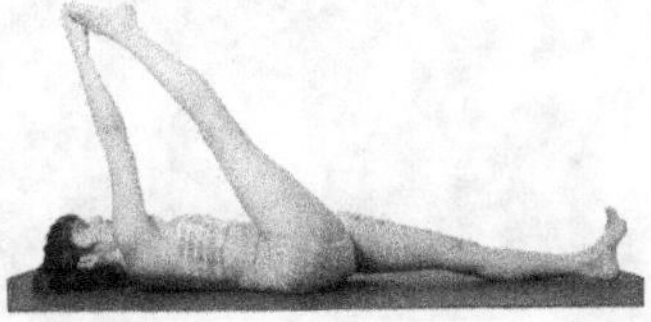

Return to Setup position with vigor.

— Sweep your right leg up to the vertical line with a sure move. Actively grip your big toe, extend your right leg, and anchor your left side.

— Stop in place and use the momentum of your transition to do justice to the illustrious Setup position.

SUPTA PĀDĀṄGUṢṬHĀSANA (Lying Down Hand to Big Toe Posture)

13 TRAYODAŚA
13TH POSITION, EXHALE

Exhale

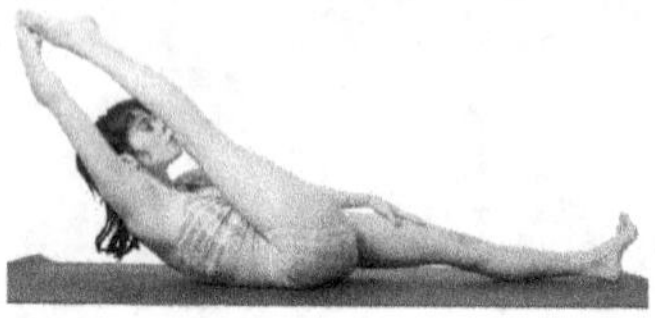

Come up; touch head to shin.

— Lift up your torso with gusto, pull down with your right arm, and touch your head to shin.

14 CATURDAŚA
14TH POSITION, INHALE

Inhale

Strike Setup position.

— Lower your head and torso to the ground and recreate the root position for the fourth and final time on the first side.

— Retain your grip on the big toe, kick up brilliantly with your right leg, and resist with your strong right arm.

— Swiftly align your head, torso, pelvis, and left leg along the horizontal axis.

Vinyāsa Meta View
The Royal Road is one name the Yogīs give to the Central Axis. Focusing your mind inward and locating the core of your body is like walking a great, winding road to the center of yourself, where sacred mysteries meant only for you await your discovery.

Exhale

Return to supine Samasthiti.

— Release your big toe, swing your leg down to Supta Samasthiti, and animate your body in a flash.

15 PAÑCADAŚA
15TH POSITION, INHALE

Inhale

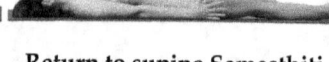

Swing left leg up; strike Setup position, second side.

— Lift up your left leg and catch your big toe with your fingers.

— Extend your left leg with an upward thrust of astounding power. Work to touch the sky with your toes and brace your left arm with a matching counterforce.

— Root down through your right leg and right arm.

16 ṢOḌAŚA
16TH POSITION, EXHALE

Exhale, 5 to 8 Breaths

Come up into a forward bend.

— Vigorously lift up your head and torso, touch chin to shin, and pull down with your left arm.

— Raise your upper body away from the earth and strengthen your arms, legs, and belly.

State of the Āsana

SUPTA PĀDĀṄGUṢṬHĀSANA

Left Side — 5 to 8 Breaths
Dṛṣṭi: Pādayorāgrai *(Foot)*

17 SAPTADAŚA
17TH POSITION, INHALE

Inhale

Come down and honor the Setup position.

— Lower your head and torso to the ground.

— Grip your big toe with new vigor and kick up through your left leg with maximal force as you brace your left arm.

— Lower your chin, cast a fiery gaze down the length of your body, and pull up your navel.

18 AṢṬADAŚA
18TH POSITION, EXHALE

Exhale, 5 to 8 Breaths

Circle your left leg out to the side.

— With a sure gesture, sweep your left leg to the side and touch your left foot to the ground beside you.

— Command your leg movement. Kick out through your left foot and lengthen your leg as you take it out to the side and down.

— Upon arrival: send an intelligent wave of force out from the origin of your leg (ball of femur in hip socket) to the extremity (pointed toes). Watch the outward-bound, ray-like force shoot through your leg bones from hip to toes and continue traveling out beyond your body into space towards infinity.

State of the Āsana

SUPTA PĀDĀṄGUṢṬHĀSANA

Left Side — 5 to 8 Breaths
Dṛṣṭi: Pārśva *(Side)*

19 EKONAVIṂŚATI
19TH POSITION, INHALE

Inhale

Swing left leg up to the center and strike Setup.

— Raise your left leg up to the vertical line with a clear move.

— Lengthen the leg, strengthen the arm, and firmly grip the big toe.

— Brace your right arm and stamp down your right leg with your right hand.

— Keep your chin level, cast your gaze down, internalize your senses, and bring the power of the Setup position into focus.

SUPTA PĀDĀṄGUṢṬHĀSANA (Lying Down Hand to Big Toe Posture)

20 VIṂŚATI
20TH POSITION, EXHALE

Exhale

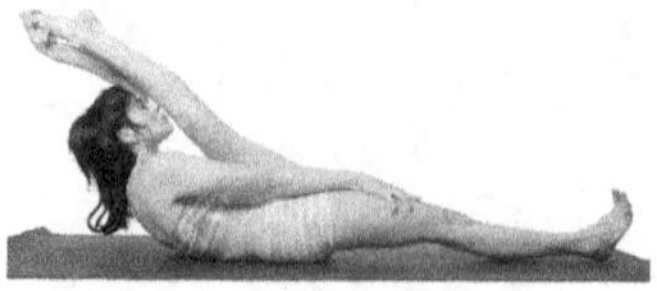

Perform a pure lift-up move and touch head to shin.

- — Lift up your head and torso with a power surge and draw your body up from the ground.
- — Touch your head to your leg and pull down with your left arm.
- — Root your right thigh and lengthen your right leg.

21 EKAVIṂŚATI
21ST POSITION, INHALE

Inhale

Return to Setup position.

- — Lower your head to the ground and strike the root pose instantly.
- — Grip your big toe, swiftly kick up through your left leg, and brace your left arm.
- — By charging up your torso, pelvis, and legs with physical actions, transform the middle line that spans the length of your torso from tail to head into a great river of light that flows freely and shines brightly within you.

22 DVĀVIṂŚATI
22ND POSITION, EXHALE

Exhale

Lower left leg and strike supine Samasthiti.

- — Sweep your left leg down, charge up your limbs, galvanize your center, and transform your stick-shaped body into a shaman's staff.

23 TRAYOVIṂŚATI
23RD POSITION, INHALE

Inhale

Perform Chakrāsana, a backwards somersault.

- — With a great rhythm, hoist your legs and arms overhead, lift your hips, and plant your hands on the ground underneath your shoulders.
- — Push off the ground with your hands and strengthen your arms as your legs and hips pass over you.
- — Tuck your chin, drive your legs back, and come to the destination of Caturaṅga Daṇḍāsana.
- — Remember that using a combination of momentum and arm strength is the key to protecting your neck in this transition.

24 CATURVIMŚATI
24TH POSITION, EXHALE

Exhale

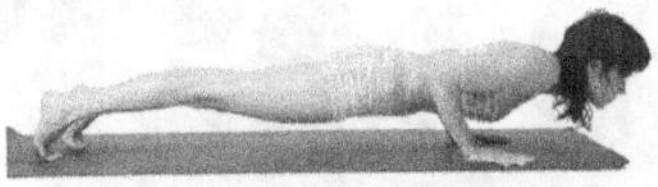

Four-Limbed Staff Pose.

— When you arrive in position, stop cleanly and hover just above the ground.

— Hold steady in the quintessential strength pose.

— Your strong body, awakened by earth, water, fire, air, and space makes for a perfect devotional offering to the secret, miraculous Source of All.

Vinyāsa Meta View
Meditation on the Water element: When you move into your pose, move like a river. Flow like water, smooth and steady, without ceasing. Adapt, bend, be flexible. Equally meet any and all features. Flow fast or slow, be narrow or wide, tiny or great. Work, work, work. Find ways to let water inform the spiral gestures of your arms, legs, spine, and mind. Learn to swirl and eddy with graceful determination and perpetual softness. Patiently and persistently liquify, nourish, and replenish. Cut through the stuck earth of your habit-ridden body and mind. Meander purposelessly while unerringly following your trustworthy inner compass. Be true to your great yearning to merge with the deepest Source. Rejoice in tasting the nectar of life while you are breathing and be ready to flow on to the other side at the end of your journey here.

25 PAÑCAVIMŚATI
25TH POSITION, INHALE

Inhale

Rise up and coil your spine into an arch.

— With rhythm, lift up your head in a semicircle, straighten your arms with a press move, and gracefully arch your spine.

— Stretch back through your legs from hips to toes, lift your inner thighs, and fully extend your ankles.

26 ṢAḌVIMŚATI
26TH POSITION, EXHALE

Exhale

Come to Adho Mukha Śvānāsana.

— Thrust back powerfully with your lower body and ride the momentum all the way to Downward Dog.

— Pause at the end of your movement, ground your thighbones, and lengthen the backs of your legs.

— Lift your sitting bones and free your buttocks.

— Tilt your pelvis to neutral on the diagonal line that spans your pelvis, spine, and arms.

Water Element

FULL VINYĀSA

27 SAPTAVIMŚATI / INHALE — ARDHA UTTĀNĀSANA
28 AṢṬĀVIMŚATI / EXHALE — UTTĀNĀSANA
SAMASTHITI

UBHAYA PĀDĀṄGUṢṬHĀSANA (Both Big Toes Pose)

7 SAPTA

7TH POSITION, INHALE

Exhale

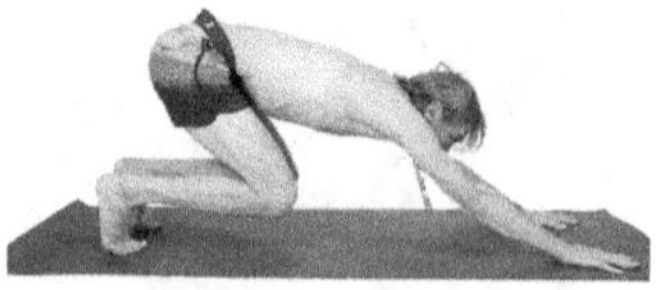

Crouch low.

— Hunker back patiently, like a stealthy cat anticipating a surprise attack. Get low to the ground, love the earth with your stance, clear your mind, and be ready for a sudden strike.

Inhale

Charge forward feetfirst.

— Slingshot your body forward with a committed leap, no holding back.

Vinyāsa Meta View

With your transition and pose announce to the universe and all its inhabitants, "Here I am, on this earth, laying it all on the line, striking my most excellent form at this time! My pose is mine and no one else's. I stand behind my actions. I offer my most complete expression of what I deem to be good, proper, beautiful, and worthy. And I am content."

Exhale

Supta Samasthiti.

— Lie down in Supta Samasthiti and pause. Root your limbs, awaken your center, and create Space within the cave of your mouth *(Khecarī Mudrā)*.

Vinyāsa Meta View

Two meditations from the Vijñāna Bhairava for exploring the Space Element within the microcosm of your body:

Dhāraṇā #22

For the yogī who firmly contemplates the void above (cave of the palate), the void at the base (cave of the sacrum), and the void in the heart (cave of the heart), there arises freedom from thought constructs (vṛtti) and communion with Śiva, God of Yoga, who transcends all thought constructs (nirvṛtti).

Dhāraṇā #25

The yogī should contemplate the skin part of the body as a dividing wall or boundary. Within the boundary there is nothing substantial, only pure space. Meditating like this, the yogī reaches a state of consciousness which transcends the illusory world of material objects.

8 AṢṬAU

8TH POSITION, INHALE

Inhale, Exhale

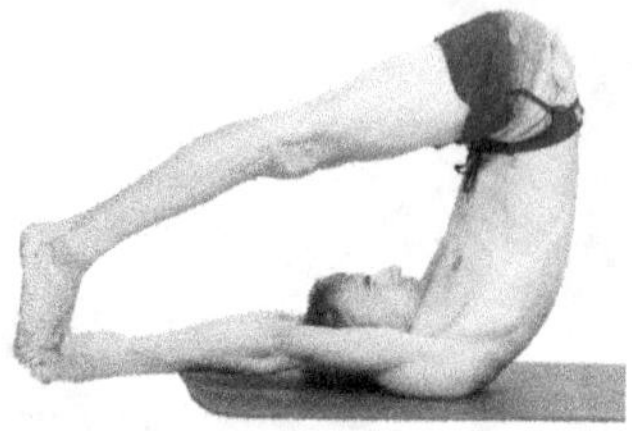

Swing legs and arms overhead; grip big toes.

— Hoist your legs and arms overhead with plenty of momentum.

— Bring your feet to the ground behind you and firmly grip your big toes with your fingers.

— Shift your weight back towards your legs and strengthen your extended arms.

— Brace your pelvis, lift up your sitting bones, and make your spine tall.

FULL VINYĀSA

SAMASTHITI

1 EKAM / INHALE — ŪRDHVA HASTĀSANA

2 DVE / EXHALE — UTTĀNĀSANA

3 TRĪṆI / INHALE — ARDHA UTTĀNĀSANA

4 CATVĀRI / EXHALE — CATURAṄGA DAṆḌĀSANA

5 PAÑCA / INHALE — ŪRDHVA MUKHA ŚVĀNĀSANA

6 ṢAṬ / EXHALE — ADHO MUKHA ŚVĀNĀSANA

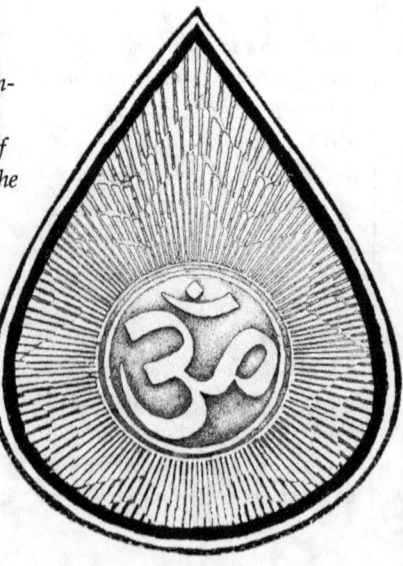

Space Element

9 NAVA
9TH POSITION, INHALE

Inhale, 5 to 8 Breaths

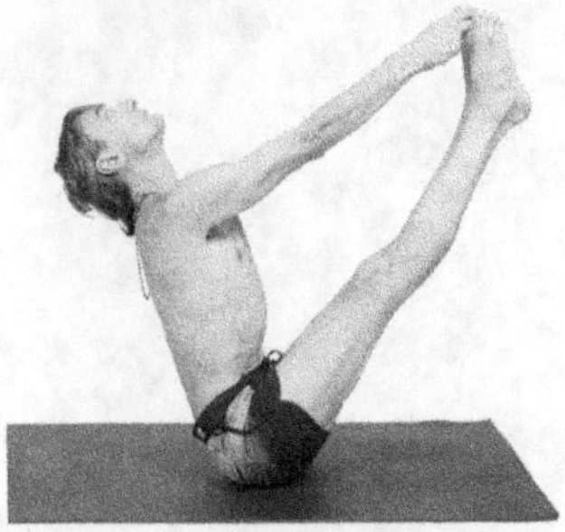

Roll forward, balance, and pull back on toes.

— Propel your legs forward with a powerful throw.

— Generate enough momentum to roll across your spine and up to a clear stopping place on the edge of imbalance.

— To stop and balance in midair after you've fully committed to rolling forward is tricky, but you can use the following three actions like brakes to stop your body in place at will:

1) Grip your big toes firmly as you lengthen your legs.
2) Pull back strongly through your fully extended arms.
3) Lean back through your head and chest.

State of the Āsana

UBHAYA PĀDĀṄGUṢṬHĀSANA

5 to 8 Breaths or more
Dṛṣṭi: Ūrdhva *(Upward)*

10 DAŚA
10TH POSITION, EXHALE

Exhale

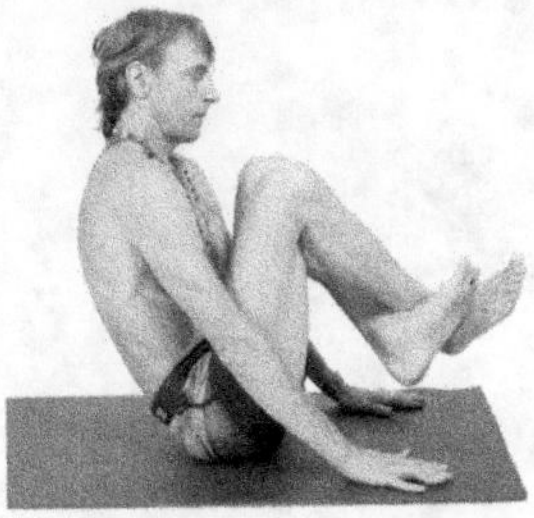

Crouch!

— Release the grip on your feet. Lower your hands to the ground in front of your hips and make ready for a power lift.

Inhale

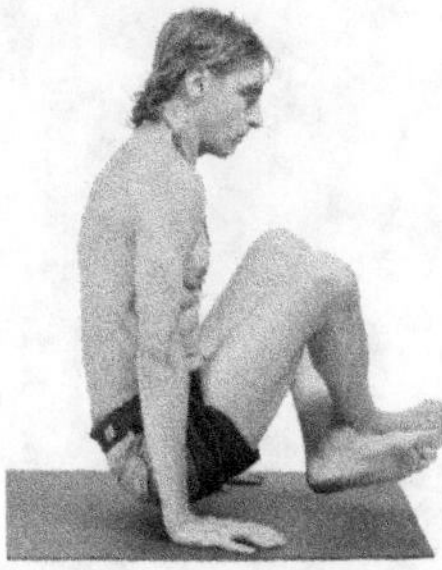

Stamp down and lift up.

— Strike the ground with your hands and swiftly lift up your hips.

— Suck your feet under you, bend your elbows, and lean forward.

11 EKĀDAŚA
11TH POSITION, EXHALE

Exhale

Jump back.

— Pivot on your arms, dive your upper body forward as though doing a face-plant, and drive your legs back with control.

UBHAYA PĀDĀṄGUṢṬHĀSANA (Both Big Toes Pose)

Exhale (continued)

Stop instantly in Caturaṅga Daṇḍāsana.

— Make your whole body strong as steel and as pliable as a willow reed.

12 DVĀDAŚA

12TH POSITION, INHALE

Inhale

Rocket upper body to the peak; anchor legs.

— To come into your pose, pretend your nose is a pencil point and use it to draw a shapely circle across the sky as you lift up your head and spine.

— As you circle your head up, arch your spine and press your arms straight.

— Perform the following actions to support the circular gesture of your spine and the mighty expansion of your chest:

- Root down with your hands.
- Make your arms tall and strong.
- Reach back through your legs resolutely.

13 TRAYODAŚA

13TH POSITION, EXHALE

Exhale

Sweep back to Downward Dog in a flash.

— Catch a wave of momentum and take a smooth ride back to Down Dog.

— Pause and absorb your whole consciousness in shape-making. Transform your body into a Yantra, a Magical Shape that holds the power to captivate your attention. With your form, express geometrical precision and transport yourself to sacred realms within the Heart Lotus, beyond fear or your thinking mind.

FULL VINYĀSA

14 CATURDAŚA / INHALE — ARDHA UTTĀNĀSANA
15 PAÑCADAŚA / EXHALE — UTTĀNĀSANA
SAMASTHITI

ŪRDHVA MUKHA PASCHIMOTTĀNĀSANA (Upward Facing Western Stretch Pose)

7 SAPTA

7TH POSITION, INHALE

Exhale

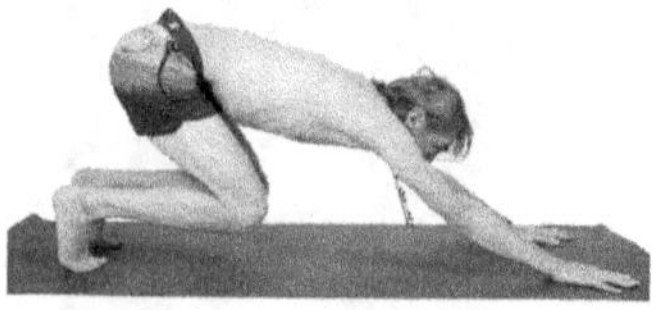

Stamp hands, squat low, and root hips back.

— Sweep your out-breath down the length of your spine and infuse your center with vitality. Crouch in earnest, a hunter on the hunt for a sublime form.

Inhale

Spring forward playfully.

— Leap forward in an instance of total action. Find a pure movement not tainted by deliberation or doubt or any thought at all.

— Land your feet well forward of your hands and come to your destination with supreme confidence.

Exhale

Lie down with control.

— Lie down flat on your back with your feet together; visualize Samasthiti, the root of all poses.

8 AṢṬAU

8TH POSITION, INHALE

Inhale, Exhale

Swing limbs overhead, catch big toes, and crouch.

— Hoist your legs and arms overhead with a surge of power and touch your toes to the ground behind you.

— Firmly grip your outer feet with your hands.

— Shift back, lengthen your legs, and brace your arms.

— Lift up your pelvis and make your spine tall.

— Build up energy; store up enough force in your bones to launch a marvelous rolling move.

FULL VINYĀSA

SAMASTHITI

1 EKAM / INHALE — ŪRDHVA HASTĀSANA

2 DVE / EXHALE — UTTĀNĀSANA

3 TRĪṆI / INHALE — ARDHA UTTĀNĀSANA

4 CATVĀRI / EXHALE — CATURAṄGA DAṆḌĀSANA

5 PAÑCA / INHALE — ŪRDHVA MUKHA ŚVĀNĀSANA

6 ṢAṬ / EXHALE — ADHO MUKHA ŚVĀNĀSANA

9 NAVA
9TH POSITION, INHALE

Inhale

Roll forward, make a clean stop, and balance.

— Propel your legs forward with firepower and roll your spine across the ground like a free-turning wheel.

— As you come upright, stop with certainty at the right moment and achieve a dynamic balance point.

— Kick your legs forward, pull back with your extended arms, and lean your upper body back.

— Transform a dicey predicament into an immovable spot.

Exhale, 5 to 8 Breaths

Fold forward and strike the precarious jackknife form.

— Lift up your spine, pull down through your arms, and draw your head and torso to meet your fixed legs.

— Enjoy adamant rootedness in a challenging pose and learn the secret that the edge of imbalance is the safest, most secure, most alive place to be.

State of the Āsana

ŪRDHVA MUKHA PASCHIMOTTĀNĀSANA

5 to 8 Breaths or more
Dṛṣṭi: Nasagrai *(Nose)*

10 DAŚA
10TH POSITION, INHALE

Inhale

Grip feet, lean back, and strike Setup position.

— Keep a hold on your feet, extend your arms, lean back, and stop distinctly in the Setup position; love this wondrous mainstay of the practice.

— Strengthen your arms and thrust up through your legs until your toes touch the sky-dome.

— Pull up your navel and expand your chest infinitely.

— Do your best to engage all of your parts in a coordinated act of pure effort, yet remain without ambition for predetermined results.

Exhale

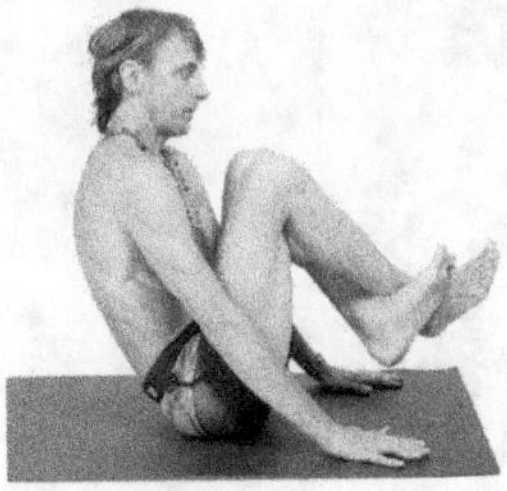

Crouch and make ready.

— Release the grip on your feet and plant your hands on the ground in front of your hips.

— Galvanize your forces and build up energy. Get ready to use rhythm, timing, and momentum to your advantage.

ŪRDHVA MUKHA PASCHIMOTTĀNĀSANA (Upward Facing Western Stretch Pose)

11 EKĀDAŚA
11TH POSITION, INHALE

Inhale

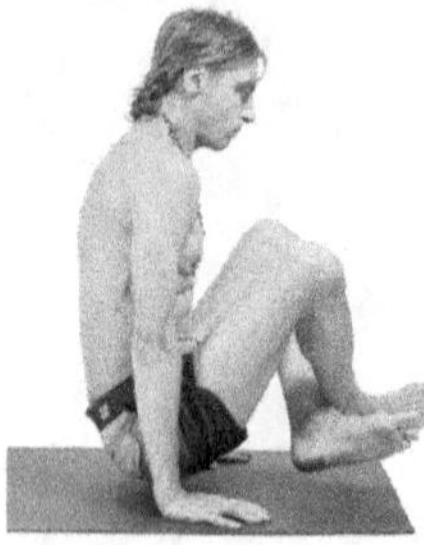

Lift up as a total act.

— Strike the ground with your hands, lift up your hips, and whip your feet under you without touching them to the ground.

12 DVĀDAŚA
12TH POSITION, EXHALE

Exhale

Jump back.

— Bend your elbows and balance in a compact body shape.

— Pivot on your arms, lower your head and chest towards the ground, drive your feet back, and extend your legs.

Exhale (continued)

Caturaṅga Daṇḍāsana.

— Shazam! Materialize the great Plank Form.

— Hold steady for a beat or two and draw upon the great store of vitality housed in every tiny corner of your subtle body. Then, you'll easily honor this foremost Yantra.

13 TRAYODAŚA
13TH POSITION, INHALE

Inhale

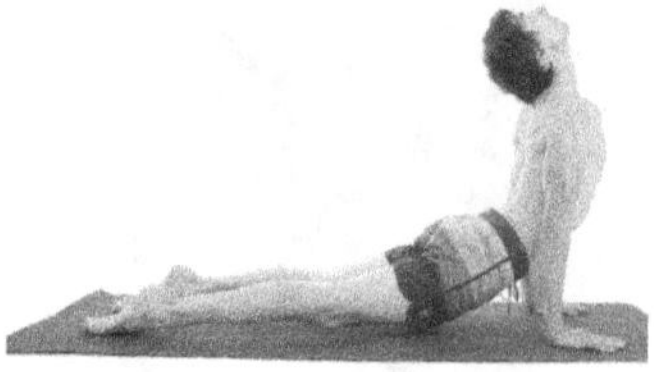

Spring up from the ground and bow spine.

— Perform the following movements in rapid succession:

- Push your toes back across your mat.
- Lift up your head in a circle.
- Press your arms straight.
- Fully extend your legs and point your toes.
- Open your chest in a mighty gesture of expansion.
- Take your head back with the abandon of an enchanted dancer.

14 CATURDAŚA

14TH POSITION, EXHALE

Exhale

Sweep hips back with skillful precision.

— Use this transition to send Life Energy rushing along the center line of your body to the root of your spine (*Mūlādhāra*).

— Stop when your legs and your spine / arms achieve an A-frame shape with your pelvis tilted to neutral on the diagonal, forming the angle at the peak.

— Pull up your navel and see if you can catch the elusive Belly Flying Up Gesture, a powerful yoga ally indeed.

FULL VINYĀSA

15 PAÑCADAŚA / INHALE — ARDHA UTTĀNĀSANA
16 ṢOḌAŚA / EXHALE — UTTĀNĀSANA
SAMASTHITI

SETU BANDHĀSANA (Bridge Pose)

7 SAPTA
7TH POSITION, INHALE

Exhale

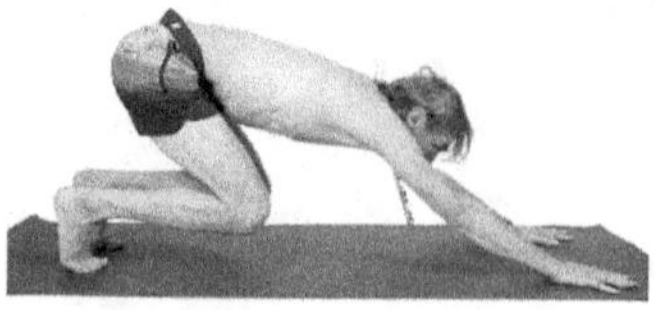

Crouch down low; exhale thoroughly.

— Sink your hips down toward the earth and hunker back.

— Root down your hands and strengthen your arms.

— Pull up your navel and concentrate Prāṇa in your center.

— Appreciate the process of getting ready to spring.

Inhale

Jump forward.

— Leap forward with a mighty expansion of your lungs. Manifest your intention to land your feet well forward of your hands.

Exhale

Strike Supta Samasthiti.

— Lie back by engaging your core muscles.

— Visualize your head, torso, pelvis, legs, and arms in the magical power shape of a Daṇḍa *(Stick, Staff, Wand, Pillar of Light).*

8 AṢṬAU
8TH POSITION, EXHALE

Free Breathing, Exhale

Set legs, arch spine, plant head, and cross arms over chest.

— From your lying down position, turn your feet out and walk them back toward your hips.

— Stamp your feet, lift your knees, adduct your thighs, and brace your legs.

— Keep your hips down as you press the ground with your elbows, lift up your head, and dome your chest.

— Take your head back and then down to the ground.

— Cross your arms over your chest and grip the area above your collarbones with your fingers.

— Hug your arms to your chest and pull down through your forearms from fingers to elbows.

— Pause, charge up your limbs with vital force, expand your chest, and make ready for a dynamic lift-up move.

FULL VINYĀSA

SAMASTHITI
1 EKAM / INHALE — ŪRDHVA HASTĀSANA
2 DVE / EXHALE — UTTĀNĀSANA
3 TRĪṆI / INHALE — ARDHA UTTĀNĀSANA
4 CATVĀRI / EXHALE — CATURAṄGA DAṆḌĀSANA
5 PAÑCA / INHALE — ŪRDHVA MUKHA ŚVĀNĀSANA
6 ṢAṬ / EXHALE — ADHO MUKHA ŚVĀNĀSANA

9 NAVA
9TH POSITION, INHALE

Inhale, 5 to 8 Breaths

Lift hips, brace arms, root legs, and strike Bridge Pose.

— With a burst of power, stamp down your feet, lift up your spine, lengthen your legs, and brace your arms.

— As you ascend to the peak of your Bridge pose, hug your chest with your arms and draw your upper spine into a deep coil within your torso.

— Upon arrival in your pose:

- Ground your head in tandem with rooting your feet.
- Continuously lengthen your legs.
- Pull down through your arms from fingers to elbows.
- Expand your chest and subtly deepen your spinal arch.

Vinyāsa Meta View
Visualize your body as an ancient, arched stone bridge. Your head and feet are the solid foundational piers embedded in the ground on either side of the water. Your torso, pelvis, and legs form the strong arched structure that spans across the stream.

State of the Āsana

SETU BANDHĀSANA

5 to 8 Breaths
Dṛṣṭi: Nasagrai *(Nose)* or Broomadhya *(Eyebrow Center)*

10 DAŚA
10TH POSITION, EXHALE

Exhale

Lower hips; return to Setup position.

— Bend your knees and lower your hips to the ground.

Exhale (continued)

Lie down and prepare to somersault.

— Quicken your whole body in Supta Samasthiti. Transform your core into a Pillar of Light *(Suṣumṇā Nāḍī)*.

— With swiftness of mind and body, get ready for dynamic action.

11 EKĀDAŚA
11TH POSITION, INHALE

Inhale

Perform a backward somersault *(Chakrāsana)*.

— Swing your arms, legs, and hips overhead and plant your hands on the ground under your shoulders.

— Generate plenty of momentum and push off the ground with your hands as your hips and legs pass overhead.

— Tuck your chin and drive your legs through to their destination.

— *Note:* as you execute your move, use a combination of momentum and arm strength to protect your neck.

SETU BANDHĀSANA (Bridge Pose)

Exhale

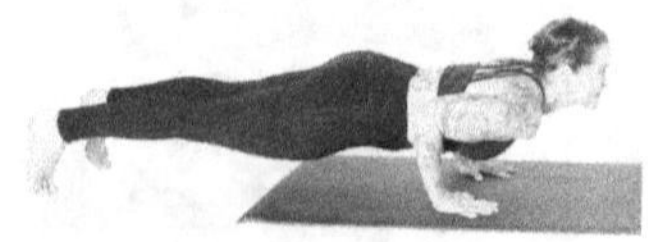

Strike Four-Limbed Staff Pose, the mighty strength builder.

— Stay put in the Horizontal Staff Pose and grow strong.

Vinyāsa Meta View
Summoning your strength in this auspicious shape gives you these two Siddhis (Magical Powers):

Yama Siddhi, the Power to say NO and refuse to—

1) *Cause harm.*
2) *Be untrue.*
3) *Waste your creativity.*
4) *Fall into envy or unthankfulness.*
5) *Be possessive or indulge to excess.*

Niyama Siddhi, the Power to say YES and commit to—

1) *Cultivate purity in your actions.*
2) *Be content any time under any circumstances.*
3) *Sustain a strong yoga practice.*
4) *Study ardently and meditate upon the yoga texts.*
5) *Align yourself with the Sacred Source beyond your ego.*

12 DVĀDAŚA
12TH POSITION, INHALE

Inhale

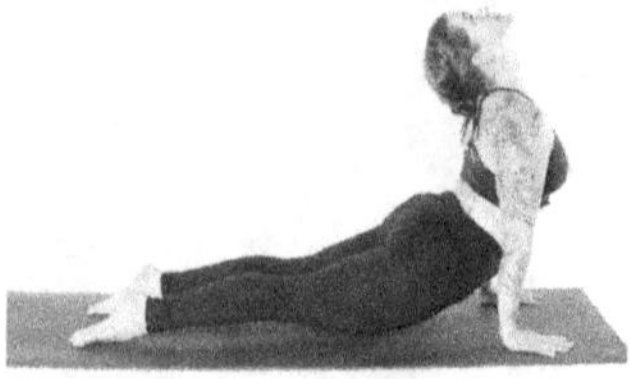

Lift up head and press arms straight.

— Apply skillful timing when you perform the following actions:

- Circle your head up to the end point.
- Coil your spine into a mighty arch within your torso.
- Push down into the ground strongly with your hands and lengthen your arms.
- Stubbornly root your legs.

13 TRAYODAŚA
13TH POSITION, EXHALE

Exhale

Drive hips back with a sweep.

— Ride the powerful backward thrust of your hips and glide to Down Dog effortlessly.

— Upon arrival, take an extra breath or two.

— Follow the Exhalation Force *(Apāna Vāyu)* along your spine to its end point at the base of your pelvis.

— Follow the Inhalation Force *(Prāṇa Vāyu)* up your spine from the base of your pelvis to the top of your chest.

— The wise yogī who skillfully directs the two opposite breathing forces up and down the spine attains the power to act skillfully and the courage to entrust all results to the secret Sacred Source.

FULL VINYĀSA

14 CATURDAŚA / INHALE — ARDHA UTTĀNĀSANA
15 PAÑCADAŚA / EXHALE — UTTĀNĀSANA
SAMASTHITI

ŪRDHVA DHANURĀSANA (Upward Bow Pose)

7 SAPTA
7TH POSITION, INHALE

Exhale

Stamp hands, brace arms, and hunker back.

— Crouch low in a primal position.

— Come home to the origins of your own body and find the source of all beautiful movement.

Inhale

Leap forward all at once.

— Use discernment to jump your feet purely forward.

— Send your legs traveling through space with effortless lightness.

Exhale

Lower head and torso to the ground.

— Lie down and contemplate your body in Samasthiti as a glorious Pillar of Light.

8 AṢṬAU
8TH POSITION, EXHALE

Free Breathing, Exhale

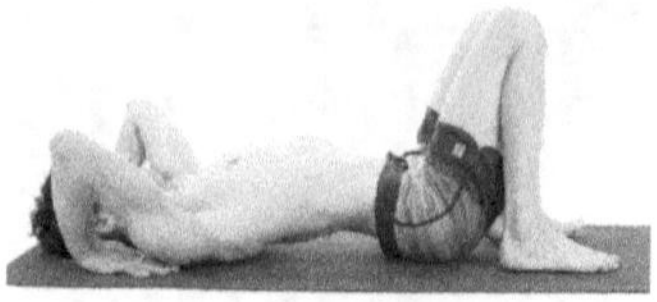

Plant hands and feet, brace limbs, and prepare to push up.

— Bend your knees and bring your feet back to your sitting bones.

— Lift your arms overhead and place your hands under your shoulders.

— Stamp down your hands, brace your arms, and suck your elbows towards each other.

— Stamp down your feet, brace your legs, and suck your knees towards each other.

— Don't hurry through the Setup position; take the time to store up energy in your limbs and benefit from anticipating action.

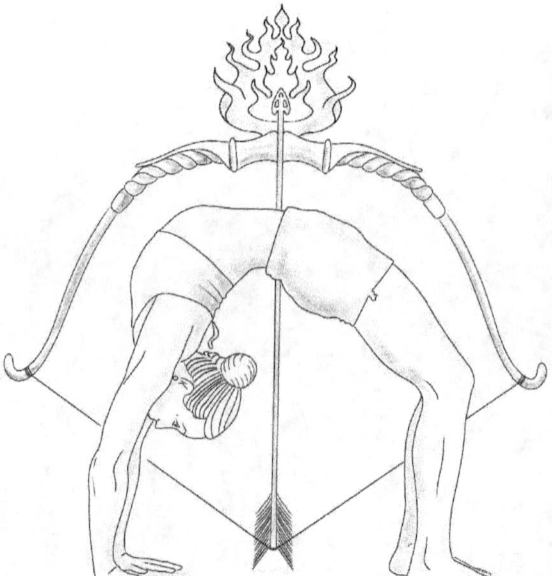

FULL VINYĀSA

SAMASTHITI
1 EKAM / INHALE — ŪRDHVA HASTĀSANA
2 DVE / EXHALE — UTTĀNĀSANA
3 TRĪṆI / INHALE — ARDHA UTTĀNĀSANA
4 CATVĀRI / EXHALE — CATURAṄGA DAṆḌĀSANA
5 PAÑCA / INHALE — ŪRDHVA MUKHA ŚVĀNĀSANA
6 ṢAṬ / EXHALE — ADHO MUKHA ŚVĀNĀSANA

9 NAVA
9TH POSITION, INHALE

Inhale, 5 to 8 Breaths

Lift up pelvis, press arms straight, and arch spine.

— Stamp down your hands and feet with spirit, thrust upwards through your pelvis, and sweep your spine up into a tall arch.

— Upon arrival, shift slightly towards your legs and vertically line up your knees over your ankles.

— Powerfully brace your legs, then shift towards your arms.

— Press your arms straight and attempt to line up your shoulders over your elbows and wrists.

— Maximally lift up your spine and create a dynamic arch within your torso, like bending a bow by pulling back the bowstring to shoot an arrow.

Vinyāsa Meta View
Transform your spine into a mighty bow. Become like Śiva who drew back his mighty bow and shot an arrow across the cosmos to pierce the three aerial cities of the demons, winning him the name Tripurāntaka (Slayer of the Three Demon Cities).

State of the Āsana

ŪRDHVA DHANURĀSANA

5 to 8 Breaths
Dṛṣṭi: Broomadhya
(Eyebrow Center)

10 DAŚA
10TH POSITION, EXHALE

Exhale

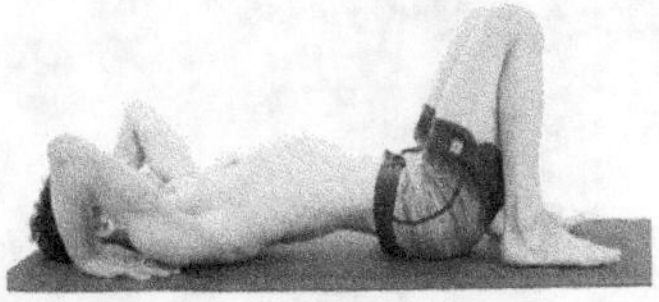

Return to Setup position; prepare to lift up again.

— Come down: bend your elbows slowly, tuck your chin, and lower your pelvis and torso to the ground with control.

— Get ready to come up again: plant your hands and feet, brace your arms and legs, and flush the air out of your lungs.

— Then come up: lift up your sacrum, press your arms straight, and draw your spine up into a mighty bow shape within your torso.

— After five to eight breaths, come back down to the Setup position.

— Do three to ten backbends. Be sure to go through the whole process of creating your Setup position, coming up with a supremely confident move, staying for several breaths, and skillfully returning to the Setup position.

Exhale (continued)

Pause in Supta Samasthiti.

— After your last backbend, lie down and pause.

— Devote yourself to this version of the Stick Shape with the know-how of a yogī and get ready to somersault.

11 EKĀDAŚA
11TH POSITION, INHALE

Inhale

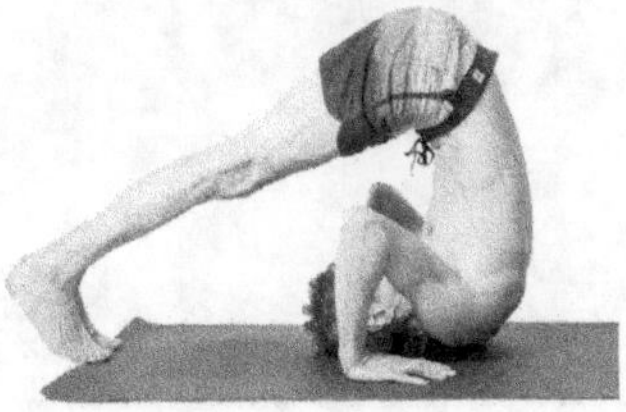

Backwards somersault.

— Roll your legs and hips overhead with a playful, momentum-generating throw. Lift your arms and plant your hands on the ground under your shoulders.

— As your legs and hips pass over your head and shoulders, tuck your chin and push off your hands.

— Rely on the strength of your arms to take weight off your neck as you drive your legs all the way through to their end point.

— As you learn to perform Chakrāsana *(Backwards Somersault)*, allow your body to be led into action by the rhythm of your gesture and let fly a freewheeling Vinyāsa.

Vinyāsa Meta View
As an alternative to somersaulting, simply roll to the side, sit up, and strike Caturaṅga Daṇḍāsana.

ŪRDHVA DHANURĀSANA (Upward Bow Pose)

Exhale

Caturaṅga Daṇḍāsana.

— Strike a perfectly straight daṇḍa *(staff)* by investing your legs, arms, pelvis, and torso with great stopping power.

— Find out for yourself why the stick pose is a main source of strength for a yogī.

12 DVĀDAŚA
12TH POSITION, INHALE

Inhale

Lift head, open chest, and anchor legs.

— Come to the peak of your position and pause. Feel the grounding power of your limbs and the resulting dynamic action of bowing your spine within your torso.

13 TRAYODAŚA
13TH POSITION, EXHALE

Exhale

Propel hips back and make the inverted V shape.

— Transition skillfully, arrive in Adho Mukha Śvānāsana, and strike an immovable spot.

— Only a devoted Haṭha Yogī properly appreciates the magic of this unusual yet potent meditation seat.

Vinyāsa Meta View
Use your stay in this pose to contemplate the Supreme Self that dwells within your body and from which springs the entire universe. This Sacred Source is the Changeless Reality. It transcends your senses, is uncaused, indefinable, has neither eyes nor ears, neither hands nor feet, is all-pervading, subtler than the subtlest, the Everlasting Source of All. That, and not anything else, is your boundless essence.

FULL VINYĀSA
14 CATURDAŚA / INHALE — ARDHA UTTĀNĀSANA
15 PAÑCADAŚA / EXHALE — UTTĀNĀSANA
SAMASTHITI

SĀLAMBA SARVĀṄGĀSANA (All Limbs Pose)

7 SAPTA
7TH POSITION, INHALE

Exhale

Crouch.

— Stamp down your hands and brace your arms as you lower your hips and coil your body into a shape built for springing.

Inhale

Shoot legs forward to a light landing.

— Jump feetfirst and suck your thighs to your chest, like a diver making a half-pike move.

— As you jump, stabilize your hips in direct contrast to throwing your legs forward.

Exhale

Come to Supta Samasthiti.

— Lie down. Withdraw your senses inward, internalize your awareness, and listen to the sound of your breath inside your body.

8 AṢṬAU*
8TH POSITION, INHALE

Inhale, 15 Breaths or more

Lift legs to vertical and stamp hands onto back of torso.

— Sweep your legs and pelvis up from the ground with a mighty hoist-up move.

— Stack your ankles, knees, and hips over your shoulders.

— Plant your hands on your back as low as possible, preferably onto your ribs.

— Suck your elbows towards each other and make your upper arm bones parallel.

— Press into your back strongly with your hands and root down through your arms.

— Sink your torso into your hands and arms while sucking your spine forward like doing a backbend.

— Lengthen your legs, reach up through the bones, and touch your toe tips to the stars.

— To awaken your center: activate your buttocks, abdomen, and the fronts and backs of your thighs.

— Perform Jālandhara Bandha *(Chin Lock)* by lifting your chest to meet your chin. Relax your throat.

State of the Āsana

SĀLAMBA SARVĀṄGĀSANA

15 Breaths or more
Dṛṣṭi: Nasagrai *(Nose)*

FULL VINYĀSA

SAMASTHITI
1 EKAM / INHALE — ŪRDHVA HASTĀSANA
2 DVE / EXHALE — UTTĀNĀSANA
3 TRĪṆI / INHALE — ARDHA UTTĀNĀSANA
4 CATVĀRI / EXHALE — CATURAṄGA DAṆḌĀSANA
5 PAÑCA / INHALE — ŪRDHVA MUKHA ŚVĀNĀSANA
6 ṢAṬ / EXHALE — ADHO MUKHA ŚVĀNĀSANA

The order of the vinyāsa numbers above reflects the full vinyāsa count and this explains the seemingly irregular pattern of numbers.

9 NAVA*
9TH POSITION, EXHALE

Exhale, 8 Breaths or more

Hinge at hips, lower legs, and clasp hands.

— From Shoulder Stand, work these key points to create an effective transition into Halāsana:

- Swoop your legs down with command and touch your feet to the ground with control.
- Keep your arms, torso, and pelvis fixed in position as you move your legs through space with economy.
- For the leg action, think of the balls of your femurs in the hip sockets as the central hub of a wheel and your descending legs as spokes turning on the hub.
- Maintain your tall spine and release your hands from your back as you swoop your extended legs down with speedy confidence.

— As your feet come to the ground, extend your arms behind you, clasp your fingers, and stamp down your arms firmly from your shoulders to your fingers. Stabilize your neutral pelvis as you kick strongly through your feet and maximally lengthen your legs.

State of the Āsana

HALĀSANA *(Plow Pose)*

8 Breaths or more
Dṛṣṭi: Nasagrai *(Nose)*

9 NAVA*
9TH POSITION, EXHALE

Exhale, 8 Breaths or more

Bend knees and squeeze ears with inner legs.

— From Halāsana, bend your knees and bring them back to either side of your head.

— Extend your arms, clasp your fingers, and root down from your shoulders to hands.

— Stabilize your hips and firm your legs.

— Squeeze your ears with your inner knees to seal in Prāṇa and withdraw your senses inward.

— This unusual form that is named Ear Pressure Pose is a gift from Haṭha Yoga to help you create absorption and know the splendors of the Middle Channel, Suṣumṇā Nāḍī, home of the great Kuṇḍalinī Śakti.

State of the Āsana

KARṆAPĪḌĀSANA
(Ear Pressure Pose)

8 Breaths or more
Dṛṣṭi: Nasagrai *(Nose)*

9 NAVA*
9TH POSITION, EXHALE

Inhale

Return to Shoulder Stand proper and pause.

— From Karṇapīḍāsana, sweep your legs and hips up to the vertical axis and firmly plant your hands on your back.

— Stack your ankles, knees, and hips directly over your shoulders.

— Establish your body in the form of a daṇḍa by stabilizing your legs, pelvis, torso, and arms.

— Press your back with your hands as you push your torso into your hands.

— The classic vertical Shoulder Stand is an important Setup position that enables you to take Lotus by the use of your legs only, without help from your hands.

Exhale, 8 Breaths or more

Take Lotus and lower thighs to hands.

Flip Move instructions for taking Padmāsana in Shoulder Stand:

— Externally rotate your right thigh and flip your right foot into Half Lotus. Then, externally rotate your left thigh and flip your left foot into Full Lotus.

— *Pro tip:* lift your right knee up toward vertical before flipping your left foot into place.

Upon achieving Lotus:

— Release your hands from your back, extend your arms, and lower your knees to meet your hands.

— Brace your arms to stop the downward movement of your legs and balance in a middle position.

— Create a Mudrā *(Energetic Seal)* by pressing down with your legs and pushing up with your arms.

— Utilize the play of opposing forces to perform the Belly Flying Up Gesture. Hollow your belly to clear your mind of extraneous thoughts.

State of the Āsana

ŪRDHVA PADMĀSANA
(Inverted Lotus Pose)

8 Breaths or more
Dṛṣṭi: Nasagrai *(Nose)*

SĀLAMBA SARVĀṄGĀSANA (All Limbs Pose)

9 NAVA*
9TH POSITION, EXHALE

Exhale, 8 Breaths or more

Lower thighs and wrap arms around legs.

— From Ūrdhva Padmāsana, lower your knees to either side of your head.

— Wrap your arms around your thighs and clasp your fingers. Shift your weight onto your shoulders and upper back to take pressure off your neck.

— Hug your legs with your arms, draw your thighs closer to you, and make a compact shape.

— Turn inward. Become a yogī shaman. Withdraw into the interior of your body. Seek healing medicine and renewal. Bring sacred visions back from your depths and fearlessly share your truths with the world.

State of the Āsana

PIṆḌĀSANA *(Embryo Pose)*

8 Breaths or more
Dṛṣṭi: Nasagrai *(Nose)*

9 NAVA*
9TH POSITION, EXHALE

Exhale, 8 Breaths or more

Roll down; anchor seat and arch spine.

— From Piṇḍāsana, with your legs in Lotus, come down and bring your seat to the ground.

— Partially sit up, then lower your head and torso back, press your elbows into the ground, and lift up your chest into a high dome shape.

— Bring your head back and down to the ground.

— Catch your feet with your hands.

— Weight your pelvis, ground your thighs, pull on your feet with your hands, and ground your head.

— With your lower body tethered to the earth, expand your chest greatly and coil your upper spine into your chest.

— Express your form by being aware of the gesture of your spinal column at the center of you. Expertly transport yourself beyond the mundane to the sacred world that is home to a yogī.

State of the Āsana

MATSYĀSANA *(Fish Pose)*

8 Breaths or more
Dṛṣṭi: Broomadhya
(Eyebrow Center)

9 NAVA*
9TH POSITION, EXHALE

Exhale, 8 Breaths or more

Reach up through arms and legs on the diagonal.

— From Matsyāsana, retain your dome-shaped chest as you lift your knees and release your legs from Padmāsana *(Lotus).*

— Extend your legs and arms brilliantly upward and outward on parallel diagonal lines.

— Use the twin forces of kicking away with your legs and reaching away with your arms to open your chest and enhance your spinal arch.

— Visualize light shooting through your limbs and out into space.

— By the purity of your efforts, transform your spine into a colorful rainbow arch and courageously light up any darkness within you.

State of the Āsana

UTTĀNA PĀDĀSANA
(Extended Legs Pose)

8 Breaths or more
Dṛṣṭi: Broomadhya
(Eyebrow Center)

10 DAŚA
10TH POSITION, INHALE

Inhale

Swing legs and hips overhead with gusto.

— From Uttāna Pādāsana, hoist your legs overhead and perform a backwards somersault.

— Push off the ground with your hands, strengthen your arms, and tuck your chin as your hips and legs pass over you.

— Generate enough power to carry you all the way to your end point.

Exhale

Stop suddenly and strike Four-Limbed Staff Pose.

— Arrive at your destination of Caturaṅga. Hold steady and swiftly add the following refinements:

- Root down into the earth with your hands and feet.
- Strengthen your arms and legs.
- Tap the great vitality housed in your center.

11 EKĀDAŚA

11TH POSITION, INHALE

Inhale

Come up with power and press the arms straight.

— Lift up your head in a circle, open your chest, and extend your arms.

— Stubbornly root your legs to increase your ability to arch your spine.

Vinyāsa Meta View

Use this pose to learn an essential backbend principle:

Root your limbs to free your spine.

A yogī who delves deep enough into this pose, adding stopping power to the limbs in contrast to extending the spine, not only achieves Meru Daṇḍa Siddhi (Spine Control Power) but also becomes an alchemist who can transform seemingly debilitating limits into important avenues of creative expression.

12 DVĀDAŚA

12TH POSITION, EXHALE

Exhale

Glide to Downward Dog dynamically.

— Swing your hips back to Down Dog on a sure trajectory and pause.

— Make pilgrimages to the three sacred caves situated at intervals along your spinal axis *(Meru Daṇḍa):*

- The first is the cave of your sacrum, in the lower regions below your navel.
- The second is the cave of your heart, in the middle region within your chest cavity.
- The third is the cave of your palate, in the upper regions within your sinuses and skull.

— Your breath and your mind are the vehicles you use to travel to these remote power caves. Breathe along the whole length of your spine to map your way.

— Enjoy occupying these great, spacious caverns that are located within your own body and you'll begin to follow your most worthy desires in this life.

**The order of the vinyāsa numbers above reflects the full vinyāsa count and this explains the seemingly irregular pattern of numbers.*

FULL VINYĀSA

13 TRAYODAŚA / INHALE — ARDHA UTTĀNĀSANA
14 CATURDAŚA / EXHALE — UTTĀNĀSANA
SAMASTHITI

ŚĪRṢĀSANA (Head Balance Pose)

7 SAPTA
7TH POSITION, INHALE

Exhale

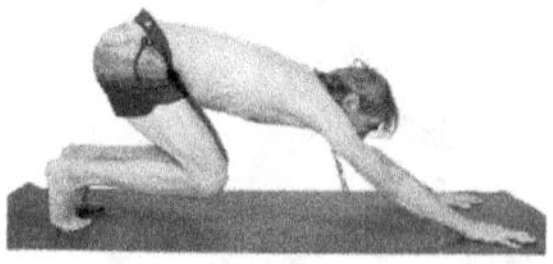

Hunker down, galvanize center, and exhale boldly.

— Squat generously, come down low to the ground, invigorate your limbs, and make ready for action.

Inhale

Hop to kneeling.

— Step or hop forward to a kneeling position and begin the process of creating the all-important Setup position.

Free Breathing, Exhale

Root limbs, make spine tall, and strike Setup position.

— Bring your forearms to the ground with your elbows separated to shoulder width apart.

— Clasp your fingers snugly and place your head on the ground just in front of your hands.

— Lift up your hips, extend your legs, and brace your upper back.

— Walk your feet forward and stop in place when your hips are vertical over your shoulders.

— Pause. Stamp down your arms, lift up your shoulders, and invest your upper back with great stopping power.

— Lift up and separate your sitting bones and "un-tilt" your pelvis to neutral.

— Go up on your tippy toes; powerfully extend your legs from hips to toes.

— Get ready to swing your legs up to the vertical axis with targeted dynamism.

— *Note:* activating your limbs and making sure your arms bear the majority of your weight in Śīrṣāsana is essential for protecting your neck and retaining the natural curve of your cervical spine.

8 AṢṬAU
8TH POSITION, INHALE

Inhale, 25 Breaths or more

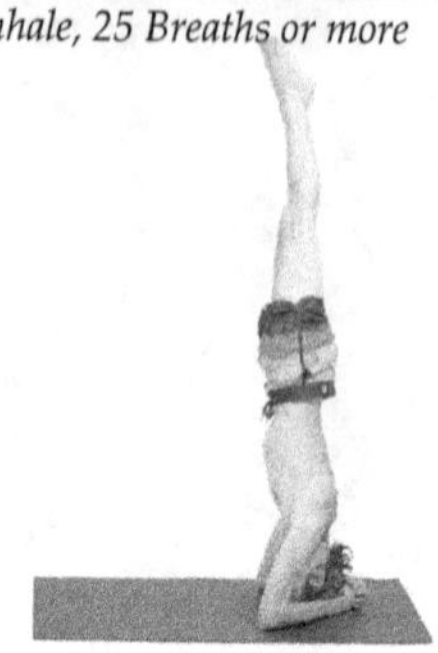

Root arms and sweep legs up to vertical with economy.

— Hoist up your legs without any doubt; move at the same speed from start to finish and stop with precision when your body masses line up over each other.

— Upon arrival in position, activate your body from head to feet.

— Root your forearms, lift up your shoulders, and add great stopping power to your upper back.

— Widen your mid-back and tuck in your front lower ribs.

— Lengthen your coccyx, suck up your navel, and stabilize your pelvis at neutral.

— Ground your femur bones; this means firmly press your thighbones back and lodge the long shafts of the bones deeper into your thighs.

— Reach up brilliantly through your legs; send rocket launch forces up through the bones from hips to feet. Use your unceasing efforts to lengthen your legs as a physical method to contemplate the infinite power of love.

State of the Āsana

ŚĪRṢĀSANA

25 Breaths or more
Dṛṣṭi: Nasagrai *(Nose)*

Vinyāsa Meta View

Droṇa, the renowned archery master, gave the following lesson to the five Paṇḍava brothers in the art and skill of archery. He tied a wooden fish high on a tree above a pool of water and asked each student to strike their stance and aim the bow and arrow at the fish's eye while looking only at its reflection in the water below.

As each student took his stance, Droṇa asked, "Before you shoot, what all do you see?" The first brother began with, "I see the sky, the tree, the ..." but before he could finish, Droṇa had him sit down. The next archer was told to take up his stance. One by one, each offered a similar answer: "I see the branch of the tree, the fish, the..." and each one was instructed to sit down. Finally, when Arjuna, the ace archer, was asked the same question, he stated without hesitation, "I see the eye of the fish." Guru Droṇa exclaimed with delight, "Shoot!" Arjuna's arrow unwaveringly pierced right through the eye of the fish.

Let this story from the Mahā- bhārata remind you to target your movement with great precision before you act.

FULL VINYĀSA

SAMASTHITI
1 EKAM / INHALE — ŪRDHVA HASTĀSANA
2 DVE / EXHALE — UTTĀNĀSANA
3 TRĪṆI / INHALE — ARDHA UTTĀNĀSANA
4 CATVĀRI / EXHALE — CATURAṄGA DAṆḌĀSANA
5 PAÑCA / INHALE — ŪRDHVA MUKHA ŚVĀNĀSANA
6 ṢAṬ / EXHALE — ADHO MUKHA ŚVĀNĀSANA

9 NAVA
9TH POSITION, EXHALE

Exhale, 8 Breaths or more

Swing legs down to a halfway point.

— Bring your legs from vertical to horizontal in a single downward swoop synchronized with your exhalation.

— Keep your legs brilliantly extended as you descend and draw a quarter circle in the air with your toes.

— Stop your legs in place cleanly at the halfway point.

— Root down through your arms and stabilize your three main body masses as you brilliantly kick away through your feet and lengthen your legs with great determination.

State of the Āsana

ARDHA ŚĪRṢĀSANA
(Upward Staff Pose)

8 Breaths or more
Dṛṣṭi: Nasagrai *(Nose)*

Inhale

Return to vertical and stop with precision.

—Hinge at your hips, root your arms, and keep your head, torso, and pelvis vertically aligned as you sweep your feet back up and stay for a moment or two.

— A connoisseur of Śīrṣāsana comes up and goes down into the pose by playing with the opposing forces of Tamas Guṇa *(Quality of Heaviness)* in the upper body and Sattva Guṇa *(Quality of Lightness)* in the lower body. In other words, adding great weight and grounding power to your arms brings freedom and lightness to your legs.

10 DAŚA
10TH POSITION, EXHALE

Exhale

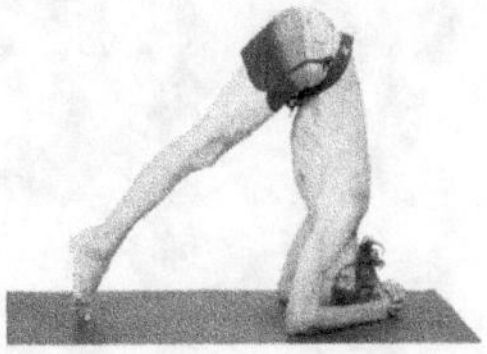

Sweep legs down; return to Setup position.

— Cast your legs away from your stable body masses as you descend and send roots into the ground through your arms.

— Make both your movement and your breath steady from start to finish.

— Learn to hinge at your hips and isolate the movement of your legs. Visualize the ball of your femur in the hip socket as the hub of a wheel and your leg as a spoke that moves up or down as a result of the turning of the hub at the center of the wheel.

Vinyāsa Meta View
Utilize all upside-down positions to make a study of gesturing with your legs. Draw inspiration from a ballet dancer who expresses uncanny exuberance and intelligence through her powerful and graceful leg gestures.

Free Breathing

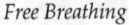

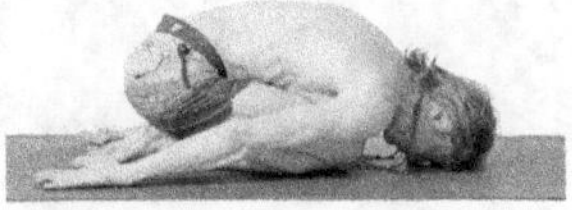

Keep head down; lower hips to heels.

— Bring your feet to the ground, bend your knees, lower hips to heels, and come to Bālāsana *(Child's Pose).*

— Release your neck and rest for a few breaths.

— Direct the flow of your inhalation to the backside of your body and expand your back ribs as you pull in air against resistance from your constricted throat. Use the breath to massage the adrenal glands that are situated on top of your kidneys.

ŚĪRṢĀSANA (Head Balance Pose)

11 EKĀDAŚA
11TH POSITION, EXHALE

Exhale

Take Caturaṅga Daṇḍāsana with a skillful strike.

— Stamp down your hands and feet; firmly brace your arms and legs.

— Get enchantingly low to the ground and hover with poise.

12 DVĀDAŚA
12TH POSITION, INHALE

Inhale

Stamp down hands, lift up spine, and straighten arms.

— Rear up from the earth and arch your spine like a cobra standing up for a strike.

— Bow or coil your spine within your torso as you straighten your arms and lift up into position.

— By your dedication to arching your spine in this pose, become a yogī who masterfully plays with the great spiral forces of creation and dissolution.

13 TRAYODAŚA
13TH POSITION, EXHALE

Exhale

Send hips back with skillful force.

— Transition to Downward Dog with confidence and find a welcome home base.

— Linger in an immovable spot for an extra breath or two and sip the nectar of pure consciousness.

FULL VINYĀSA

14 CATURDAŚA / INHALE — ARDHA UTTĀNĀSANA
15 PAÑCADAŚA / EXHALE — UTTĀNĀSANA
SAMASTHITI

YOGA MUDRĀ / PADMĀSANA / UTPLUTHIH

(Union Seal Pose / Lotus Pose / Sprung Up Pose)

7 SAPTA

7TH POSITION, INHALE

Exhale

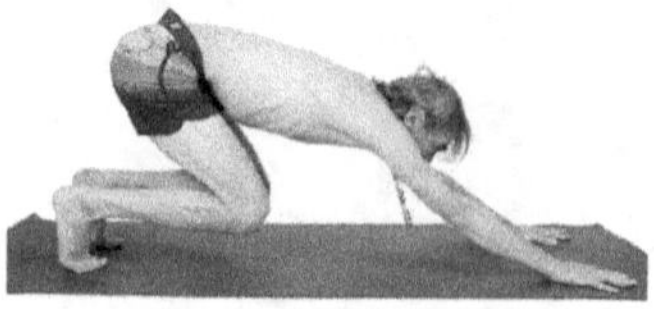

Take to the Crouch.

— Hunker back with your haunches low to the ground. Wait patiently; build up tension like a motionless cat on the verge of a surprise attack.

Inhale

Leap forward to Daṇḍāsana.

— With suddenness, spring playfully and involve your whole body in the act. Know that to bring your whole heart and a wink to each tiny move makes you a yogī.

8 AṢṬAU

8TH POSITION, INHALE

Free Breathing

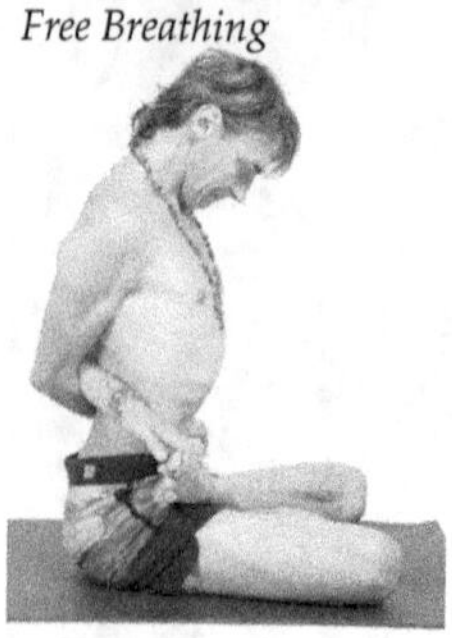

Take Lotus and bind feet with hands; strike Setup position.

— To take Lotus, externally rotate your right leg and bring your right foot back to your navel. Externally rotate your left leg; bring your left foot over the top of your right thigh and towards your navel.

— Lean forward and swing your left arm around behind you; use your left hand to catch your left foot. Next, swing your right arm around behind you and use your right hand to catch your right foot. Then sit upright and pause.

— *Note:* in Ashtanga, Baddha Padmāsana is a Setup position for transitioning into Yoga Mudrā, but feel free to stopover and stay for some time in this excellent pose.

— Experience the set of Mudrās, Energetic Seals, that are born from folding your legs in Lotus, crossing your arms behind you, and binding your feet with your hands. Use this unique position to store up plenty of force within your legs, arms, and spine in anticipation of folding forward to Yoga Mudrā.

9 NAVA

9TH POSITION, EXHALE

Exhale, 10 Breaths or more

Fold forward with a poised swoop.

— Project your spine forward into space as you come down. Trust your rooted legs to support your spine's spirited flight.

— Use core strength to remain in control of your descent all the way to its end and touch your chin or forehead to the ground lightly.

— As you come to a stop, weight your pelvis and legs like a ship's anchor on the seafloor.

— Alternate between subtly lengthening your spine and surrendering the weight of your body masses to the ground beneath you.

— Use Ujjāyī *(Sound Breathing)* to breathe deeply. Guide the piston-like action of your diaphragm up and down your torso with each exhale and inhale. Amplify the contraction and expansion rhythm of your breath one cycle at a time.

State of the Āsana

YOGA MUDRĀ

10 Breaths or more
Dṛṣṭi: Broomadhya
(Eyebrow Center)

FULL VINYĀSA

SAMASTHITI
1 EKAM / INHALE — ŪRDHVA HASTĀSANA
2 DVE / EXHALE — UTTĀNĀSANA
3 TRĪṆI / INHALE — ARDHA UTTĀNĀSANA
4 CATVĀRI / EXHALE — CATURAṄGA DAṆḌĀSANA
5 PAÑCA / INHALE — ŪRDHVA MUKHA ŚVĀNĀSANA
6 ṢAṬ / EXHALE — ADHO MUKHA ŚVĀNĀSANA

**The order of the vinyāsa numbers above reflects the full vinyāsa count and this explains the seemingly irregular pattern of numbers.*

10 DAŚA*
10TH POSITION, INHALE

Inhale

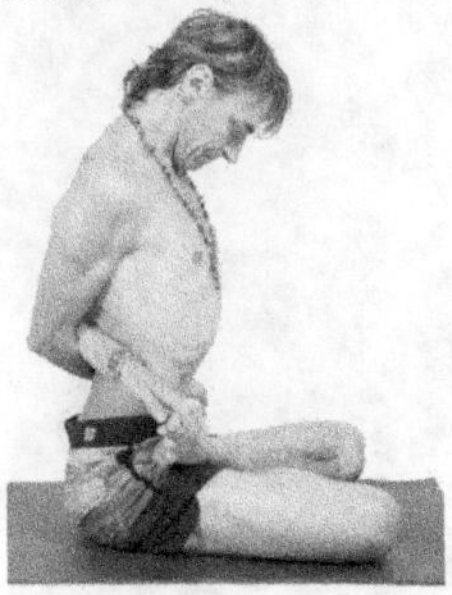

Sit up and retain Bound Lotus Setup position.

— Root down your legs and sweep your body upright in time with drawing in a smooth, sure inhalation.

— Take a moment to focus on the Mudrā of gripping your feet with your hands.

— Anchor your seat, pull up your navel, and float the core of your heart.

— Bow your forehead and lock your chin down to your lifted chest *(Jālandhara Bandha).*

— Cast a steady gaze down; look inside your torso towards your Heart Center.

8 AṢṬAU*
8TH POSITION, INHALE

Inhale, 25 Breaths or more

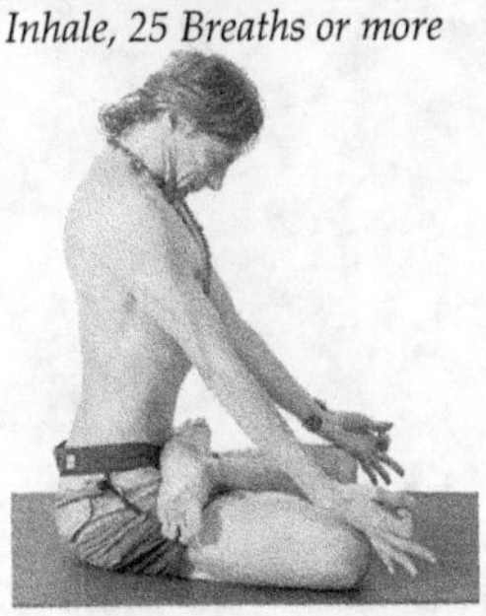

Release arms and strike a skillful Prāṇāyāma seat.

— Sit tall, extend your arms, and touch your thumbs to your index fingers to create an auspicious Mudrā *(Jñana Mudra).*

— Work with Ujjāyī *(Victorious)* breathing. Control your glottis, constrict your throat, and regulate the flow of air into and out of your lungs. Cultivate a steady, agreeable sound. Vary the tone, length, speed, and forcefulness of each inhale and exhale.

— For your inhalation, pull in your breath against resistance from your narrowed throat and for your exhalation, gently push or squeeze the air out of your lungs against resistance from your throat. Direct the flow of your out-breath down the length of your spine to the root of your pelvis and guide the in-breath up from the base of your pelvis to the top of your chest.

— Work with the three main Bandhas *(Mūla, Uḍḍīyāna, and Jālandhara)* as you sit and breathe.

State of the Āsana

PADMĀSANA

25 Breaths or more
Dṛṣṭi: Nasagrai *(Nose)*

8 AṢṬAU*
8TH POSITION, INHALE

Inhale, 25 Breaths or more

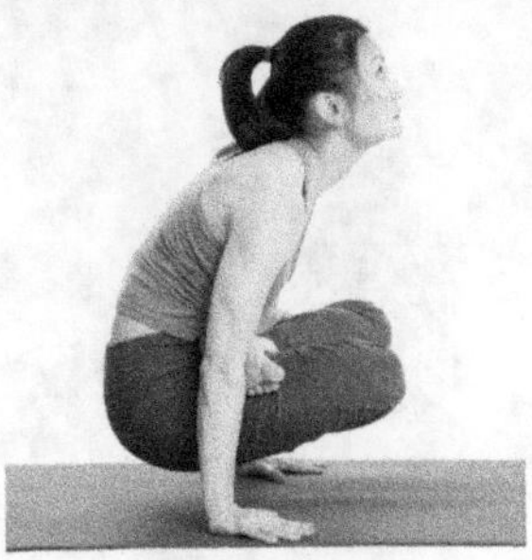

Strike down, lift up, and hold.

— Press your hands down, clear your lower body off the ground, and hold steady while breathing freely.

— Stamp the earth with your hands and root down through the whole length of your arms.

— Lift up your hips, thighs, and knees with sustained determination.

— Subtly lift up your pelvic floor, pull up your navel, and supercharge your center.

— Actively recruit strength from every corner of your being. Marvel at the power of your own body while also humbling yourself before greater forces of the cosmos.

— Enjoy the supreme challenge of finishing your practice with an act of pure effort, a test of your physical and mental strength.

State of the Āsana

UTPLUTHIH

25 Breaths or more
Dṛṣṭi: Nasagrai *(Nose)*

9 NAVA
9TH POSITION, INHALE

Exhale

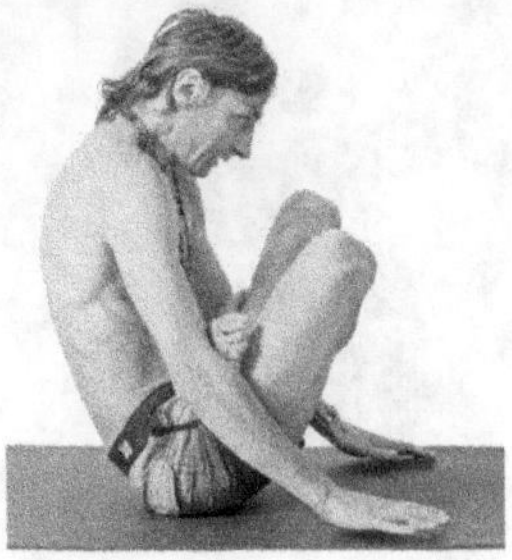

Prepare to jump back with legs in Padmāsana.

— Lower your hips to the ground keeping your legs folded in Lotus; plant your hands on the ground in front of your hips. Lift up your knees and get ready for a powerful strike-and-lift move.

YOGA MUDRĀ / PADMĀSANA / UTPLUTHIH

(Union Seal Pose / Lotus Pose / Sprung Up Pose)

Inhale

Inhale and lift up with a burst of power.

— Stamp down with your hands, lift up your hips, swing your legs under you, and lean your upper body forward.

10 DAŚA

10TH POSITION, EXHALE

Exhale

Jump back and release Lotus.

— Bend your elbows, pivot on your arms, and continue to lower your head towards the ground. Release your Lotus in mid-flight, as nimbly as a frog, and extend your legs behind you.

Exhale (continued)

Caturaṅga Daṇḍāsana.

— Use this challenging pose to practice stopping in place instantly.

— By repeating the small task of creating a clean stop at the end of each transition, gradually you can win Nirodha Siddhi: the superpower of being able to stop all motion or activity at will.

11 EKĀDAŚA

11TH POSITION, INHALE

Inhale

Ground limbs, lift head, arch spine.

— Lift up your head and spine; straighten your arms by pressing down into the earth with your hands.

— Expand your chest magnificently, stubbornly root your legs, and fill up your lungs as if sipping the finest nectar.

12 DVĀDAŚA

12TH POSITION, EXHALE

Exhale

Send hips back with a playful throw.

— Expertly swing your hips back; strike a dynamic pose.

— Perform Uḍḍīyāna Bandha, the Belly Flying Up Gesture by doing these steps:

- Brace your limbs and send your out-breath shooting along your spine to the root of your pelvis.
- Then, before you breathe in, pull your belly up into a hollow with surprising swiftness.
- As your belly flies up, watch all thoughts vanish from the field of your mind with the suddenness of a whipcrack.

FULL VINYĀSA

13 TRAYODAŚA / INHALE — ARDHA UTTĀNĀSANA
14 CATURDAŚA / EXHALE — UTTĀNĀSANA
SAMASTHITI

ŚAVĀSANA (Corpse Pose)

7 SAPTA
7TH POSITION, INHALE

Exhale

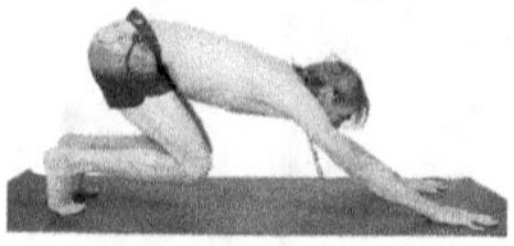

Crouch.

— Commit yourself wholly to one final crouch.

— Prepare to jump through with style and take Śavāsana.

Inhale

Spring!

— Leap forward with great speed, and yet don't hurry. Slow down time itself by becoming fully absorbed in the primal dance of the Crouch and Spring!

Exhale

Lie down in Supta Samasthiti.

— Before relaxing your body, strike a vigorous supine version of Samasthiti. Lengthen and strengthen your legs and arms, curl your tailbone, and lift the pit of your abdomen to set your pelvis to neutral. Elongate your spine, stabilize your ribs, float the core of your heart, and level your chin.

— Internalize your mind and senses and enjoy the splendor of awakened Kuṇḍalinī *(Life Force)* flowing within Suṣumṇā Nāḍī, the Most Glorious Prāṇic Channel, situated at the center of you.

8 AṢṬAU
8TH POSITION, EXHALE

25 Breaths or more

Relax limbs and body masses; take rest.

— Separate your legs and arms.

— Lengthen your tailbone and gently lift up your navel.

— Widen your mid-back and draw your front ribs down without strain.

— Level your chin and allow the natural curve of your cervical spine to take shape.

— Surrender the weight of your whole body to the earth. Release your head, torso, pelvis, arms, and legs.

— Relax your brain and jaw; soften your lips and tongue.

— Awaken your palate and allow vast space to open within you.

— Make a pilgrimage to the cave of your heart. Wander within the cave; hunt for your own true Self, Atman, the Ultimate You, who dwells there in secret. The ancients say this Changeless One has the size of a thumb and dwells eternally within the heart of every being.

State of the Āsana

ŚAVĀSANA

25 Breaths or more

FULL VINYĀSA

SAMASTHITI
1 EKAM / INHALE — ŪRDHVA HASTĀSANA
2 DVE / EXHALE — UTTĀNĀSANA
3 TRĪṆI / INHALE — ARDHA UTTĀNĀSANA
4 CATVĀRI / EXHALE — CATURAṄGA DAṆḌĀSANA
5 PAÑCA / INHALE — ŪRDHVA MUKHA ŚVĀNĀSANA
6 ṢAṬ / EXHALE — ADHO MUKHA ŚVĀNĀSANA

CLOSING PRAYER

Om

Svastiprajābhyah paripālayantām

Nyāyena mārgena mahim mahīśah

Gobrāhmanebhyah śubhamastu nityam

Lokāh samastāh sukhinobhavantu

Om shanti shanti shantih

—

Om

May all be well with humankind

May the leaders of the Earth protect it by keeping on the right path

May there be goodness for those who know the Earth to be sacred

May all beings be happy and free; may my thoughts, words, and actions contribute to this happiness and freedom

May we find Cosmic peace, Planetary peace and Inner peace

Om, peace, peace, peace

ĀSANA NAMES OF THE PRIMARY SERIES

Sūrya Namaskāra & Standing Postures	*V*	*S of A*
Sūrya Namaskāra A *Sun Salutation A*	9	6
Sūrya Namaskāra B *Sun Salutation B*	17	14
Pādāṅguṣṭhāsana *Big Toe Pose*	3	2
Pāda Hastāsana *Hand to Foot Pose*	3	2
Utthita Trikoṇāsana *Extended Triangle Pose*	5	2 , 4
Parivṛtta Trikoṇāsana *Revolved Triangle Pose*	5	2 , 4
Utthita Pārśvakoṇāsana *Extended Side Angle Pose*	5	2 , 4
Parivṛtta Pārśvakoṇāsana *Revolved Side Angle Pose*	5	2 , 4
Prasārita Pādottānāsana A *Wide-Legged Intense Forward Bend Pose*	5	3
Prasārita Pādottānāsana B *Wide-Legged Intense Forward Bend Pose*	4	3
Prasārita Pādottānāsana C *Wide-Legged Intense Forward Bend Pose*	4	3
Prasārita Pādottānāsana D *Wide-Legged Intense Forward Bend Pose*	5	3
Pārśvottānāsana *Side Intense Forward Bend Pose*	5	2 , 4

Primary Series	*V*	*S of A*
Utthita Hasta Pādāṅguṣṭhāsana *Extended Hand to Big Toe Pose*	14	2, 4, 7, 9, 11, 14
Ardha Baddha Padmottānāsana *Half Bound Lotus Stretching Pose*	9	2 , 7
Utkaṭāsana *Fierce Pose*	13	7
Vīrabhadrāsana A - B *Warrior Pose*	16	7, 8, 9, 10
Daṇḍāsana *Staff Pose*	16	7
Paschimottānāsana A - B *Intense Western Stretching Pose*	16	8 , 9
Purvottānāsana *Intense Eastern Stretching Pose*	15	8
Ardha Baddha Padma Paschimottānāsana *Half Bound Lotus Western Stretching Pose*	22	8 , 15
Triaṅga Mukhaikapāda Paschimottānāsana *Three Limbs Face One Leg Western Stretching Pose*	22	8 , 15
Jānu Śīrṣāsana A - B - C *Head to Knee Pose*	22	8 , 15
Marīchyāsana A - B *Great Sage Pose*	22	8 , 15
Marīchyāsana C - D *Great Sage Pose*	18	7 , 12
Nāvāsana *Boat Pose*	13	7
Bhujapīdāsana *Arm Pressure Pose*	15	8
Kūrmāsana / Supta Kūrmāsana *Tortoise Pose / Laying Down Tortoise Pose*	16	7 , 8
Garbha Piṇḍāsana / Kukkuṭāsana *Embryo in the Womb Pose / Rooster Pose*	15	8 , 9

V — Vinyāsa Count
S of A — State of the Āsana

	V	S of A
Baddha Koṇāsana A - B *Bound Angle Pose*	16	8 , 9
Upaviṣṭha Koṇāsana A - B *Seated Angle Pose*	15	8 , 9
Supta Koṇāsana *Lying Down Angle Pose*	16	8
Supta Pādāṅguṣṭhāsana *Lying Down Hand to Big Toe Posture*	28	9, 11, 16, 18
Ubhaya Pādāṅguṣṭhāsana *Both Big Toes Pose*	15	9
Ūrdhva Mukha Paschimottānāsana *Upward Facing Western Stretch Pose*	16	9
Setu Bandhāsana *Bridge Pose*	15	9

Finishing Postures	V	S of A
Ūrdhva Dhanurāsana *Upward Bow Pose*	15	9
Sālamba Sarvāṅgāsana *All Limbs Pose*	14	8
Halāsana *Plow Pose*	15	9
Karṇapīdāsana *Ear Pressure Pose*	15	9
Ūrdhva Padmāsana *Inverted Lotus Pose*	15	9
Piṇḍāsana *Embryo Pose*	15	9
Matsyāsana *Fish Pose*	15	9
Uttāna Pādāsana *Extended Legs Pose*	15	9
Śīrṣāsana *Head Balance Pose*	14	8
Ardha Śīrṣāsana *Upward Staff Pose*	15	9
Yoga Mudrā *Union Seal Pose*	14	9
Padmāsana *Lotus Pose*	14	8
Utpluthih *Sprung Up Pose*	14	8
Śavāsana *Corpse Pose*	8	8

GLOSSARY

A

Agastya A great Yogī, a hero who successfully protects and defends the gods and humanity from the demonic forces that periodically gain power. Agastya is particularly known for his Herculean digestive powers.

Akimbo With hands on the hips and elbows turned out.

Apāna Vāyu The downward, contractile energy pattern that is associated with exhalation.

Armpit Chest The upper part of the chest cavity, the area of your chest that spans from the armpits to the collarbones, important to distinguish in order to avoid flaring the front lower ribs when attempting to open the chest.

B

Bandha Energetic Lock, examples include the three most famous: Mūla *(Root, pelvic floor lock)*, Uḍḍīyāna *(Flying Up, abdomen lock)*, and Jālandhara *(Water Bearer, chin lock)* Bandhas.

Bhakti Devotion to God, one of the four main branches of Yoga that consist of Haṭha, Bhakti, Karma, and Jñāna Yogas.

Bhūtas The elements Earth, Water, Fire, Air, and Space are building blocks of the material world that the yogī works to know intimately, emulate, harness the power of, embody, manifest, and express.

Buddhi Intellect, Higher Faculty of Awareness, Intelligence, Intuitive or Higher Mind, Discriminative Faculty of the mind, one of the three main aspects of the mind that are made up of Buddhi, Ahaṅkāra, and Manas.

C

Chakra Energy Center, Lotus, Whirling Wheel of Life, examples include the seven famous chakras: Mūlādhāra, Svādhiṣṭhāna, Maṇipūra, Anāhata, Viśuddha, Ājñā, and Sahasrāra, situated along Suṣumṇā Nāḍī *(Most Glorious Prāṇic Channel)* within the Subtle Body *(Prāṇamaya Kosha)*.

Catvāri The number four in Sanskrit, an alternate name for Caturaṅga Daṇḍāsana *(Four-Limbed Staff Pose)*. Caturaṅga Daṇḍāsana is the 4th Vinyāsa of Sūrya Namaskāra A.

Central Axis or Median Plane The medial line that divides the physical body vertically into equal right and left halves, also sometimes refers to the central Prāṇic Channel, Suṣumṇā *(Most Glorious)*, a main component of the Subtle or Energy Body *(Prāṇamaya Kosha)*.

Central Prāṇic Nāḍī, Glorious Channel, Central Channel Synonyms for Suṣumṇā Nāḍī, the main Prāṇic Channel of the Subtle or Energy Body *(Prāṇamaya Kosha)* that spans from Mūlādhāra *(Root Support)* at the base of the pelvis to Sahasrāra *(Thousand-Petaled Lotus Flower)* at the crown of the head.

Coccyx Tailbone, joined at the very end of the sacrum *(back of the pelvis)*, two to four tiny, partially fused vertebrae.

Crouch To bend your knees and lower yourself so that you are close to the ground, to hunker down into a poised stance that readies you for dynamic, speedy, and nimble action, like a sprinter on the starting block, an animal preparing to strike, or a yogī getting ready to leap from Downward Dog to Daṇḍāsana in preparation for doing a seated posture.

D

Daṇḍa Staff, Stick, Rod, Lever, a technical and poetic image for the Central Axis of the body. A main image for creating a relationship of integrity between the three main body masses in every pose, beginning and ending with Samasthiti, the one universal posture that is the mother of all other poses.

F

Femur Bone Also called the thighbone, upper bone of the leg, this is the longest and strongest bone of the body. Controlling, grounding, enjoying, and becoming absorbed in this bone is the key to mastery of Āsana and Haṭha Yoga.

G

Gesture Purposeful, expressive, or strategic movement, an action that expresses feelings, intentions, or something meaningful in a somatic language, a synonym for Vinyāsa as in each Vinyāsa is a gesture.

God Eternal One, Sacred Immutable Being, Cosmic Person, the Infinite, Sacred Trickster, Secret One, the Self-Luminous Being, Divine, Sacred Source, Supreme Self, Changeless Reality, Self.

H

Heart Cave A technical and poetic reference to the Energetic Plexus located at the Heart Center *(Anāhata Chakra)*. Visualizing the chest area as a Sacred Cave that contains vast space and also houses the Self enables the yogī to create powerful, expressive postures and clear the mind of all distractions.

I

Indriyas Senses in yoga. There are ten senses: eyes, ears, nose, mouth, and skin and also voice, locomotion *(legs)*, grasping *(arms)*, genitals, and organs of elimination. The yogī aims to reclaim and interiorize the senses, to steady and control each of these organs in order to use them for accurately perceiving the sacred dimension of reality that is hidden behind the false appearance of the visible world.

J

Jālandhara Bandha Water Bearer Lock, Chin Lock, one of the three famous Bandhas *(Mūla, Uḍḍīyāna, and Jālandhara)* used by Haṭha Yogīs to control the body and mind. To perform this Bandha, lift up the chest into a mighty expansion and lower the jaw towards the top of the chest (notch between the collarbones). The idea is to lift the chest and bow the forehead with a clear, rhythmic move as a way of catching, trapping, or confining the upward-rising energy *(Prāṇa Vāyu)* that manifests with the inhalation. Jālandhara is also a symbolic gesture of prayer and receptivity, a bowing to the Sacred Source that abides in the Heart Center.

K

Khecarī Mūdra Space Making Seal, an energetic seal located at the palate. To awaken the palate is to create discernment and open up the interior spaces of the body and mind. All yoga techniques are said to be subordinate to Khecarī Mudrā, the chief of all Mudrās.

Kuṇḍalinī Coiled, Serpentine, a technical and poetic term for Prāṇa, Life Force, the invisible energetic substratum of all the forms in the material world. Also a term for the Goddess Śakti, the consort of Śiva.

L

Lotus of the Heart Synonym for the Anāhata Chakra, the energy plexus located at the Heart Center within the Subtle Body.

M

Mahā Mudrā Great Seal, Great Gesture, a Prāṇāyāma technique of expelling the air out of the lungs, retaining the breath, simultaneously locking the three main Bandhas *(Mūla, Uḍḍīyāna, and Jālandhara)*, and causing Prāṇa to flow up the Middle Channel in a dazzling display of glorious light.

Māyā Illusory World, Magic, false appearance of the visible, material world, spiritual ignorance.

Middle Channel, Middle Axis Different names for Suṣumṇā *(Most Glorious Prāṇic Channel)*.

Mudrā Energetic Seal, Gesture, a main branch of Haṭha Yoga that consists of subtle techniques such as Bandhas, strategic dynamic movements, and purposeful internal actions.

Mūla Bandha Root Lock, an energetic lock or sealing in of Prāṇa, at the base of pelvis, a physical contraction of the pelvic floor, a pulling up of Prāṇa, Life Force, from the base of the spine as a means of trapping, confining, conserving, or redirecting upward the downward-flowing Contraction Energetic Force *(Apāna Vāyu)* that manifests with the exhalation.

Mūlādhāra Root Support, an energy center or chakra that is the foundation of the Subtle Body, place where Śakti or Life Force originates deep in the center of the body, corresponds to the physical area of the pelvic floor. The aim of the yogī in practice is to wake up Śakti within Mūlādhāra and cause her to fly up the Middle Channel to reunite with Śiva within Sahasrāra *(Thousand-Petaled Lotus Flower)*, the energy center at the crown of the head.

N

Nāḍī Tube or channel-like conductor for carrying Prāṇa *(Life Force)*.

Nirodha Cessation, Stopping, to Arrest, refers to clearing the mind, causing a cessation of activity within the field of the body / mind.

P

Palate The roof of the mouth, location of the sacred energy center known as Khecarī Mudrā *(Space Making Seal)* also a person's appreciation of taste and flavor, especially when sophisticated and discriminating.

Palate Cave A technical and poetic reference for the mouth as a sacred cave called Khecarī *(Space Maker)*. Visualizing the cavernous structure of the mouth as a mystical, energetic center enables the yogī to manifest and express the element of Ether or Space at will and gain the prize of unbiased discernment.

Prāṇa Life Force, the invisible, energetic substratum that gives rise to all material forms.

Prāṇa Vāyu The upward, expansive Energy Pattern that is associated with the inhalation.

GLOSSARY

Prāṇāyāma Breath Control, un-restraining the breath, controlling the Prāṇa or Life Force, the Fourth Yogic Limb of Ashtanga Yoga.

Pratibhā In a flash, instantaneously, in the time it takes to snap the fingers, like a lightning strike.

Pṛthivī The Sacred Earth Goddess who generously supports every posture or attitude, the Inexhaustible Source of Abundance, the One Source that the yogī trusts implicitly and turns to for support eternally.

S

Sacral Cave A technical and poetic reference, cave-shaped sacrum that makes up the back of the pelvis. Visualizing this area as a sacred cave enables the yogī to create powerful, expressive movements and postures.

Sacrum Shaped like a shield or downward-pointing arrow, this bone is located at the base of the lumbar vertebrae and is connected to the pelvis.

Sagittal or Medial Plane A vertical plane running top to bottom that divides the body into right and left halves.

Sahasrāra Chakra Thousand Petals, the Seventh Chakra *(Energy Plexus)* situated at the crown of the head within the Subtle Body *(Prāṇamaya Kosha).*

Śakti Life Force, Prāṇa, Kuṇḍalinī, Feminine Divine, Serpentine Primal Energy, Śiva's consort.

Sattva Guṇa Quality of Lucidity, of the three Guṇas or Qualities (along with *Tamas and Rajas*) that join together in infinitely varied combinations in order to manifest all the forms of the material world. Sattva is light, white, and cohesion; it is the contractile, inward-driving, galvanizing Centripetal Force. Sattva Guṇa is also a synonym for Buddhi, Higher Mind, Intellect, Power of Discernment, or Lucidity.

Side or Frontal Plane A vertical plane running from side to side, divides the body or any of its parts into anterior *(front)* and posterior *(back)* portions.

Śiva Auspicious, God of Yoga, King of Tamas Guṇa *(Quality of Inertia),* one of the trinity of Hindu Gods that include Brahma, Viṣṇu, and Śiva.

Spring To jump, leap, or move suddenly forward, to go into action decisively without a trace of doubt or hesitation, to create an event of supremely confident, pure movement.

Suṣumṇā Nāḍī The main Prāṇic Channel of the Subtle or Energy Body *(Prāṇamaya Kosha)* that spans from Mūlādhāra *(Root Support)* at the base of the pelvis to Sahasrāra *(Thousand Petals)* at the crown of the head.

T

Tapas Heat, Shining, Friction, Intense Spiritual Practice, Vision Questing, Asceticism, Restraint, Yoga Practice, building up heat through directing the mind and senses inward and keeping the consciousness riveted in the present moment.

Three Main Body Masses The head, torso, and pelvis. Having the skill and kinesthetic intelligence to maintain a relationship of integrity between your three main body masses is an essential key to mastery in Āsana and Haṭha Yoga.

Transverse or Horizontal Plane A horizontal plane that divides the body into upper *(superior)* and lower *(inferior)* halves.

Tripurāntaka Means the Slayer of the Three Demon Cities. This is an alternate name given to Śiva, God of Yoga, because he shot an arrow at the perfect time so that it simultaneously pierced the three aerial cities, thereby destroying a powerful demon stronghold.

U

Uḍḍīyāna Bandha Belly Flying Up Lock, an energetic lock or sealing of Prāṇa created by pulling up the navel and hollowing out the entire abdominal cavity as means of catching, trapping, confining, or redirecting upward the downward-flowing Contraction Force *(Apāna Vāyu)* of the exhalation.

Ujjāyī Upward, Expansive, Victorious Breath, sound breathing, the most basic Prāṇāyāma technique that involves constricting the throat in order to control the in and out flow of the breath.

V

Vertical Axis/Vertical Line/Spinal Axis A synonym for the Central Axis of the physical body, can also refer to Suṣumṇā Nāḍī *(Most Glorious Prāṇic Channel).*

Y

Yantra Restraining Instrument, a branch of Yoga devoted to creating meditation through focusing on visual forms. Japa Yantra is to repeatedly contemplate a form in order to extract insights and wisdom. To do an āsana is to create a Yantra, a mathematically precise form that clears the mind of extraneous thoughts and helps the yogī perceive the Sacred Reality behind the false appearance of all physical things.

EIGHT LIMBS OF YOGA

Yama	Restraint, Power to Say NO
Niyama	Observance, Power to Say YES
Āsana	Posture
Prāṇāyāma	Breath Control
Pratyāhāra	Withdrawal of the Senses
Dhāraṇā	Concentration
Dhyāna	Meditation
Samādhi	Absorption

Yamas
Ahimsā—*Non-harming, positive relationship to one's anger*
Satyā—*Truthfulness, sincerity of heart, faithful to principles, virtuous*
Asteya—*Non-stealing, non-imitation, trusting your giftedness*
Brahmacharya—*Responsibly harnessing one's creative energy*
Aparigraha—*Non-possessiveness, radical self-sufficiency*

Niyamas
Śaucha—*Somatic and psychic purity*
Santoṣa—*Contentment, equanimity*
Tapas—*Discipline, intense spiritual practice*
Svādhyāya—*Self-inquiry, study of sacred texts, recitation of Mantras*
Īśvara-Praṇidhāna—*Dedicating oneself to the Supreme Soul*

DṚṢṬI (GAZE)

Agrataḥ	Forward
Aṅguṣṭā Ma Dyai	Toward the thumb(s)
Broomadhya	Toward the eyebrow center
Hastāgrai	Toward the hand
Nābi Chakra	Toward the navel
Nasagrai	Down the nose
Pādayorāgrai	Toward the foot/feet
Pārśva	Side
Ūrdhva	Upward

NUMBERS IN SANSKRIT

1	Ekam	**11**	Ekādaśa	**21**	Ekaviṃśati
2	Dve	**12**	Dvādaśa	**22**	Dvāviṃśati
3	Trīṇi	**13**	Trayodaśa	**23**	Trayoviṃśati
4	Catvāri	**14**	Caturdaśa	**24**	Caturviṃśati
5	Pañca	**15**	Pañcadaśa	**25**	Pañcaviṃśati
6	Ṣaṭ	**16**	Ṣoḍaśa	**26**	Ṣaḍviṃśati
7	Sapta	**17**	Saptadaśa	**27**	Saptaviṃśati
8	Aṣṭau	**18**	Aṣṭadaśa	**28**	Aṣṭāviṃśati
9	Nava	**19**	Ekonaviṃśati		
10	Daśa	**20**	Viṃśati		

The God Śiva is named both Yogeśvara *(Lord of Yoga)* and Bhūteśvara *(Lord of the Five Elements)*—this is perfectly logical to a lover of the great art of Āsana.

ABOUT THE AUTHOR

DAVID GARRIGUES

Since 1991, David has maintained an enthusiastic daily personal practice that is dedicated to Āsana and Prāṇāyāma study in the Ashtanga tradition. His intense commitment to practice and to teaching inspires his students who form a diverse, soulful, open-hearted, and serious global learning community.

David was introduced to yoga at the age of sixteen when a friend taught him the classic set of postures known as Sūrya Namaskāra *(Sun Salutations)*. David maintained a self-taught practice for more than a decade before everything changed when he met Marie Svoboda, Seattle's "Grand Dame of Yoga," in 1991. Attending her classes lit an everlasting fire for yoga in him and he immersed himself in a blazing, resolute study of yoga. During this time David also had the great fortune to study intensively with senior BKS Iyengar teacher, Aadil Palkhivala, attending weekly classes and participating in many intensives and teacher trainings.

David met Pattabhi Jois in 1993 and over the next sixteen years he traveled to Mysore, India more than twelve times to study with the great yoga master. In 1996, Pattabhi Jois granted David a teaching certificate; David is among a small group of Ashtanga Yoga teachers who received a teaching certificate directly from Sri K. Pattabhi Jois. David returned to Seattle and opened the first-ever Ashtanga Yoga studio there.

David now lives in Philadelphia and is an internationally recognized yoga teacher and creator of the Āsana Kitchen video instruction series, one of the leading online yoga learning resources on YouTube. David travels extensively throughout the US, Europe, and India offering workshops, in-depth studies, and retreats. He has numerous online courses and is the author of many books, *Vāyu Siddhi: Secrets of Yogic Breathing, Maps and Musings: Writings that Celebrate Haṭha Yoga and the Quest for Self Knowledge, Ecstatic Discipline: 46 Poems for Lovers of Haṭha Yoga, Teaching Yoga With Verbal Cues,* and *Ashtanga Yoga Vinyāsa.*

David's mission is to help students of yoga flourish within the living, contemporary lineage of Ashtanga Yoga. He aims to be part of the circle of Haṭha Yoga lovers who are devoted to applying the teachings of Ashtanga Yoga in ways that promote physical, psychological, and spiritual growth in themselves and others.

Photographer, Ariel Dubov

MODEL BIOGRAPHIES

JOY MARZEC

They say Ashtanga is for the "hard cases"—for the people who can only survive in the world if they have a daily Yoga practice. I am one of those people. I need to practice each day. It sets me right, makes me less anxious, gives me courage to risk, risk, risk. I was introduced to Yoga at sixteen, started practicing Ashtanga at nineteen, and started studying with David at twenty-two. From the first moment I met David, I knew him. He got me and I got him. David's approach to Ashtanga has always made sense to me. "The practice needs to serve you," he says. Through the daily grind of Tapas, I have learned what it means to have the discipline of a mental attitude.

A significant part of my life has been about supporting David in his teaching vision. I have produced his video courses, workshops, books, app, and the Asana Kitchen subscription channel. In return, he has supported my filmmaking. I am so grateful to the universe for bringing us together. I couldn't ask for a better partner in crime.

Photographer, Joe Longo

JOANNA DARLINGTON

Joanna began studying several styles of yoga āsana in 2003, including Iyengar, restorative, and eventually discovering and maintaining a primary focus in the Ashtanga Vinyāsa system. Using the Ashtanga curriculum, she continually endeavors to deepen her study of Haṭha Yoga.

For more than a decade she has focused her teaching on helping students discover alignment and strength in their own individual practice. This involves keen observation of and input from each student concerning their particular circumstances, abilities, and limitations. Joanna feels that with compassion comes understanding, and a mutual understanding forms a stable base for deep learning and absorption. She is senior apprentice to her teacher, David Garrigues and follows his lineage, continuing to share the teachings as they have been passed down to her. When Joanna is not teaching, she continues to assist David during his weekend workshops and Mysore intensives both across the US and abroad, and firmly believes that people of all shapes, sizes, and levels can benefit from this practice. You can follow her teaching at joannadarlington.com.

Photographer, Gabriella Marks

LAURA FRIDAY

Laura Friday is a sixty-eight-year-old yogī who has been practicing yoga for fifteen years and exploring Ashtanga for the last ten years. She is a mother, friend, musician, teacher, gardener, cat and nature lover, and basketball player. Her yoga practice feeds every part of who she is, and every part of who she is feeds her yoga practice.

For more information on her yoga classes go to www.laurafriday.com.

Photographer, Barbara Swenson Photography

ARTIS SMITH

Artis was first introduced to yoga in the early 1990's. At that time, he was more interested in the meditative aspects and not focused on āsana. For about seven years, Artis studied Soto Zen Buddhism at the Atlanta Soto Zen center. Following his studies, he moved to the Virginia Beach area where he was first introduced to the physical āsana practice of yoga. After his first class, he was hooked and started teacher training soon after. Artis received his teaching certification from Atma Bodhi Yoga in Virginia Beach, VA in 2014 and his teacher training certification in Ashtanga Vinyāsa Yoga from Manju Jois in 2015. Artis's primary teacher at this time is David Garrigues. Artis has completed a teacher's track training with Garrigues and attended four workshops with him. Artis has been teaching for six years: five years in Virginia Beach and a year in Atlanta. He is excited to be back in Augusta, GA, his hometown, sharing the benefits of yoga with the community.

The true way to happiness is through service to others.

Photographer, Rick Milton

DEREKA ANNE

Dereka first found her way into the yoga room in November 2016. She pursued the yogic path with passionate curiosity, which inspired her to travel around the world in search of something yet to be discovered. This journey led her to find the Ashtanga lineage where she has had the privilege of practicing with many notable teachers, one of whom is David Garrigues. Dereka has been a student of David's since 2018 and under his guidance has explored new dimensions of her practice. Her love and passion for the method continue to grow as she has found that through yoga, she has the ability to explore the depths of this incarnation of self.

You can follow Dereka's journey at derekaanneyoga.com.

Photographer, Taylor Shirk.

DEEPA RAO

For Deepa, the seed of Yoga was planted in school. Already practicing Ashtanga when she came to David Garrigues, she grew immensely with his compassionate guidance. She works on the mat like a research scientist applying her discoveries to all that is life—music, writing, and teaching yoga. She is an independent advertising professional based in Mumbai.

Photographer, Nitin Sapkale

JESSICA SANDHU

Jessica Sandhu is a yoga teacher and health coach based in Washington, D.C. She has been practicing yoga since the age of twenty-two, using it to help ease lower back pain and emotional stress. She utilizes yoga and health coaching as tools to help others find balance and peace in their lives on and off the mat.

You can learn more about Jessica and her work at jessicasandhu.com.

Photographer, Reema Desai

Additional thanks to models Rahul Urs, Michael Joel Hall, Lynn Qu, and Julia Lopez for their beautiful photos!

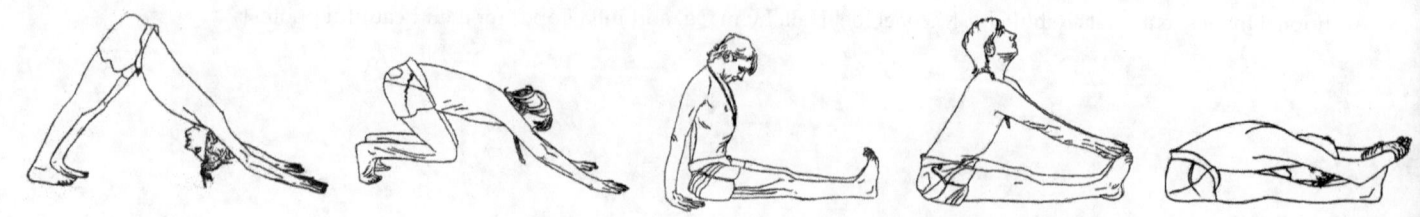

www.ingramcontent.com/pod-product-compliance
Lightning Source LLC
Chambersburg PA
CBHW080840120626
46553CB00009B/2507
* 9 7 9 8 2 1 8 1 3 1 1 3 5 *